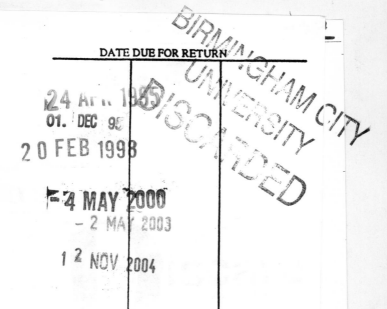

Shakespeare's Plays in Performance

In grateful memory

of

LEONARD RICE-OXLEY

tutor and friend

Shakespeare's Plays in Performance

John Russell Brown

EDWARD ARNOLD (PUBLISHERS) LTD.
LONDON

First published 1966

Printed in Great Britain by
W. & J. Mackay & Co Ltd, Chatham

Contents

Acknowledgements

THE author gratefully acknowledges permission to publish in revised form material that has appeared elsewhere: Edward Arnold (Publishers) Ltd., publishers of *Stratford-upon-Avon Studies* for Chapters VI, VII and IX; the Shakespeare Association of America, Inc., publishers of *Shakespeare Quarterly*, for the Appendix; the Speech Association of America, publishers of the *Quarterly Journal of Speech*, for part of Chapter II; the Syndics of the Cambridge University Press, publishers of *Shakespeare Survey*, for Chapters XI, XII and XIII; Tulane University, publishers of *Tulane Drama Review*, for Chapter XIV, *Directions for 'Twelfth Night'* (this last chapter in its original form is copyright, 1961, by *Tulane Drama Review*, appearing in Vol. 5, No. 4, June 1961, of that periodical; Chapter IV is a complete reworking of ideas first expressed in two articles in *Tulane Drama Review*.

A passage from *Lichtenberg's Visits to England*, tr. Margaret L. Mare and W. H. Quarrell (1938) is reprinted by courtesy of the Clarendon Press; one from Bernard Shaw's theatre criticism by permission of the Public Trustee and the Society of Authors; one from M. Saint-Denis, *Theatre: the Rediscovery of Style* (1960), by courtesy of the author; and one from T. S. Eliot's 'Seneca in Elizabethan Translation', published in *Elizabethan Dramatists* and *Selected Essays of T. S. Eliot*, by permission of Faber and Faber Ltd. and Harcourt, Brace and World, Inc.

Unless otherwise stated, quotations are taken from Peter Alexander's edition of the *Complete Works* (1951).

Illustrations are reproduced by the courtesy of the Birmingham Reference Library (XIII), la Comédie de l'Est, Strasbourg (XVIII), Mr. Gordon Craig (IX–XII), the Governors of the Royal Shakespeare Theatre (I, VIII, XVII, XXII–XXXVII, XXXIX, XL and XLIII–XLVI), the Harvard Theatre Collection (VII), the Mander and Mitcheson Theatre Collection (IV and V), the Scottish Tourist Board (XXXVIII), *Plays and Players* (incorporating *Theatre World*) (XVI), and the Trustees of the National Portrait Gallery (II); and of the following photographers: J. F. W. Cocks (VIII), Gordon Goode (XXII–XXXVII, XXXIX and XL), Angus McBean (XVII and XLI–XLVII), and Houston

Rogers (VI, XIV, XV and XIX-XXI). Mrs. Maureen Hill, Miss R. Waveney Payne, Miss Eileen Robinson and Miss Helen Willard have given generous assistance in procuring photographs for this book.

The author gratefully acknowledges the skilled and patient help of Mr. David Borland who criticised the first drafts of many of the chapters of this book.

List of Plates

Figures i to iv on pp. 134 and 135 are drawn by Colin Winslow

Introduction

WHY are Shakespeare's plays so actable? How do they draw and hold their audiences? How can we gain an impression of performance from reading a text? How should the plays be staged in our theatres to present the fullness of Shakespeare's imagination? These are some of the questions that led me to write this book, to try one approach and then another, to experiment in stage-productions and in research and argument. A knowledge of what precisely can and should happen when a play is performed is, for me, the essential first step towards an understanding of Shakespeare, and perhaps the most difficult and fascinating of all.

I start with the text and the actor, which is the closest point of contact between Shakespeare and those who perform his plays. Problems of style and interpretation are at once encountered, and confusions due to changes in taste and conditions of performance. While general considerations prepare for the more particular, every chapter in the first part of the book is basically concerned with how an actor must respond to the text and what revaluations of that text are accomplished by his performance. I have tried to look and listen, as well as read, to respond to entire characterisations as well as momentary and immediate effects, and to remember the excitement of great and original performances.

Most of my examples throughout the book are taken from the 'early middle' period—from *Romeo and Juliet, Richard the Second, The Merchant of Venice* and later comedies, from *Julius Caesar* and *Hamlet*. I do not wholly avoid the challenge of later plays, but the comparative clarity of those I have chosen for sustained comment permits a bolder handling; and yet their artistry is so assured that debate about the extent of Shakespeare's achievement is unnecessary. They are also free from authorship problems, and were first printed from manuscripts close to Shakespeare's own.

After actors, I consider the stage and stage-action—again in conjunction with a close study of texts. Here it is necessary to treat plays individually and to find appropriate terms for complex and continually changing phenomena. We are considering the 'form and pressure' of a dramatic image in which poetry, ambiguities, moral concepts and characterisations are inextricably involved with visual and temporal effects—compositions in form, colour and rhythm, devices of scale, contrast, repetition, sequence, tension and tempo. Gordon Craig's *On the Art of the Theatre* has this advice for a director of Shakespeare's tragedies:

> Let me tell you at the commencement that it is the large and sweeping impression produced by means of scene and the movement of the figures which is undoubtedly the most valuable means at your disposal.

There is so much else that asks for immediate attention in Shakespeare's texts that Craig explains:

> I say this only after very many doubts and after much experience.[1]

In this part of my book I try to show the power of the 'large and sweeping impressions' of setting and movement, and to indicate what stage effects are required by the dialogue in addition to those described in the brief and often unreliable stage-directions.

In a third section I then proceed to the audience and very briefly discuss the nature of its response.

In a final section I consider particular English productions from recent years. In this way I can show what today's theatre directors and actors have discovered about how to present the plays. In one chapter I argue that the visual style of a production using elaborate twentieth-century stage-equipment can be determined largely by a study of minute textual details.

There are several other books I could have written on my theme. Each chapter might have been a disputation with established literary opinion. Or I could have recorded contemporary productions and shown the range of their achievement, or collected evidence from theatre history; either way I would have written about effects that can certainly be achieved in performance. More technically, I could have documented my own experiments in production and what I lost in width of reference offset by precision of detail. Or I might have been entirely speculative, considering ideal productions in theatres from the

[1] Op. cit. (ed. 1957), p. 21.

Elizabethan or any other age; but so the actors' complete embodiment of Shakespeare's roles would have been forgotten.

The book I have chosen to write is both speculative and practical. I have tried to use the practical achievements of others and, by repeated resource to the text of the plays, to seek more clues to the stage reality that lies there waiting to be awakened. I have seldom argued about specific interpretations but the whole book advocates a decisive movement away from literary criticism towards theatrical study; and its last chapters and appendix call for textual and historical study to reinforce the imagination and expedience that customarily sustain the production of Shakespeare in our theatres.

PART ONE

The Text and the Actors

I

Verbal Drama

★

OPENING Shakespeare's *Works* every reader is liable to attend to the words only; they are cunning and wonderful, and absorb immediate interest. Our minds can be pleasurably entangled, at any point, in a subtle net of ambiguities, complexities and levels of meaning, of word-music and allusiveness; and having caught us in one segment, the whole play, or several plays, can be animated by our efforts to understand. Shakespeare's verbal art is, in fact, a trap; it can prevent us from inquiring further.

Perhaps rhetorical passages are the strongest barriers. Figurative argument marching vigorously within a metrical form towards some culminating statement both convinces and arrests as we read: so in *Henry the Fifth*:

> Therefore doth heaven divide
> The state of man in divers functions,
> Setting endeavour in continual motion;
> To which is fixed as an aim or butt
> Obedience; for so work the honey bees,
> Creatures that by a rule in nature teach
> The act of order to a peopled kingdom.
> They have a king, and officers of sorts,
> Where some like magistrates correct at home;
> Others like merchants venture trade abroad;
> Others like soldiers, armed in their stings,
> Make boot upon the summer's velvet buds,
> Which pillage they with merry march bring home
> To the tent-royal of their emperor; . . .
>
> (I. ii. 183ff.)

And further traps are hidden even here, for we must keep alert if we are to remember the whole argument when the next two lines catch us with their euphony, allusiveness, and completeness:

SPP—B

> Who, busied in his majesty, surveys
> The singing masons building roofs of gold, . . .

The 'singing masons . . .' draws our attention away from neighbouring lines, becoming independent of the immediate context; our imagination feeds fully, and other business seems impertinent.

Or a conceit can dominate our thoughts by its mere elaboration; so in *Much Ado*, Hero sends Margaret to Beatrice:

> . . . say that thou overheard'st us;
> And bid her steal into the pleached bower,
> Where honeysuckles, ripened by the sun,
> Forbid the sun to enter—like favourites,
> Made proud by princes, that advance their pride
> Against that power that bred it. There will she hide her
> To listen our propose.
>
> (III. i. 6–12)

At first we may be puzzled by unnecessary decoration—'Why not identify the bower simply?' we ask; but then the words claim our further consideration, and literary criticism and historical research occupy our thoughts. Yes: *steal* and *honeysuckles* are appropriate to the close, sweet yet familiar entanglement that will follow. *Ripened by the sun* is a contrast to Beatrice's earlier, 'Thus goes every one to the world but I, and I am sunburnt' (II. i. 286–7).

The *honeysuckles* on the pleached bower are also *proud*; and so Hero, again contrasting natural growth, will soon arraign Beatrice:

> But nature never fram'd a woman's heart
> Of prouder stuff than that of Beatrice.
> Disdain and scorn ride sparkling in her eyes,
> Misprising what they look on; and her wit
> Values itself so highly that to her
> All matter else seems weak. She cannot love, . . .
>
> (III. i. 49–54)

The *honeysuckles, ripened by the sun*, are like Beatrice in denying the full nature of the *power* that made them *favourites*. Nor must we miss the topicality of this decorative conceit: favourites *were* powerful at the court of Elizabeth I in 1598–9 when *Much Ado* was written. The great Lord Burghley died on 13 September 1598, and for some years his son, Robert, had been rising to influence challenged by the more military and handsome Earl of Essex. Francis Bacon warned the Earl not to force the issue:

> My Lord, these courses be like to hot waters, they will help at a pang: but if you use them, you shall spoil the stomach, and you shall be fain still to make them stronger and stronger, and yet in the end they will lose their operation.

And there were lesser favourites like Sir Christopher Hatton—'a mere vegetable of the Court, that sprung up at night'—Sir Walter Raleigh, or the Queen's godson, Sir John Harington. Power could suddenly be lost: when Harington returned from Ireland knighted by Essex, the Queen exclaimed, 'By God's Son! I am no Queen; that man is above me' and banished the comparatively innocent godson from Court. When Hero likens honeysuckles to proud favourites her words draw our attention until we observe the whole play in little: pride *versus* nature, in Beatrice, Benedick, Don John and Dogberry ('I am a wise fellow; and, which is more, . . . as pretty a piece of flesh as any is in Messina . . .'); a reminder of the impermanence of pride, and honeysuckles and favourites.

One decorative passage can send us to more words, to the course of the play's action, and back again to words; we stay fascinated in the verbal contrivance and have little leisure to ask how important this steeplechase is for the comedy as a whole. Books have been filled with accounts of these pursuits: Shakespeare's use of language and his imagery, his themes perceived in the 'poetic texture' of the dialogue. While none of these studies would claim to be inclusive or final, all suggest that a careful study of words reveals a coherent 'attitude to life' which is a hidden, unifying influence on the structure and substance of the plays.

In the eighteenth century, before literary criticism grew subtle and hardworking, a fascination with Shakespeare's words led to numerous collections of the 'beauties of Shakespeare'. So when the poet, Pope, prepared an edition of the plays, he helped his readers and showed his own discrimination by marking with asterisks the finest passages. Now that we no longer quote a splendid passage and leave its wings unmeasured by criticism, we are still liable to be held by the words and pride ourselves on showing the relevance and complexity of any highly wrought passage.

* * *

But there are many other elements in a drama that must be appreciated—those which are not so easily reached through the printed page—and the very words themselves can be fully known only if they are considered in their dramatic context. They must be heard in sequence, supported by actors' impersonations, related to the physical and visual elements of performance; and so, perhaps, revalued.

For example, theatre history reminds us of numerous lines that would yield a lean harvest to literary investigation, but have inspired successive audiences to wonder and applause. Notable in the earlier plays is Richard III's 'A horse! a horse! my kingdom for a horse!' (V. v. 7), or Petruchio's response to the Shrew's last speech, 'Why, there's a wench! Come on, and kiss me, Kate.' (V. ii. 180); dramatic considerations of physical action and bearing, intonation and emphasis, a new simplicity and weight of utterance, carry these moments. In *Henry the Fourth, Part II* the crucial moment in the last long interview between the dying king and Prince Hal is the simple, incomplete verse-line, 'O my son' (IV. iv. 178), which every actor of the role in my experience has made more affecting than the other hundred and fifty lines of the duologue. *Hamlet* has many such lines: 'Go on; I'll follow thee' to the Ghost, and 'O God!', 'Murder!', 'My uncle!' (I. iv. 79 and 86, and I. v. 24ff.). When Hamlet first calls the Ghost 'father' many actors have found that the text asks for particular emphasis:

> Kean, we are told, was no longer frightened. Booth 'dropped on one knee . . . and bowed his head, not in terror, but in awe and love.' At the sight of the spirit, Salvini's face was 'illumined with an awe-struck joy'; and his Hamlet, 'spontaneously, and one would almost say unconsciously, uncovers his head.'[1]

The theatrical fact of the silent Ghost meeting Hamlet is large and, in ways that the reader might never guess, the text grows in performance to answer it. Later, Hamlet's first words in his mother's closet, 'Now, mother, what's the matter?' and, near the end of the same scene, his repeated 'Good night, mother.' (III. iv. 8 and 159ff.) are powerful beyond literary analysis. Such uncomplicated, forceful lines are in the comedies too, in Rosalind's 'And so am I for no woman' (*As you Like It*, V. ii. 81ff.) or Benedick's 'This can be no trick' (*Much Ado*, II. iii. 201). All these live only in their dramatic context, nourished by timing,

[1] A. C. Sprague, *Shakespeare and the Actors* (1948), p. 140.

surprise, repetition, change of dramatic idiom, physical performance, mood, grouping.

In the greatest tragedies Shakespeare seems especially concerned to build theatrical intensity and revelation with the barest verbal material. Obviously, Lady Macbeth's sleep-walking scene verbally echoes important themes and introduces staggering images and juxtapositions of ideas, but its full power is not easily revealed by literary analysis. According to the Doctor and Gentlewoman her 'Oh, oh, oh!' (V. i. 49) is the emotional climax revealing a heart 'sorely charg'd': her fullest suffering lies beneath the words that somnambulism releases. For a literary analyst, Macbeth's last couplet:

> Lay on Macduff;
> And damn'd be him that first cries 'Hold, enough!'
> (V. viii. 33–34)

has a metrical obviousness and traces of fustian; it gains stature and meaning only in enactment, by a physical resurgence and concentration. Here is a report of Irving's Macbeth in *The Academy* of 2 October 1875:

> What one finds so good in his Fifth Act, is not only the gradations of abjectness and horror, as evil news follow on evil news, but the self-control that has long deserted him, gathered together at last; and the end, whatever the end may be, accepted with some return of the old courage, only more reckless and wild; for it is the last chance and a poor one . . .
>
> Mr. Irving's fight with Macduff illustrates quite perfectly, in its savage and hopeless wildness, the last temper of Macbeth.

These are effects that are supported by the text but can be realised only in performance.

King Lear alone could provide weighty evidence of the need to pass beyond literary analysis: 'Come, boy' and 'I shall go mad!' to the fool—the 'tone in which Garrick uttered' these last words 'absolutely thrilled' his audience;[2] and:

> I will say nothing.
>
> Didst thou give all to thy daughters?
>
> Come, unbutton here.

[2] W. Clark Russell, *Representative Actors* (n.d.), p. 110.

Give me thy arm;
Poor Tom shall lead thee

Then kill, kill, kill, kill, kill, kill!

Come, come; I am a king,
My masters, know you that.

Then there's life in't. Nay, an you get it, you shall
get it by running. Sa, sa, sa, sa.

Do not laugh at me;
For, as I am a man, I think this lady
To be my child Cordelia.
—— And so I am, I am.

Thou'lt come no more,
Never, never, never, never, never.
Pray you undo this button. Thank you, sir.
Do you see this? Look on her. Look, her lips.
Look there, look there![3]

Words like *laugh* and *man, my child* and *I am,* or *never, see* and *look* and even *button* will yield to literary analysis and show something of the relevance of these passages; and so will their syntax and metre. But Cordelia's 'And so I am, I am' or Lear's 'Look there, look there!' demand theatrical criticism to explain the rightness, delicacy and overwhelming intensity of feeling that accompanies the monosyllables in performance. These are the moments that stay with the audience long after the play is finished.

* * *

A dramatic text is spoken and heard; some words may be, as it were, in capital letters, some may be written very small indeed, some almost illegibly—quite different from the uniform scale of a printed page. In non-dramatic forms of writing such effects may sometimes be managed, but for a play in performance they are necessary, and greatly magnified. Listen to anyone's speech: the words 'I will' spoken very quickly have a different meaning and are almost opposite in aural effect compared with the same words spoken very slowly and quietly. Or coming after a long sentence and complicated interplay of syntax and

[3] I. v. 47; II. iv. 285; III. ii. 38; III. iv. 48 and 107; IV. i. 79–80; IV. vi. 188 and 201–5; IV. viii. 68–70; V. iii. 307–11.

metre, they will sound differently and mean differently from the same words in a nimble prose exchange. (Alterations of pitch or stress, or of tone and texture, also modify them.) In such ways the literary meaning and metrical effect of a printed text develop through performance into something far more complicated.

The first rule for reading the text of a play is to remember that dramatic energy is dynamic not static, that the dramatist has tried to control the tempo of performance in the smallest detail, to prepare, sustain and release moments of large emotion and alternately lead forward and hold back the audience's attention. The second rule is to remember the actor, whose sensibility and physical performance support the words, and the other actors on stage with him.

Short but sustained speech will illustrate the dynamic qualities of theatrical writing; for example, Oberon's reply to Puck just before day comes to the wood outside Athens in *A Midsummer Night's Dream*:

> But we are spirits of another sort:
> I with the Morning's love have oft made sport;
> And, like a forester, the groves may tread
> Even till the eastern gate, all fiery red,
> Opening on Neptune with fair blessed beams,
> Turns into yellow gold his salt green streams.
> But, notwithstanding, haste, make no delay;
> We may effect this business yet ere day.
>
> (III. ii. 388–95)

The plot is scarcely forwarded by the information of the first six lines, but much else is accomplished. Time and the general situation are established with talk of the 'eastern gate, all fiery red.' And the gold and fiery light of the sun in opposition to cold water, repeats an important theme in the play, echoing earlier references to a 'cold fruitless moon', 'salt tears', 'the moon, the governess of floods, Pale in her anger', or the sea's 'contagious fogs'. But to understand its theatrical effect enactment must be considered as well: these ideas are not neatly defined, but placed and imaged so that the warmth and yellow radiance transfigure the salt and green sea; the sun overpowers the sea with the long, tidal reach of syntax, so making the green one gold. When the actor speaks the lines this metrical effect is inescapable; rhythm, pitch, stress and phrase ensure its communication. So, too, the character Oberon grows, the long, controlled sound of his speech giving him an authority which he has no need to claim—often a main consideration in the balance of an acted scene. The control is astonishing: after the quick descriptive clause of 'like a forester', another adverbial clause follows and within that yet another with 'Opening on Neptune with fair blessed beams'; he has leisure, even, for the double epithet of 'fair blessed' at its close, before the strong and simple verb of the main clause is supplied in 'Turns'. The impression of controlled power in Oberon depends largely on temporal and musical means and on the clarity of performance; and because these are usually unrecognised in operation by the audience, they work with seeming inevitability—this, again, is part of their effect, giving an impression of reserved power.

The influence of these six lines extends beyond the time in which they are spoken. They accentuate, by contrast, the renewed speed of Oberon's concluding couplet when he leaves without doubting Puck's response, and the energy, compactness and outspokenness of Puck left alone on the stage:

> Up and down, up and down,
> I will lead them up and down . . .

Their reverberations continue when the lovers enter, for the young men's unsustained rhythms in asserting power, by contrast with both Puck and Oberon, will sound shallow and insecure:

> Where art thou, proud Demetrius? Speak thou now . . .

Out of dramatic context, both rhythm and vocabulary might be called direct and efficient, but theatrical enactment must revalue this.

When we progress beyond the meaning of words and our own appreciation of rhythm and texture, to their enactment, we move quickly from the printed page to the whole stage, from variations of tempo and emphasis to physical movement, silence, posture, grouping, the potential surprise of an entrance or exit, emotional performances. We must continue to ask 'What is the effect?' in preference to 'What is the meaning?' When at last we ask the second question we have to account for impressions which quotation of the text alone can never represent.

* * *

The dynamic nature of theatrical energy ensures that a dramatist must be specially concerned with metre and prose rhythms. (The lameness of translated plays is some indication of the importance of an author's time-control through speech.) Someone who did not understand a word of English could hear Cordelia's answer to Lear in performance and gain some impression of her physical involvement and the extremity, purity and strength of her feeling. The rhythms of her short speech must answer and satisfy the rhythms of his longer speech:

> Do not laugh at me;
> For, as I am a man, I think this lady
> To be my child Cordelia.
> —— And so I am, I am.

To manage the proper rhythmic balance, the two impersonators of these roles must be closely and silently attuned to each other's performance and, therefore, they will communicate a shared, delicate and intuitive sympathy; how this reaches the audience is not easily explained, but it is an effect good actors can command in such a context. Metre and syntax instigate, and release, the physical and emotive elements of performance.

In Shakespeare's day this generative power of words in a theatrical context could be controlled surely by virtue of the firm metrical base of blank-verse. When he began to write, the iambic beat was over-assertive; in his preface to *Menaphon* (1589), Thomas Nashe criticised dramatists who indulged the 'spacious volubility of a drumming decasyllabon.' But other writers besides William Webbe, in his *Discourse of English Poetry* (1586), judged that the 'natural course of most English verses seemeth to run upon the old iambic stroke',[4] and most sought to refine rather than replace its 'measure' or 'certain frame'.

By accepting a far more regular metre than would be tolerated to-day, the Elizabethans discovered a manner of speech that was both forcible and subtle. As Sir Philip Sidney put it, each syllable could be 'peysed', or weighed:

> The Senate of Poets hath chosen verse as their fittest raiment . . . not speaking (table-talk fashion or like men in a dream) words as they chanceably fall from the mouth, but peysing each syllable of each word by just proportion according to the dignity of the subject.[5]

[4] *Elizabethan Critical Essays*, ed. G. G. Smith (1904), i. 273.
[5] *Idem*, i. 160.

For play-writing, metre was almost universal: Hamlet asks the players for 'temperance' and 'smoothness' even in the 'very torrent, tempest, and, as I may say, whirlwind of your passion' (III. ii. 6–8) and this implies rigorous verbal accomplishment for both actor and author. Joseph Hall's *Virgidemiarum* (1598) pictures some dramatists watching a play and following the actors in a manuscript as if it were a musical score:

> Meanwhile our poets in high parliament,
> Sit watching every word, and gesturement,
> Like curious censors of some doughty gear,
> Whispering their verdict in their fellow's ear.
> Woe to the word whose margent in their scroll
> Is noted with a black condemning coal.
> But if each period might the synod please—
> Ho! bring the ivy boughs, and bands of bays.
>
> (I. iii. 45–53)

Blank verse gives the necessary control, power and coherence for physical enactment to grow out of the speaking of the text. The control comes by 'peysing' each syllable and varying the interplay of syntax and metre. Impressions of emotion grow by breaking a regular confinement, or by extending over many lines a single unit of rhythmic design. And coherence derives from the regularity sustained beneath all manner of irregularities, the now discreet and scarcely heard 'drumming' of the iambic pentametres. Metre enables a dramatic poet to influence the dynamics of production and the actors' performances.

In *Romeo and Juliet* Friar Lawrence enters the play alone, carrying a basket:

> The gray-ey'd morn smiles on the frowning night,
> Check'ring the eastern clouds with streaks of light;
> And fleckel'd darkness like a drunkard reels
> From forth day's path and Titan's fiery wheels.
> Now, ere the sun advance his burning eye
> The day to cheer and night's dank dew to dry,
> I must up-fill this osier cage of ours
> With baleful weeds and precious-juiced flowers.
>
> (II. iii. 1–8)

Thematically the soliloquy is significant. In the previous scene the sun had been associated with Juliet as Romeo exclaims:

What light through yonder window breaks?
It is the east, and Juliet is the sun.

(II. ii. 2–3)

Later Juliet is to call Romeo 'thou day in night', a light so fine that it will draw worship away from the 'garish sun' (III. ii. 17–25). At the end of the play, the Prince also speaks of the dawn:

A glooming peace this morning with it brings,
The sun for sorrow will not show his head.

(V. iii. 304–5)

The night, too, recurrs as an image throughout the play, in Romeo's foreboding and Juliet's invocation of 'gentle night' and 'loving black-brow'd night', and repeatedly in Romeo's dying speech in the 'palace of dim night' when Juliet's

beauty makes
This vault a feasting presence full of light.

(V. iii. 74–120)

Here then, with his first entry, the Friar is presented verbally, as if he willingly accepts the alternation of night and day and of good and evil: thematically a position of strength. But by temporal effects his soliloquy means much more. Its antitheses fit neatly into the metrical line-units, and the rhyme. The iambics of the first couplet are regular except for the easy reversal in the first foot of the second line—'Check'ring'—and the stronger reversal in the first line: 'The gray-ey'd morn *smiles* on the frowning night'. Notice how well-contained the 'frowning night' is, at the metrically regular end of the line; and how the potential threat is then dispersed in the belittling 'Check'ring' placed strongly in the first reversed foot of the next line. By all these means, the couplet is a stage-direction: Friar Lawrence's movements have a regular pace; he is neat; he is smoothly and pleasantly optimistic; he is gentle. The next line gives more power to darkness by comparing it with a 'drunkard' reeling, but still this reaction is not developed; here the notion is reduced in scale by 'fleckel'd' and quenched by the overwhelming metrical strength of 'From forth day's path' at the beginning of the next line, and by the additional description in 'Titan's fiery wheels'. The image of a drunkard being almost run over by a chariot is potentially brutal; but the 'drunkard' is lost from consciousness in considering the course of the sun, and the Friar immediately veers to another aspect of his concerns, introduced with a regular pentametre without the trace of a caesura which earlier had contributed to an impression of neatness: 'Now ere the sun advance his burning eye'. 'Burning eye' suggests some danger but this is turned to favour and to prettiness in the double antitheses and early caesura of the next line: 'The day to cheer and night's dank dew to dry.' Here is an indication of thought and feeling that must suggest physical bearing; the Friar's temperament is nervous but habitually controlled by an easy intellectual optimism; he recognises danger but dismisses it from his consideration by thoughts of the good. His posture, facial expressions, tone of voice expressing all this will add to the theatrical effect, especially as he is a new character alone on the large open stage, an object of intense scrutiny. So in performance, the Friar's acceptance of the 'alternation of night and day, and of good and evil' is not the position of strength the printed text might suggest: he is, also, somewhat shallow and petty.

In the Ball Scene of *Romeo and Juliet*, Act I Scene v, metrical variety indicates the individual bearing of the actors and also major elements in stage-management. It starts with grumbling and emphatic prose for the servants suggesting a Breughel-like detail and scale. Then comes the more sustained but short-phrased, almost puffing, emphasis of Capulet managing his guests; he is largely monosyllabic, directly physical in detail, repetitive and, for a time, alliterative:

> Welcome, gentlemen! Ladies that have their toes
> Unplagu'd with corns will have a bout with you.
> Ah ha, my mistresses! which of you all
> Will now deny to dance? She that makes dainty,
> She I'll swear hath corns; am I come near ye now?
> Welcome, gentlemen!

and then he retires into the longer phrases of personal reminiscence. Romeo's question to a nameless servant:

> What lady's that which doth enrich the hand
> Of yonder knight?

is smoothly sustained in image and rhythm; the simple reply, 'I know not, sir', does not deflect him; he modifies his image, and rhymes with his own last word:

> O, she doth teach the torches to burn bright!

Metrical regularity is emphasised by alliteration and then a more powerful irregularity with 'burn bright!' at the end of the line. His imagery changes again, but in sustained response and guided by the rhymed couplets. Tybalt interjects in another rhythm, sharp and athletic:

> This, by his voice, should be a Montague.
> Fetch me my rapier, boy, What, dares the slave. . . .

He changes from soliloquy to dialogue without embarrassment, and his speech builds quickly in emphatic statement. When he is questioned by Capulet his anger is sustained largely by repetition; he then becomes more brief and leaves with new, incisive threats.

The following dialogue between Romeo and Juliet is in complete contrast: they share a sonnet, its rhymes, form and images. The two lovers are strangely singled out from the other dancers and the sonnet, with its dominant image of worship, is their own predestined dance—impelled, gentle, mutual and awed; it requires a separation from the scene's ordinary pace—its blank verse and couplets—which they alone know. Through its verbal exchanges they move towards their kisses, first palm-to-palm and then lip-to-lip. Without such a presentation these intimate actions would have been lost in the crowded, animated scene, or might have been exaggerated by the actors in an effort to give them dramatic forcefulness; as Shakespeare directs through his metrical dialogue, the kisses have their own silence because our attention waits upon them for the completion of the sonnet. Even the words are revalued by their metrical setting: if the lovers did not have to share the rhythms and form of the sonnet, their conceits might ring too keenly; but, secure in the privacy of the sonnet, the wit can sound tender and contented as, perhaps, off-stage only intimate love-talk can be.

* * *

Similes, metaphors and other figures of speech, when read in conjunction with the rhythm and tempo of speech, can indicate physical performance. The Friar's changing imagery suggests a timorous nature, Romeo's sustained imagery an absorption in a single feeling. But, perhaps more powerfully, images also display a general, overall excitement, a state of being in which fantasy becomes real.

When we read a printed text we pick our way slowly through the conceits—as we have attended to Hero's talk of honeysuckles. But the actor has assimilated all this—or should have done—so that in speaking the difficulties disappear and excitement takes their place. Hero is a young girl in love, about to talk of love and to give thoughts of love to her cousin, who has derided love; lightly spoken her speech is alive with feeling as well as thought.[6] (The metre helps, too; notice the way in which 'like favourites' starts its new, energetic development at the end of a line after the period had seemed to be complete.) In Anthony Mundy's *Zelauto* (1580), a novel which Shakespeare almost certainly read while preparing to write *The Merchant of Venice*, a young man becomes satisfied that his lady is concerned for him; he is said to look 'smug' and then:

> his conceits began to come so nimbly together, that he now rolled in his rhetoric, like a flea in a blanket.
>
> (Sig. P3)

However complex Shakespeare's imagery can seem, and however long a reader may pour over the words, from the stage it is often a wide-spreading vigour and enjoyment that is the dominant impression communicated to the audience.

Two testimonies are useful here. First Bernard Shaw inveighing against academic critics and elocution teachers:

> Powerful among the enemies of Shakespear are the commentator and the elocutionist: the commentator because, not knowing Shakespear's language, he sharpens his reasoning faculty . . . instead of sensitizing his artistic faculty to receive the impression of moods and inflexions of feeling conveyed by word-music; the elocutionist because . . . he devotes his life to the art of breaking up verse in such a way as to make it sound like insanely pompous prose. The effect of this on Shakespear's earlier verse, which is full of the naïve delight of pure oscillation, to be enjoyed as an Italian enjoys a barcarolle, or a child a swing, or a baby a rocking-cradle, is destructively stupid.
>
> (Review of *All's Well, Saturday Review*, 2 Feb., 1895)

The second is from the publishers of the first edition of *Troilus and Cressida* in 1609 who wrote in their preface that Shakespeare had:

> such a dexterity, and power of wit, that the most displeased with plays are pleas'd with his comedies. And all such dull and heavy-witted wordlings, as were never capable of the wit of a comedy,

[6] See chapter XI, pp. 171–72.

> coming by report of them to his representations have found that wit there, that they never found in themselves, and have parted better witted than they came; feeling an edge of wit set upon them, more than ever they dream'd they had brain to grind it on. So much and such savoured salt of wit is in his comedies, that they seem (for their height of pleasure) to be born in that sea that brought forth Venus.

Alive in performance, Shakespeare's most conceited and obscure passages can represent enjoyment or vigour or confidence or sexual excitement—all powerful over an audience; they may also suggest sensitivity, gentleness, deep involvement—the kind of feelings which do not startle an audience but affect them slowly. The reader misses all this because he does not assimilate the conceits and rhetoric as an actor does, nor hear them as one part of the actor's performance.

The remainder of the first part of this book offers some ways of defining and measuring the actors' necessary contribution.

II

Acting

★

THIS chapter is a digression. I have already made assumptions about an actor's response to Shakespeare's text that some scholars would challenge by reference to Elizabethan conditions of performance and so I want to examine these assumptions before proceeding further.

It used to be possible to quote Hamlet's advice to the players, point out that no extravagances were to be used, and leave the rest to the actor to interpret in the tradition of his art, but today many scholars believe that actors must rediscover a lost technique in order to present Shakespeare's plays. Many would say that Elizabethan acting was 'fundamentally formal' and only 'shaded by naturalism from time to time'.[1] 'Formal acting' has not been properly defined but is assumed to be the opposite of 'natural', and to make no attempt to give an impression of real life. It gives first place to literary qualities: 'poetry and its decent delivery' are considered 'the only real essentials of Elizabethan drama'.[2]

The quest for a historically correct acting style for Shakespeare is comparatively new, and an authoritative, complete and balanced treatise is yet to be published. But in the meantime, what guidance can scholarship give to actors, producers and readers of Shakespeare's plays?

It seems to me that the subject has been approached from an unfortunate angle and that, in consequence, the evidence has been distorted and misapplied. Briefly, I believe that 'formalism', as it is generally understood in this context, was fast dying out in Shakespeare's age, and that a new naturalism was the kindling spirit in his theatre. This was not what we understand by naturalism today, but it did aim at an illusion of real life. I want to reverse the statement which I have quoted above, and to say that Elizabethan acting aimed at an illusion of life, although vestiges of an old formalism remained. If I am right,

[1] S. L. Bethell, 'Shakespeare's Actors', *R.E.S.*, new series, i (1950), 205.
[2] Ibid.

actors today have a better chance of interpreting Shakespeare than those who were his contemporaries, for modern traditions are based on a thorough-going naturalism unknown to Elizabethans. If the relics of formalism are properly respected, we can realise the illusion of life with a new delicacy and completeness.

* * *

To prove my point, I would have to examine in detail, and in chronological sequence, the whole *corpus* of Elizabethan drama. All I can do here is to counter some of the arguments which might be brought against my statement, and present some evidence which I do not think has been sufficiently discussed.

The earliest advocates of formal acting base their statements on Elizabethan stage-conditions; for example, after describing the circled audience and the gallants sitting on the stage, S. L. Bethell maintained that

> . . . even with the abundance of make-up, scenery, and properties in use today, it would have been impossible for actors so closely beset with audience, to create and sustain an illusion of actual life, especially as they performed in broad daylight.[3]

Obviously these conditions made it difficult to sustain an illusion of real life, but nevertheless it was certainly attempted and achieved. Thomas Heywood in his *An Apology for Actors* (1612) writes,

> . . . turn to our domestic histories: what English blood, seeing the person of any bold Englishman presented, and doth not hug his fame, and honey at his valor, pursuing him in his enterprise with his best wishes and, as being wrapt in contemplation, offers to him in his heart all prosperous performance, *as if the personator were the man personated*?[4]

John Webster, in the Character of 'An Excellent Actor' (1615), uses almost the same words: 'what we see him personate, we think truly done before us.'[5] John Fletcher was praised for giving opportunity for a similar illusion:

[3] *Shakespeare and the Popular Dramatic Tradition* (1944), p. 31. See also M. C. Bradbrook, *Themes and Conventions of Elizabethan Tragedy* (1935), pp. 20–21.

[4] Sig. B4; the italics are mine.

[5] John Webster, *Works*, ed. F. L. Lucas (1927), iv. 43.

How didst thou sway the theatre! make us feel
The players wounds were true, and their swords, steel!
Nay, stranger yet, how often did I know
When the spectators ran to save the blow?
Frozen with grief we could not stir away
Until the Epilogue told us 'twas a play.[6]

Prolonged death speeches must have made the simulation of real life very difficult—*The Knight of the Burning Pestle* ridicules their excesses—but Burbage evidently could achieve it; not only did the audience think he actually died, but the dramatic illusion extended to the other actors in the scene with him:

Oft have I seen him play this part in jest,
So lively, that spectators and the rest
Of his sad crew, whilst he but seem'd to bleed,
Amazed, thought even then he died in deed.[7]

From such descriptions, we must assume that Elizabethan actors aimed at an illusion of real life and that the best of them achieved it.

(Even when scholars accept such a statement, they still write down the acting as 'formal'. So Professor Harbage maintained that

> we are told *what* the actor did (in the estimation of the spectator), but not *how* he did it. Since the conventions of formal acting will be accepted as just while formal acting prevails, testimony like the above is nugatory.[8]

This argument satisfies the evidence if, on other grounds, the acting is known to have been 'formal'. But even if this is granted, the fact remains that an illusion of life was attempted; if our actors are more thorough in this respect, may they not be interpreting the plays in the new spirit in which they were written?)

Arguments for formal acting which are based on the plays themselves are difficult to answer directly without a detailed, chronological study. But one may notice, in general, that much of the evidence is taken from early plays, the famous Towton scene in *III, Henry VI* (II. v) being always to the fore. The formal, didactic arrangements of such scenes died out as the Morality plays, on which they seem to be

[6] F. Beaumont and J. Fletcher, *Comedies and Tragedies* (1647), Sig. f2v.
[7] Quoted from Sir E. K. Chambers, *The Elizabethan Stage* (1923), ii. 309.
[8] A. Harbage, 'Elizabethan Acting', *PMLA*, liv (1939), 692; the evidence he quotes includes the verses on Burbage quoted above.

based, disappeared also; it is not representative of the first decade of the seventeenth century. Direct address to the audience is another feature of Elizabethan plays which has been adduced in support of formal acting; such speeches have been thought to shatter 'all possibility of dramatic illusion.'[9] Here it is admitted that Shakespeare's plays do not provide any strikingly clear example, yet even if such were found it would not be an insurmountable obstacle to the simulation of real life on the stage. There was no gap between audience and stage in the Elizabethan theatre, so actors did not address the audience as if it were in another world. There was a reciprocal relationship; the audience could participate in the drama as easily as the actors could share a joke or enlist sympathy. The very fact that it is difficult to distinguish direct address from soliloquy, and soliloquy from true dialogue, shows that contact with the audience was quite unembarrassed. They shared a sturdy illusion of life.

The use of verse in Elizabethan drama has also been taken for a sign that acting was formal; for instance, it has been said of the sonnet embedded in the dialogue of *Romeo and Juliet* (I. v. 91ff.):

> Shakespeare's purpose can only be achieved if his audience is allowed to respond to the figures, the images, and the metrical pattern of these fourteen lines. There is no need to imitate dialogue realistically.[10]

But once more the development of new styles in writing and acting must be taken into account. When Jonson wrote *Timber*, the style of Marlowe already belonged to another age:

> The true artificer will not run away from nature, as he were afraid of her; or depart from life, and the likeness of truth; but speak to the capacity of his hearers. And though his language differ from the vulgar somewhat; it shall not fly from all humanity, with the *Tamerlanes*, and *Tamer-Chams* of the late age.[11]

Once the idea of development is accepted, the debatable question about

[9] S. L. Bethell, op. cit., p. 86.

[10] B. L. Joseph, *Elizabethan Acting* (1951), p. 129.

[11] *Works*, ed. C. H. Herford and P. and E. Simpson, viii (1947), 587. Jonson's editors date *Timber* between 1623 and 1635 (xi (1952), 213); but C. J. Sisson has shown that the work was probably composed as lecture notes while Jonson was acting as deputy for Henry Croke, the Professor of Rhetoric at Gresham College, in 1619 (*T.L.S.*, September 21, 1951).

Elizabethan acting ceases to be 'Was it formal or natural?'; it is rather, 'Which was the new, dominant style, the fashionable mode in which they would strive to produce even old plays or recalcitrant material?' I believe that the comparison between the style of Marlowe's age and that of Jonson's points in one direction only. It had become possible to speak the verse as if it were meant—as if, at that instant, it sprang from the mind of the speaker. Shakespeare's mature style has the best of two worlds: there is the eloquence, precision, structual strength and melody of verse, but there is also the immediacy and movement of actual speech. The dramatist has achieved the ideal which Puttenham sought in the courtly poet; he is now

> a dissembler only in the subtleties of his art; that is, when he is most artificial, so to disguise and cloak it as it may not appear, nor seem to proceed from him, by any study or trade of rules, but to be his natural.[12]

'Artificial' language must seem a 'natural' idiom. This new dialogue needed a new style of acting; as the verse became less obviously formal and declamatory, so did the acting. Both aimed at an illusion of 'natural' life.

★ ★ ★

One piece of external evidence has been generally accepted as an indication of formal acting. This is the Elizabethan comparison between the actor and the orator. The *locus classicus* is the Character of 'An Excellent Actor':

> Whatsoever is commendable in the grave orator, is most exquisitely perfect in him; for by a full and significant action of body, he charms our attention.[13]

A later statement is Richard Flecknoe's *A Short Discourse of the English Stage* (1664) which says that Richard Burbage

> had all the parts of an excellent orator (animating his words with speaking, and speech with action).[14]

[12] *The Art of English Poesie* (1589); G. Gregory Smith, *Elizabethan Critical Essays* (1904), ii. 186–7.

[13] Cf. A. Harbage, op. cit., pp. 701–2; B. L. Joseph, op. cit., *passim*; and S. L. Bethell, 'Shakespeare's Actors', op. cit., p. 202.

[14] Quoted from E. K. Chambers, op. cit., iv, p. 370. There has been some argument about the validity of this evidence; see A. Harbage, op. cit., p. 695 and S. L. Bethell, 'Shakespeare's Actors', op. cit., pp. 200–1.

The use of the word *action* to describe the bodily movements of both orator and actor shows how accepted was the comparison between the two kinds of artist.

From this evidence several deductions might be made: first, the actor used a declamatory voice as distinct from a conversational; secondly, he observed the phrasing, figures, and literary quality of his lines in the manner laid down for the orator; and thirdly, he used 'action' to enforce the meaning of his lines rather than to represent the emotion of a character or an involvement in business appropriate to the imagined situation. It has been suggested that John Bulwer's *Chirologia* and *Chironomia*, two books of manual signs for the use of orators, published in 1644 and written by a specialist in the teaching of the deaf, might represent the 'actions' used on the Elizabethan stage.[15] But the deductions can go further, and the actor is sometimes endowed with the intentions of the orator; it is thought that he excited the emotions of his audience rather than expressed those of the character he was representing. Under such conditions a play would be a number of speeches, rather than an image of actual life. It has even been suggested that, in Dr. Johnson's words, an Elizabethan went to the theatre in order to

> hear a certain number of lines recited with just gesture and elegant modulation.[16]

Obviously one cannot deny the comparison between actor and orator, but this does not imply that the comparison held at all points; both artists spoke before the audience and used gestures—and there the comparison might rest. Distinctions between the two were clearly recognized by Elizabethans. So Abraham Fraunce, speaking of the orator, says that gesture should change with the voice,

> yet not parasitically as stage players use, but gravely and decently as becometh men of greater calling.[17]

[15] So B. L. Joseph, op. cit. Even as an indication of an orator's art the books are, however, suspect, for Bulwer himself confesses that 'I never met with any rhetorician or other, that had pictured out one of these rhetorical expressions of the hands and fingers; or met with any philologer that could exactly satisfy me in the ancient rhetorical postures of *Quintilian*' (*Chironomia*, p. 26; quoted from Joseph, ibid., pp. 45–47).

[16] B. L. Joseph, op. cit., p. 141.

[17] *The Arcadian Rhetoric* (1588), Sig. I7^v.

The distinction may not be flattering to the actor but it is plain enough. Thomas Wright's *The Passions of the Mind* (1604) makes another distinction; here the orator is said to act 'really' to 'stir up all sorts of passions according to the exigency of the matter,' whereas the player acts 'fainedly' in the performance of a fiction 'only to delight' (p. 179).

Rhetoric was taught in Elizabethan schools and universities where 'pronunciation'—or delivery—received its due attention. Indeed, Heywood in his *Apology* shows that acting was used as a means of training the young orator. If the arts of acting and oratory were truly similar, here would be an excellent 'school' for actors; but clearly it was not: scholars learned a style of acting for oratory that was condemned on the public stage. So, in *II, The Return from Parnassus* (*c.* 1602), Kempe, the professional actor, criticises the scholar-players as those who

> never speak in their walk, but at the end of the stage, just as though in walking . . . we should never speak but at a style, a gate, or a ditch, where a man can go no further.
>
> (IV. iii.)

Kempe criticises them because they did not act as men do in real life. Richard Brome makes a similar distinction against scholar-players in *The Antipodes* (1640):

> Let me not see you act now,
> In your Scholastic way, you brought to town wi' ye,
> . . . I'll none of these absurdities in my house.
>
> (II. ii)

The gestures described in Bulwer's books for orators could be among the scholastic absurdities which Brome inveighs against. In Campion's *Book of Airs* (1601), criticism is precise:

> But there are some, who to appear the more deep and singular in their judgement, will admit no music but that which is long, intricate, bated with fuge, chain'd with syncopation, and where the nature of every word is precisely express'd in the note, like the old exploided action in comedies, when if they did pronounce *Memeni*, they would point to the hinder part of their heads, if *Video* put their finger in their eye.[18]

Here, rhetorical gestures are considered both scholastic ('deep and

[18] To the Reader; *Works*, ed. P. Vivian (1909).

singular') and old-fashioned; clearly Campion thought they were not in use in the up-to-date theatres of London.

Perhaps the distinction between actor and orator is most clearly stated in Flecknoe's praise of Burbage which has already been quoted:

> He had all the parts of an excellent orator . . ., yet even then, he was an excellent actor still, never falling in his Part when he had done speaking; but with his looks and gesture, maintaining it still unto the height . . .

Flecknoe says, in effect, that though Burbage had the graces of an orator, *yet even then he was an excellent actor*—in spite of some likeness of his art to oratory.

Earlier in the same passage, Flecknoe had claimed that Burbage

> was a delightful Proteus, so wholly transforming himself into his part, and putting off himself with his clothes, as he never (not so much as in the tyring-house) assum'd himself again until the play was done.

Such absorption in a role has nothing to do with oratory; it is closer to the acting techniques of Stanislavski. The actor obliterated his whole consciousness and outward bearing in those of his part, and did not merely declaim his lines with formal effectiveness. The Prologue to *Antonio and Mellida* (first performed in 1599) gives a similar impression where actors are shown preparing for their parts and speaking extempore in the appropriate 'veins'. An incidental image in *Coriolanus* implies the same technique:

> You have put me now to such a part which never
> I shall discharge to th' life
>
> (III. ii. 105–6)

In the event, Coriolanus was unable to do as Burbage did and wholly transform himself into his assumed character.

* * *

There are many extant descriptions of Elizabethan acting but the value of this evidence is commonly belittled because it is written in the same technical language as the criticism of rhetoric and oratory. So Hamlet's advice to the players is dismissed as 'a cliché from classical criticism, equally applicable to all the arts.'[19] Or again, it is claimed that

[19] A. Harbage, op. cit., p. 690.

> the poet has put into the mouth of his Prince nothing that conflicts with the directions normally provided by the teachers of rhetorical delivery.[20]

But the fact that the same language was used to describe acting and oratory does not mean that those arts were identical. The language of criticism was in its infancy and it was perhaps inevitable that acting should be dependent on the technical vocabulary of a more systematic art.

Descriptions of acting use many words and phrases from the criticism of oratory, but the new context may give new pertinency. The phrase *imitation of life* is an example. It is basic to the concept of poetry as an art of imitation, a concept which was not generally understood by Elizabethans—except for Sir Philip Sidney—as referring to the poet's revelation of ideal and universal truth. The usual interpretation is seen in Sir Thomas Elyot's description of comedy as 'a picture or as it were a mirror of man's life'[21] or in Ascham's idea that drama was a 'perfect *imitation*, or fair lively painted picture of the life of every degree of man.'[22] The phrase is constantly repeated; Lodge, Jonson, and Heywood all claimed on Cicero's authority that Comedy was '*imitatio vitae, speculum consuetudinis, et imago veritatis*'.[23]

The idea of drama as a picture of life suggests a parallel in criticism of the art of painting, and here the meaning of imitation is much clearer. For instance it is implicit throughout the description of the pictures offered to Christopher Sly in the Induction of *The Taming of the Shrew*:

> —Dost thou love pictures? we will fetch thee straight
> Adonis painted by a running brook,
> And Cytherea all in sedges hid,
> Which seem to move and wanton with her breath
> Even as the waving sedges play wi' th' wind.
> —We'll show thee Io as she was a maid
> And how she was beguiled and surpris'd,
> As lively painted as the deed was done.

[20] B. L. Joseph, op. cit., p. 146.

[21] *The Governor* (1531); ed. H. H. S. Croft (1880), i. 124.

[22] *The Schoolmaster* (1570); *English Works*, ed. W. A. Wright (1904), p. 266.

[23] *A Defence of Poetry* (1579); ed. G. Gregory Smith, *Elizabethan Critical Essays* (1904), i. 81; *Every Man Out of His Humour* (1600), III. vi. 206–7; and *An Apology for Actors* (1612), Sig. F1v.

—Or Daphne roaming through a thorny wood,
Scratching her legs, that one shall swear she bleeds
And at that sight shall sad Apollo weep,
So workmanly the blood and tears are drawn.

(ii. 47–58)

'As lively painted as the deed was done' is the key to this description, and 'life-likeness' or the 'imitation of life' were constantly used in the criticism of the visual arts. So in *The Merchant of Venice*, Bassanio exclaims when he finds Portia's picture in the leaden casket, 'What demi-god Hath come so near creation?' (III. ii. 115–16), or Paulina in *The Winter's Tale*, claims that her 'statue' can show life 'Lively mock'd' (V. iii. 19). For an example outside Shakespeare, we may take Thomas Nashe's description of the floor of an Italian summer house; it was

> painted with the beautifullest flowers that ever man's eye admired; which so lineally were delineated that he that view'd them afar off, and had not directly stood poringly over them, would have sworn they had lived indeed.[24]

Imitation of life was not the whole concern of renaissance artists, but their experiments in perspective and light were at first designed to deceive the external eye; their paintings were meant to look like real life.

When the phrase is used of acting, of performing in the 'picture' that was the drama, it seems to carry the same implications of deception and appearance of reality. So Webster praises the Queen's Men at the Red Bull for their acting in *The White Devil* (1612 or 1613):

> For the action of the play, 'twas generally well, and I dare affirm, with the joint testimony of some of their own quality, (for the true imitation of life, without striving to make nature a monster) the best that ever became them.

So also, an imitation of life is praised in *The Second Maiden's Tragedy* performed in 1611:

Thou shalt see my lady
Play her part naturally, more to the life
Then she's aware on.[25]

[24] *The Unfortunate Traveller* (1594); *Works*, ed. R. B. McKerrow, ii (1904), 283.

[25] Malone Society Reprint (1909), ll. 2015–17.

Shakespeare implies the same standards in *The Two Gentlemen of Verona*:

> For I did play a lamentable part: . . .
> Which I so lively acted with my tears
> That my poor mistress, moved therewithal,
> Wept bitterly.
>
> (IV. iv. 162–7)

The idea of a play as a 'lively' picture may be seen in Rowley's verses on *The Duchess of Malfi* (1623):

> I never saw thy Duchess, till the day
> That she was lively bodied in thy play.

Most importantly the 'imitation of life' is implicit in Hamlet's advice to the players; he says that the end of playing is:

> to hold, as 'twere, the mirror up to nature; to show virtue her own feature, scorn her own image, and the very age and body of the time his form and pressure.
>
> (III. ii. 20–24)

When he criticises actors who strut and bellow, he invokes the same standard:

> I have thought some of Nature's journeymen had made men, and had not made them well, they imitated humanity so abominably.
>
> (ll. 31–34)

Hamlet applies the same criterion to acting as Bassanio did to Portia's picture—how near is it to creation?

The concept of acting as an imitation of life agrees with the other evidence I have quoted, and suggests that Elizabethan actors aimed at an illusion of real life. It does not explain *all* in the best renaissance painting or the best Elizabethan acting, but it has an important place in the artists' intentions. To describe the resultant art as formal is to deny this intention; *natural* seems a more appropriate word.

* * *

There is probably some reluctance among scholars to admit that naturalism was a keynote of Elizabethan acting. Some critics would obviously wish the plays to be acted in a formal manner. For instance it is said that a person in a play may be

> first a symbol, second a human being; . . . [and the play itself can be] primarily an argument or parable, only secondarily forced, as it best may, to assume some correspondence with the forms and events of human affairs.[26]

This is an extreme case, but there are other hints of a fear that naturalism would make Shakespeare's plays smaller, that they would lose the meaning and richness that has been found in the study. Formal acting, on the other hand, seems to offer a declamation through which technical accomplishment could be appreciated and the argument or pattern of the drama, together with its literary finesse, could stand revealed. But there is more than one kind of naturalism; there is one for the plays set in a drawing-room, and another for plays dealing with kings and soldiers, inspired prophets and accomplished courtiers. A naturalism that was true to the poetic qualities of Shakespeare's text would not disguise the high themes of tragedy or the idealism of comedy, or the subtleties of versification.

I have said that Elizabethan dramatists and actors imitated life, but this does not mean that they tried to make their plays exactly the same as real life; they did not labour, in Marston's words, to 'relate any thing as an historian but to enlarge every thing as a poet.'[27] Their plays were more exciting and colourful, more full of meaning, than real life; indeed compared with them, 'Nature never set forth . . . so rich [a] tapestry.'[28] The important fact is that the audience was encouraged to take all this as real while the performance was in progress. Within the charmed circle of the theatre, a new world might be accepted and what they saw personated could seem to be truly done before them.

George Chapman once wrote a preface to a play which had never been performed, in which he tried to analyse what his writing had lost by this misfortune. Unlike some critics, he believed that

> scenical representation is so far from giving just cause of any least

[26] Written of *Timon of Athens*; G. Wilson Knight, *The Wheel of Fire* (1930), p. 274.

[27] 'To the General Reader,' *Sophonisba* (1606); *Plays*, ed. H. H. Wood (1938), ii. 5.

[28] P. Sidney, *The Defence of Poesie* (1595); *Works*, ed. A. Feuillerat (1923), iii. 8.

> diminution, that the personal and exact life it gives to any history, or other such delineation of human actions, adds to them lustre, spirit, and apprehension.[29]

A 'personal and exact life' was what Chapman expected the actors to give to his play, and these words may serve to describe the naturalism which I believe to be the new power of Elizabethan acting. If actors in today's theatre wish to present Shakespeare's plays in the spirit in which they were written, they should respect and enjoy the magniloquence and music of the language, enter into the greatness of conception, and play all the time for an illusion of real life. They must constantly expect a miracle—that the verse shall be enfranchised as the natural idiom of human beings and that all of Shakespeare's strange creation shall become real and 'lively' on the stage. Because the Elizabethan actor was capable of this, Shakespeare, like others of his contemporaries, dared to 'repose eternity in the mouth of a player.'[30]

* * *

Several chapters that follow will be concerned, by the way, with the relative importance of the formal (or consciously artificial) elements of acting and the naturalistic as called forth by the text of Shakespeare's plays. But some further characteristics of Elizabethan actors should also be noted here as indications of the kind of presentation that is appropriate.

First, the plays were written to be boldly visual. Traces of an earlier iconographic acting and stage-management are found in Shakespeare's time. For example, in *Richard the Third*, III. ii, when Hastings is about to go to London for the last time and so walk into the trap that Gloucester has laid for him, two characters, newly introduced into the play, appear: a pursuivant and a priest, representing the affairs of the world and the affairs of heaven. They are barely identified in words because their costumes and their general bearing represent their natures; they are meaningful as soon as they are *seen*. In the same tradition are the stage-directions at the end of the 1616 version of Marlowe's *Faustus*:

[29] Dedication, *Caesar and Pompey* (1631); *Tragedies*, ed. T. M. Parrott (1910), p. 341.

[30] Thomas Nashe, Preface to Robert Greene, *Menaphon* (1589); *Works*, ed. R. B. McKerrow (1905), iii. 312.

Enter the Good Angel and the Bad Angel at several doors. . . . Music while the throne descends. . . . Hell is discovered.

Such iconographic staging was linked with new naturalism so that the stage-picture had a similar double standard as the actors' performances. On the one hand, the canopy over the open-air stage of the public theatres remained painted like a sky with stars, a 'heaven' over the stage. Ceremonies, feasts, processions and scenes of state continued to give a general meaning to the stage-action. In Henslowe's 'diary', which accounts for the back-stage efforts of several of the more popular companies at the turn of the century, lists of scenic properties include: a rock, a tomb, a Hell-mouth, the city of Rome, 'the cloth of the sun and moon', 'iii Imperial crowns; i plain crown.'[31] On the other hand, there was a pursuit of verisimilitude, such as the stage-direction in Heywood's *A Woman Killed with Kindness* (1603), mounted for one of Henslowe's companies:

Enter 3 *or* 4 *Servingmen, one with a voider and a wooden knife to take away all, another the salt and bread, another the tablecloth and napkins, another the carpet.* Jenkin *with two lights after them.*

(Scene viii)

or the scene in *Much Ado* (II. iv) in which the young ladies of Leonato's household prepare the bride for church, sending necessary messages and exchanging fashion-talk.

The most exact realism was, it is important to note, in the dress of the actors. One foreign visitor, Richard Platter, reported that, when noble lords died, their clothes were given to the servants who then sold them to actors for theatrical costumes. Certainly Henslowe's accounts show that his companies had a vast stock of costumes made of expensive 'real' material, including lace of gold, silver and copper. For Mrs. Frankford in *A Woman Killed* he bought a special black velour dress for £6 3*s*.; a single ceremonial robe cost him £19. Typical entries in the Diary are:

Lent unto Thomas dowton the 31 of Janewary 1598 to bye tafetie for ii womones gownes for the ii angrey wemen of abengton [a play by H. Porter] the some of . . . ix^{li}

Layd owt for the company the 1 of febreyare 1598 to bye A blacke velluet gercken layed thicke wth black sylke lace & A payer of

[31] *Henslowe's Diary*, ed. R. A. Foakes and R. T. Rickert (1961), pp. 319–20.

> Rownd hosse of paynes of sylke layd wth sylver lace & caneyanes of clothe of sylver at the Requeste of Robart shawe the some of . . . iiii[li] x[s]

According to one calculation Henslowe's costumes cost more money than the theatres in which they were used and stored. Such expense would be justified in his competitive world only if the maintenance of high fashion and verisimilitude were considered necessary for the actors' performances.

* * *

Shakespeare's own company of actors, first known as the Chamberlain's Men and then, on the accession of James I, as the King's Men, differed in one respect from their rivals: they proved to be a more permanent organisation. They stayed together for fifty years, until the closing of the theatres for the civil war. A large number of old and new plays appeared in their repertory: in the spring of 1613, for instance, they were responsible for the 'fourteen several plays' that were performed at Court in celebration of a royal marriage. Such experience meant that the actors would have to play 'together', and 'to each other'. Early quick-moving and ingenious comedies, like *The Taming of the Shrew* and *Comedy of Errors* obviously depend on team-work for properly sharp performance. And some tragedies, especially *Romeo and Juliet*, *King Lear* and *Coriolanus*, have concluding scenes where dramatic interest is carried as much by the characters encircling the stage as by the protagonists. More than this, many moments in every play that Shakespeare wrote repay subtle timing and interplay between characters: Orsino's silent involvement with the boy Cesario; Ophelia's taut reactions to Hamlet's passionate denunciations which indicate feelings that she does not express fully until after he has left the stage; the shifting extremes of belief and disbelief as Benedick and Beatrice learn to trust each other's hidden love. The original company of actors, knowing each other's methods—tricks of pitch, timing and tempo—may well have encouraged the writing of such corporate scenes.

The King's Men also had their undoubted 'stars', actors who drew all attention to themselves. According to Richard Flecknoe, Richard Burbage, the leading actor in Shakespeare's company, had the reputation of never leaving the stage without a round of applause—a skill that today is more common in Opera Houses than in Shakespearian theatres. The Duke of York in *Richard II* testifies that:

in a theatre, the eyes of men,
After a well-grac'd actor leaves the stage
Are idly bent on him that enters next,
Thinking his prattle to be tedious.

(V. ii. 23–26)

Burbage, Lowin, Tarlton and Kempe were widely known and had their equivalents of fans: as Hamlet welcomes his 'old friend' among the 'Tragedians of the City', so Richard Burbage was the 'old acquaintance' of the Earl of Pembroke. One dramatist likened the hero of his tragedy, *Barnavelt*, to a leading player:

> with such murmers as glad spectators in a theatre grace their best actors with, they ever heard him, when to have had a sight of him, was held a prosperous omen; when no eye gazed on him that was not filled with admiration.

(ll. 2475–82)

Clearly the major roles of Elizabethan drama supported performances that held attention by exploiting a mixture of virtuoso skills, physical attractiveness and individual personality.

* * *

In one respect the Elizabethan actors will continue to baffle our understanding: their use of boy-actors for female roles. The main obstacle here is that the conditions in which they worked can never be reproduced: the absence of actresses for comparison; the rhetorical training in schools; a system of apprenticeship to senior actors; continual work in one company for as long as eight years, graduating slowly to the heroines.

But trying to judge their performances, we should remember that contemporary accounts make no concessions—Cleopatra's jibe at the 'squeaking' boy is a special case, and remarkable as such. The evidence suggests that the boys, like their elders, aimed at an 'imitation of life'. The puritan critics of the theatre complained of their 'lewd' gestures as positive incitements to lust. In Jonson's *The Devil is an Ass* (1616), the story is told of the boy-actor, Dick Robinson, masquerading in real life as a lawyer's wife and getting away with the impersonation:

to see him behave it;
And lay the law; and carve; and drink unto 'em;
And then talk bawdy: and send frolics! O!

(II. iii)

The boys were helped, of course, by the dramatist, and in this Shakespeare was particularly careful. Many small roles, like Phoebe or Audrey in *As You Like It*, or Octavia in *Antony and Cleopatra*, derive much of their effect from stylistic contrast with the rest of the play. Even more obviously demanding roles, like Ophelia, are often given few appearances, and some of those with secondary characters or for a solo-like scene that could be intensively rehearsed on its own; Ophelia is alone with Hamlet only once, and the same is true of Gertrude. A Rosalind has to sustain long scenes, but her speeches are so witty and energetic that the audience has little leisure for idle inquisition. When, near the close, she has to show 'strange powers' Shakespeare allowed her to be self-consciously theatrical and contrived an echoing and contrasting chorus on stage. For her reappearance in female clothes he brought on three other couples so that her happiness with Orlando is supported and defined by that of others, and seen as part of a full stage-picture.

But Shakespeare used more than expert tact: he accepted the limitations of boy-actors without confining his imagination. This is shown (and its importance proved) by the many generations of actresses who have inherited the boys' roles; they may cut or underplay some of the verbal wit and refuse some of the 'formal' restrictions, but still there has been more than sufficient material in the text of the plays to awaken their full talents. These roles, like others, can sustain formalism *and* naturalism; they can be part of an ensemble effect *and* support all the star-like attractions of talented and unique performers.

* * *

Bernard Beckerman has recently tried to define by one word the style of the Elizabethans and of other actors who wish to respond fully to Shakespeare's text. Having quoted Hamlet's description of the player who

> in a dream of passion,
> Could force his soul so to his own conceit
> That from her working all his vasage wann'd;
> Tears in his eyes, distraction in's aspect,
> A broken voice, and his whole function suiting
> With forms to his conceit . . .,
>
> (II. ii. 545–50)

he suggests that the mixture of 'ceremonious acting' and 'overwhelming passion intensively portrayed' should be called 'romantic acting'.[32] But this phrase, perhaps, does not sufficiently represent the formal or representative elements, nor the ensemble effects and realistically observed details of business. I would suggest 'heroic naturalism'; that catches the opposed inspirations, but it does not sufficiently suggest the undoubted 'star' element. Too small a definitive phrase will be bound to fall short; in Shakespeare's day the actor's art had diverse influences and high achievement so that a compounded definition may be necessary. Let 'epic' stand for the ensemble and socially realistic elements, and 'romantic' for the passionate, imaginative and individual; then, perhaps, the phrase 'Epic-natural-romantic-virtuoso-formal' may be adequate.

[32] *Shakespeare at the Globe* (1962), p. 156.

III

Gestures and Business

★

THE end of Macbeth's role, as a reference to Irving has already shown, is not a speech but a wordless combat that in performance can express the last temper of the hero, his hopeless courage, pride and pain. The fight will need more time than any of his speeches in this Act and will hold the audience with its obvious excitement and danger: the tragedy is sustained at last by a piece of silent stage-business.

At the end of *Antony and Cleopatra* there are many words, but here physical enactment is a continual accompaniment, modifying and extending the verbal impression given to the audience. First the heroine is clothed in royal robe and a crown placed on her head, so that by her actions she can be seen preparing for what she calls the 'noble act' of suicide. The text suggests that the robing is effected too slowly for Cleopatra and so the glowing impression of her words mingles with physical haste and, perhaps, fumbling. She must wait for the business to be completed, until 'So, have you done?' (V. ii. 288) and then she kisses Charmian and Iras. This new business will again take some time to effect, for Cleopatra speaks specifically of a 'long farewell'. In performance both Queen and maids will share some moments of silence. Then, with no warning, Iras '*falls and dies*': this surprise movement at one and the same time alerts the audience, shows Cleopatra's composure, and suggests that her actions and words are all part of a process beyond her complete control. The thought of Antony kissing Iras reawakens Cleopatra's preparations so that now she reaches for an asp and places it at her own breast; and again she must wait, held physically still, as she calls upon the 'poor venomous fool' to 'be angry and dispatch'. Only when she feels it bite does she cry, 'Peace, peace!' For a moment she may be still again in her royal robes, but the pose is broken with another gesture as she takes another asp. She quickly completes this and begins to speak again. 'What should I stay . . .'; but then, quite suddenly, she is dead. There must be some compulsive movement at this point, for her crown is jerked 'awry'. When she is again quite still Charmian reaches up to rearrange the crown and so marks unmistakeably that Cleopatra is now like a stage-property which must be 'put right'.

For all the splendour and passion of her words, Cleopatra is presented in the final scene partly by her pose, her gestures and stage-business, and those of her attendants: these add haste, impatience, lack of full control; they accentuate the dressing-up for a royal 'act', extend the moment of shared affection between the Queen and her attendants, and express (as words do not) the pain of death; they also ensure that the audience realises quickly, before Caesar's entry, that the Queen has become a corpse.

★ ★ ★

Had Shakespeare been content to communicate by words, the actors speaking of them and his movements in sympathy with them, he would have cut off one of two hands. He would have lost the wholly physical language which is the chief means of expression in primitive theatres and has been at the service of dramatists every time an actor steps on to a stage; he would have ignored traditions of visual excitement that, as we have seen, were strong in the Elizabethan theatre. His means of expression would have lost something of its power, for physical movement is a language to which an audience responds before it can be aware of doing so, the rapid and almost unresistable communication of colour, visual form and contrast, sexual attraction or repulsion; its rhythm and changes of tempo link easily with the musical elements of verbal performance. Moreover gesture and movement form an instinctive language and is therefore capable of showing many of the psychological, physical or sociological realities that lie behind, and not infrequently enrich or deny, the more conscious interchanges of speech. Without this kind of communication Shakespeare could have named his imaginative vision but not given it tangible habitation, outline the form of what he saw in the world around and within him, but not transmitted its pressures.

In short, if we are to understand Shakespeare's plays in performance we must proceed through the text and through the physical performance that is sustained and controlled by the words, towards movement, gestures and business which can become independent of the text, limiting, denying or extending the more textual effects.

Of course it is not possible to refer to any one stage production to learn about this physical language, for plays are often distorted by irrelevant and trivial stage-business. We must look, first, for the gestures and business that can be definitely implied from the text, like Macbeth's last fight or the stage management of Cleopatra's death. This will not supply all the necessary business (as we shall see), but enough to render this the best start.

Some help will come readily from stage-directions. When Coriolanus has stood listening to Volumnia's plea for Rome and watches her kneel and rise, there is an unusually precise direction: '*He holds her by the hand, silent.*' The text of this play was probably first printed from a manuscript prepared by Shakespeare himself,[1] but even without this reassurance we may believe that the gesture is intended to show that the hero's change of mind is instinctive rather than considered and, hence, verbalised. Earlier he had risen from his seat and had remained silent while Volumnia appealed to him, so these larger physical reactions have prepared the audience's attention for the small, but deeply significant, hand movement. Or in the last Act of *Much Ado*, when a stage-direction insists that four ladies are brought forward masked, it is clear that the drama depends momentarily on stage-business. This provides a repetition of the masking for dances in Act II, the origin of many of the complications of the plot, and so the audience is suddenly faced at the end of the comedy with a visual reminder that a new succession of mistakes could take place. Words could scarcely make the point lightly enough by themselves; but, with identical visors disguising individual identities, Claudius's 'Which is the lady I must seize upon?' and Benedick's 'Which is Beatrice?' once more accentuate the importance and hazards of a choice in love; for all Benedick's new assurance he is at the ladies' mercy.

Entrances are often immediately significant in a visual way. So, for example, Granville-Barker testified that when he thought he 'knew *King Lear* well enough' through study of the text he still had not realised the effect, all words apart, that he discovered in rehearsal, when an entry very slowly brought about the meeting of 'blind Gloucester and mad Lear'.[2] Coriolanus entering in IV. iv, after being banished from Rome, is directed to appear '*in mean apparel, disguis'd and muffled*'; this is a startling change from patrician's clothes that registers at once a humiliation and shame that he had not foreseen in Rome and which

[1] Cf. W. W. Greg, *The Shakespeare First Folio* (1955), pp. 404–7.

[2] *Prefaces to Shakespeare*, 1st ser. (1927), p. xix, note.

his words in the ensuing soliloquy do not directly express. Costume again helps to make Mercade's entrance in the last scene of *Love's Labour's Lost* dramatically effective. He is dressed in black and probably moves slowly as a bearer of ill-tidings; this is in such contrast to the comic bustle already filling the stage that his entry draws immediate attention and will give to his first, simple-seeming words, 'God save you, madam!', the widest possible relevance; for a moment, before the announcement of the death of the Princess's father, the characters confront a general, intuitive fear.

'*Exeunt*' is also an important moment for business. When the tribunes stay behind after crowded scenes in *Coriolanus*, their action in drawing together in secrecy, which is emphasised by repetition, speaks visually for their mutual dependance, a motivation which in time of triumph they do not utter and may not recognise. So Shakespeare has given a sense of personal danger to the early proceedings of the tribunes and prepared the audience for their sudden collapse. In *Julius Caesar*, after the assassination in III. i, all except the conspirators flee from stage—with the further exception of Publius. Brutus directs the audience's attention to this aged and hitherto insignificant senator: suddenly he will be noticed, standing silent amid the uproar, 'quite confounded with this mutiny'. Brutus tries to reassure him and Cassius urges him to leave, but there is no verbal reply: Shakespeare has used the helpless horror-struck presence of Publius, accentuated by his absolute silence, to give a sharp contrast to the general noise and movement. Before he leaves the stage he has shown the fear in the storm, the paralysis of mind and body that the conspirators have brought about and which they will in part share at the end of the drama.

Silence is often used by Shakespeare to accentuate a reaction that can only be expressed physically. When Macduff hears that Macbeth has had his wife and children murdered, there is dialogue to support and identify the central dramatic fact of his silent gesture; it is Malcolm who speaks:

> What, man! Ne'er pull your hat upon your brows;
> Give sorrow words. The grief that does not speak
> Whispers the o'erfraught heart and bids it break.
>
> (IV. iii. 208–10)

Joy also is expressed by an inarticulate response, identified in the comments of bystanders, as Leontes and Hermione are reunited at the end of *The Winter's Tale*: 'She embraces him. . . . She hangs about his neck' (V. iii. 112–13). Again the central fact is the silent and, on this occasion, mutual gesture. Sometimes no verbal description is provided: what, for example, should be the bearing of Volumnia, after Rome has been saved by the sacrifice of her son and she enters, with Valeria and Virginia, to be welcomed by the united cheers of senators and plebeians? She is acclaimed as the 'patroness, the life of Rome!' but she does not speak a single word in her passage across the large stage (V. v). Certainly all eyes will be fixed upon her, and the performer of the role has a large opportunity to express anger, suffering, helplessness, stoic pride—whatever seems appropriate after the earlier events.

* * *

Shakespeare's reliance on silent physical reaction in this context is one measure of the trust he placed in gesture and stage-business. It also shows how much he left to the actor, for the passion given predominance here can sway the balance and meaning of the whole tragedy. And, on reflection such responsible choices are everywhere facing actors and directors in his plays: as gesture and business are important, so they crucially affect the total impression of a play.

For an example, how should Prince Hal answer in the charade episode of *Henry IV, Part I*, when he is pretending to be his father and Falstaff has been speaking in Hal's person in defence of himself?

> No, my good Lord: banish Peto, banish Bardolph, banish Poins; but, for sweet Jack Falstaff, kind Jack Falstaff, true Jack Falstaff, valiant Jack Falstaff—and therefore more valiant, being, as he is, old Jack Falstaff—banish not him thy Harry's company, banish not him thy Harry's company. Banish plump Jack, and banish all the world.
>
> (II. iv. 457ff.)

How should the answer be given: 'I do, I will?' In the 1964 Stratford-upon-Avon production, the second half of the short speech came after a moment's silence which was a 'gesture' of deliberation. The same year in a production by Joan Littlewood at the Edinburgh Festival, all four monosyllables were spoken rapidly, as Hal hastily dismounted from his improvised throne because of the knocking at the door; here, in the mounting urgency before the Sheriff enters, it was Hal's later words that gained by deliberation: 'thou art a natural coward' to Falstaff, and of himself, 'Now, my masters, for a true face and good conscience.' Which of these pieces of stage-business were correct? Should Hal dismount quickly or slowly? It has been remarked that the knocking on the door *following* 'I do, I will' (as at Stratford but not at Edinburgh) is intended to break the perplexed silence caused by Hal's speech; but the knocking was first marked in the text by the editor, Capell; neither the Quarto, printed from foul papers, nor the edited Folio version has any sign of it. As far as the original texts go Bardolph might enter without warning and interrupt Hal in the middle of a sentence. Or another completely opposite interpretation is possible: perhaps 'I *do*' should be said firmly and deliberately, *after* the 'gesture' of a direct look at Falstaff—that is, 'at this moment I most certainly do' —and then lightly, with quick movement and laughter, 'I will'—that is 'no; not yet'. (Hal certainly seems in high spirits when he next speaks: 'Heigh, heigh! the devil rides upon a fiddle-stick'.)

The main points here are that this text needs interpretation—these four monosyllables do not sufficiently control performance—that some kind of stage-business is demanded by the interruption of the charade wherever it should come, and that the stage-business and verbal interpretation together significantly alter the dramatic fact. And so in earlier examples: how much pain should be indicated when the asp bites Cleopatra, and how violently should she die? How long should Macbeth continue the fight, and how easily should he be vanquished?

There is no escape from this dilemma. Some scholars have argued that Shakespeare's plays should be performed with the minimum of business; but the text often invites unspecified gestures and movement, and we know that in Shakespeare's own day these were important elements of performance. He had inherited a visually expressive theatre and his actors were famed for their 'action'. It was reported that when a company travelled in Germany, the people not 'understanding a word they said, both men and women, flocked wonderfully to see their gesture and action'.[3] When *Othello* was performed at Oxford in 1610, a member of the audience noted that:

> Desdemona, killed by her husband, in her death moved us especially, when, as she lay in her bed, her face only implored the pity of the audience.[4]

[3] F. Moryson, *Shakespeare's Europe*, ed. C. Hughes (1903), p. 304.

[4] Cf. G. Tillotson, '*Othello* and *The Alchemist* at Oxford', *T.L.S.*, 20 July 1933.

In the text Shakespeare seems to acknowledge the power of this purely visual spectacle:

> *Look* on the tragic loading of this bed.
> This is thy work.—The *object* poisons sight . . .
>
> (V. ii. 366–7)

* * *

Acknowledging Shakespeare's occasional demand for silent physical presentation and the momentary power of gesture and business to extend or modify the verbally sustained performance, we must ask how much depends on all this. I have chosen numerous examples from *Coriolanus* to suggest a continued influence in a single play, and chapters VI and VII, by following single roles throughout their plays will show its influence on character presentation. Here I shall try to show, from *Hamlet*, that physical confrontations, a silent exeunt and a few simple gestures can work with a more verbal drama to illuminate the interplay of character and, perhaps, the presentation of story and theme.

The Closet Scene (III. iv), in which Gertrude acknowledges that Hamlet has 'cleft my heart in twain' and he gains new impetus that will alter his behaviour to the King and take him to England and back again, is generally acknowledged to be central in the tragedy. It is the most sustained and intense scene, and is an immediate contrast with the spectacle and movement of the Play Scene and Hamlet's abortive resolution to kill the King. The Ghost appears for the last time just before its climax and subsequently Hamlet appears for only three short scenes before being absent for more than five hundred lines. Its events lead directly to the catastrophe, for Claudius now takes more open measures against Hamlet and the death of Polonius provides him with a fit instrument in Laertes. But if so much is generally agreed, its sequel may be puzzling if judged by words alone. In the next two Acts Hamlet hardly speaks to his mother, the only direct duologue being in the last scene in which he says simply:

> Good madam! . . .
> I dare not drink yet, madam; by and by. . . .
> How does the Queen? . . .
> Wretched queen, adieu!

The passions of the Closet Scene, its central position and sustained and intimate excitement appear to have little consequence in the presentation of Hamlet's character, and no resolution fittingly held for the conclusion of the play.

But this is to judge by the spoken words alone. In performance, the tragedy often seems eloquently shaped: where words would have been impracticable or inadequate Shakespeare has used a physical language and the form and pressure of his tragedy unobtrusively depend upon it.

Hamlet and Gertrude meet again at Ophelia's grave. He is calm and dignified—'This is I, Hamlet the Dane'—but soon he is grappling, hand-to-hand, with Laertes. A direction in the Folio text says that he leaps into the grave; certainly Laertes cries 'The devil take thy soul' and Hamlet's response seems to grow in emotion and strength. Attempts are made to part them and, significantly, Horatio's words suggest that Hamlet is quite as incensed as Laertes:

> KING. Pluck them asunder.
> QUEEN. Hamlet! Hamlet!
> ALL. Gentlemen!—
> HORATIO. Good my lord, be quiet.

As they are forcibly restrained, Hamlet reaches a crest of verbal excitement, at least:

> Why, I will fight with him upon this theme
> Until my eyelids will no longer wag.

Then Gertrude speaks, 'O my son, what theme?' Her words are simple but momentarily they transform Hamlet so that he speaks with equal simplicity: 'I lov'd Ophelia'. The transition of mood and tone is astonishing and the audible cause of it is his mother's bare question. It could easily be unconvincing in performance, but we should also notice that Gertrude's verse-line remains incomplete, involving a break of metrical pattern and almost certainly a pause before or after: surely Hamlet must have faced his mother and in the silence responded to her physical presence. By even a slight hesitation in the course of his violent activity the audience will be encouraged to look closer and become aware of a mutual 'gesture' between the two characters, and by that means recognise an unspoken and perhaps unconscious communication.

Turning to Laertes, the apparent cause of his passion, Hamlet again speaks wildly, and the Queen, as if she does not realise the source of her earlier power, ineffectually orders the attendants to 'forbear him'. He drives the scene forward to its verbal climax:

And, if thou prate of mountains, let them throw
Millions of acres on us, till our ground,
Singeing his pate against the burning zone,
Make Ossa like a wart! Nay, and thou'lt mouth,
I'll rant as well as thou.

Then Gertrude again stills the storm and, partly by the bare-faced but effective device of repetition, the audience is drawn again to recognise the power of her physical presence over Hamlet. She speaks first to others:

This is mere madness;
And thus awhile the fit will work on him; . . .

So she fulfils Hamlet's last request in the Closet Scene by affirming that he is 'essentially in madness', not 'mad in craft', and by this act of loyalty she gains attention and holds it. Gentle words now control Hamlet so that he probably turns towards her—at least he must be still in order to listen; and by choosing a female image Gertrude seems to tell him that she herself is now true as the dove:

Anon, as patient as the female dove
When that her golden couplets are disclos'd,
His silence will sit drooping.

The text requires a quiet, low pitch and lengthened, softer rhythms, and these will best be contrived if mother and son have again confronted each other, communicating on the deepest levels of their natures. Hamlet says nothing to Gertrude, but as he turns back to face Laertes he is transformed in utterance and, therefore, bearing:

Hear you, sir:
What is the reason that you use me thus?
I loved you ever. . . .

Gertrude has nothing more to say; Hamlet has answered by his attention to her words and can speak now without passion.

The fuller issues of the situation are not forgotten, but mastered: he reasserts his full responsibility by the ironic and perhaps feignedly distracted:

But it is no matter.
Let Hercules himself do what he may,
The cat will mew, and dog will have his day.

He leaves the stage at once and in six brisk lines the King concludes the scene; the crowded stage empties silently, although Horatio, Laertes and Gertrude are each individually addressed. The mute *exeunt*, like a wave receding after breaking on the shore, gives an impression of power expended and of danger postponed by some force that has not been acknowledged verbally. Gertrude's exit, in tempo and bearing, should be contrasted with the movement of others for they have not borne the emotional centre of the scene: and here again the audience is prompted to observe the expression of feelings which are out of reach of words, of which not even Hamlet has spoken.

In the tragedy's last scene Gertrude's presence and actions are again more eloquent than her words: what she says merely directs and underlines her gestures. She crosses from her throne by the side of Claudius towards her son, gives her napkin to him and drinks to his fortune. With 'Come let me wipe thy face' she finds an intimate gesture by which she can treat him tenderly as if he were still a child, and she wholly his mother. After the narrow excitement of the duel (itself a gesture of new resolve and, later, of passion), Hamlet's first words show concern for Gertrude, and hers are an indictment of Claudius' treachery. Their verbal exchange is very brief but it must involve another confrontation, and it is from this deeply realised moment that the widest issues of the tragedy spring to life: Hamlet assumes authority and then, in passion and haste, he kills the King and ends his own part in a kind of peace.

In *Hamlet* words are spoken almost incessantly and they suggest worlds of interest. But they are not all the play; at least one strand of the story depends for its most deeply charged moments upon physical action and silent, or almost silent, confrontations.

IV
Subtext

★

ALREADY, in the presentation of Hamlet, Gertrude, Coriolanus, Volumnia, Cleopatra and Prince Hal, we have seen that Shakespeare could give dramatic expression to reactions, conscious and subconscious, that lie beneath the words that are spoken, that qualify what the text explicitly says. Despite the rhetoric, music and excitement of his words, this subtextual communication is an almost constant element of his stagecraft and one that imaginative actors delight to exploit.

So far the subtext has been observed through Shakespeare's use of gesture, stage-business and silent physical confrontations; to these means must be added the text itself: sudden shifts in subject-matter or in tone and tempo, broken syntax or metre, the introduction of unusual words or disproportionate reactions, all need to be sustained by the actor's expression of the unspoken reactions that cause them. If the text is to sound like an 'imitation of life' it needs a subtext. Here is Brutus deliberating in *Julius Caesar*:

> It must be by his death; . . . and for my part,
> I know no personal cause to spurn at him,
> But for the general: . . . He would be crown'd. . . .
> How that might change his nature, there's the question. . . .
> It is the bright day that brings forth the adder,
> And that craves wary walking. Crown him . . . that! . . .
> And then, I grant, we put a sting in him.
>
> (II. i. 10–16)

Read this aloud, conscious only of the meaning of each syntactical unit, and the consecutive meaning and development of the whole passage will hardly be communicated. At each juncture marked with three dots in the text printed above there is a transition of thought and feeling for which the words represent only the beginning and the end, the change of verbal reaction but not the process that is its cause. Why after 'It must be by his death' does Brutus continue 'and for my part'?

The text does not say—but an actor can show that the idea of Caesar's death awakens in Brutus a need to justify himself. Then, from considering political problems, Brutus simply names the crux of Caesar's ambition, 'He would be crown'd', as if he were more concerned with the person than the policy. But then from considering Caesar's 'nature', Brutus moves away again to generalities, as if too close a knowledge of the man must be avoided. If the abrupt 'that', after the precise 'Crown him', were not spoken with some strong and precise feeling, it would be a slight hesitation, out of key with the pressures of the soliloquy; it must be able to carry the transition through the reasonable qualification of 'And then, I grant' and the more evasive plural pronoun 'we', to the sharp image of 'put a sting in him'. Textually, the soliloquy is a series of disjointed statements in which lofty and political considerations are uppermost; its continuous dramatic life depends on subtextual impressions of suspicion, guilt, pride and emulation, that can be expressed physically and by variations of stress, pitch, texture, phrasing, rhythm, volume, tempo.

Shakespearian dialogue is like a stone that reveals its deep veins and rich colour only when it is carefully and appropriately polished; or like a personal letter that makes sense only to those who know the writer and can 'hear' his voice in its words; or like a map that must be read by someone familiar with the terrain. Always it demands exploration until every peculiarity of its textual surface can be sustained in dramatic reality, until the hints it contains of subtextual impulses are used to enliven and give substance to a performance and to reveal conscious and unconscious motivation.

When Juliet waits for Romeo, syntax, rhythm and imagery are clues to an impression of sexual excitement and virginal fear that should underlie the words:

> Come, night;—*and this quickly suggests the more direct idea*—come, Romeo;—*then the two ideas come together making a sharper perception*—come, thou day in night;—
>
> *and now an explanation holds this moment of awareness more leisurely but persistently, and shows its fuller implications*—For thou wilt lie upon the wings of night—*Romeo's coming is associated with* 'lying', *as on a bed and with flight, as sexual excitement is often represented in dreams*—
>
> Whiter than new snow on a raven's back—*the idea of cold virginity, has been doubly asserted in* 'white' *and* 'new snow'[1] *and the vague*

[1] The New Cambridge editors emend to 'Whiter than snow upon a raven's

threat of 'wings of night' *defined with the* 'raven' *of death.*

Then Juliet, afraid of the twin implications of sexual encounter and death, reverts quickly to the original, simpler eagerness; but now this is amplified—

Come, gentle night,—'gentle' *because night and death are now her rivals to be placated*—come, loving black-brow'd night—'loving' *and the more physical* 'black-brow'd' *associate* 'night' *with sexual concerns—*

Give me my Romeo;—*but having is now associated with loss*—and when he shall die

Take him and cut him out in little stars,—*she tries to reduce her fears by assuming the scale of nursery games, by taking refuge in childish fantasy and rivalry—*

And he will make the face of heaven so fine
That all the world will be in love with night,
And pay no worship to the garish sun.—*this thought is more extended because it is only entertained as play; but the deeper reality of her sexual involvement then takes over in an inarticulate ejaculation and she utters her longing in two close-packed metaphors, both images common in sexual fantasy and dream—*

O, I have bought the mansion of a love,
But not posses'd it; and though I am sold,
Not yet enjoy'd.

(III. ii. 17–28)

For Juliet's soliloquy, subtextual thoughts and feelings provide an impulse towards speech that supports and extends textual meanings; for Brutus' soliloquy, the subtextual impression, besides making his words seem necessary, suggests that those very words disguise the true nature of his concern with the conspiracy against Caesar. These are two, out of the many, ways in which Shakespeare used the actor's ability to give dramatic life to thoughts and feelings 'under' his dialogue.

* * *

Of course, the word 'subtext' was unknown to Shakespeare. It is not listed in *The New English Dictionary* or its *Supplement* of 1939. It comes from Stanislavski's writings about the actor and is still particu-

back', commenting 'The "new" [of Q2] is Shakespeare's false start. . . . One cannot have *old* snow on a raven's back!'; but this is to judge a tautology by literary standards (of a restricted kind), not by dramatic standards.

larly associated with the 'method' of acting that was first developed while Chekhov was writing for the Moscow Arts Theatre. Subtext was then defined as:

> the manifest, the inwardly felt expression of a human being in a part, which flows uninterruptedly beneath the words of the text, giving them life and a basis for existing. . . . a web of innumerable, varied inner patterns inside a play and a part, . . . all sorts of figments of the imagination, inner movements, objects of attention, smaller and greater truths and a belief in them, adaptations, adjustments and other similar elements. It is the subtext that makes us say the words we do in a play.[2]

The new word and its definition were so quickly adopted because they provided a more precise way of discussing the manner in which spoken stage dialogue can reveal, as ordinary speech seldom can, the innermost processes of thought and feeling, and how that dialogue is related to physical and emotional performance. Stanislavski's concept is particularly appropriate for Shakespeare's plays which for centuries have held audiences' attention by truth of utterance and reality and depth of characterisation.

At the end of the nineteenth century Henry Irving quoted Macready, the actor he most admired, to explain the importance in performance of 'the thoughts that are *hidden under words*':

> What is the art of acting? . . . It is the art of embodying the poet's creations, of giving them flesh and blood, of making the figures which appeal to your mind's eye in the printed drama live before you on the stage. 'To fathom the depths of character, to trace its latent motives, to feel its finest quiverings of emotion, *to comprehend the thoughts that are hidden under words*, and thus possess one's self of the actual mind of the individual man'—such was Macready's definition of the player's art.

In the same lecture he translated this into his own words:

> the actor who has no real grip of the character, but simply recites the speeches with a certain grace and intelligence, will be untrue. The more intent he is upon the words, and the less on the ideas that dictated them, the more likely he is to lay himself open to the

[2] C. Stanislavski, *Building a Character*, tr. Elizabeth R. Hapgood (1950), p. 113.

> charge of mechanical interpretation. It is perfectly possible to express to an audience all the involutions of thought, the speculation, doubt, wavering, which reveal the meditative but irresolute mind. . . . In short, as we understand the people around us much better by personal intercourse than by all the revelations of written words—for *words*, as Tennyson says, '*half reveal and half conceal the soul within*' —so the drama has, on the whole, infinitely more suggestions when it is well acted than when it is interpreted by the unaided judgement of the student.[3]

In an earlier age recitation of 'the speeches with a certain grace' and order and balance of deportment were more highly regarded than in Irving's or Macready's but, nevertheless, the best actors of those days were also remarkable for the impression of feeling that sustained their words and sometimes modified them. So, in 1748, it was said of Betterton's Brutus in *Julius Caesar*, that when he:

> was provok'd, in his Dispute with Cassius, his Spirit flew only to his Eye; his steady look alone supply'd that Terror, which he disdain'd an Intemperance in his Voice should rise to.[4]

Richard Steele described in *The Tatler* the 'wonderful agony' when Betterton's Othello:

> examined the circumstance of the handkerchief . . .; the mixture of love that intruded upon his mind upon the innocent answers Desdemona makes, betrayed in his gesture such a variety and vicissitude of passions, as would admonish a man to be afraid of his own heart, . . . Whoever reads in his closet this admirable scene, will find that he cannot, except he has as warm an imagination as Shakespeare himself, find any but dry, incoherent, and broken sentences; but a reader that has seen Betterton act it, observes there could not be a word added . . .[5]

Changes of taste have modified what actually happens on the stage, but the actor's pursuit of an 'imitation of life', display of 'passion' and 'natural' elocution (to use Shakespeare's phrases) and, indeed, the mere necessity to make some 'incoherent and broken' passages, like those of Brutus or Othello, comprehensible to an audience, have always led to

[3] *The Drama: Addresses* (1893), pp. 40–46; my italics.
[4] C. Cibber, *An Apology* (ed. 1740), p. 87.
[5] *The Tatler*, No. 167 (1710).

the discovery and expression of 'subtext'. Despite the comparative novelty of this word, 'that which makes an actor say his words in a play' has, for centuries, been sought out and expressed through gesture, bearing and elocution, in order to give a 'personal and exact life'[6] to Shakespeare's dialogue.

* * *

Sometimes we can observe Shakespeare's conscious experiment with these dramatic techniques, most clearly in his presentation of his characters as actors.

At the end of *Love's Labour's Lost* various country-folk speak as Worthies in a pageant. Sir Nathaniel with brave words attempts to declare 'I am Alisander': but he is mocked for his pains—'Your nose says, no, you are not'—so that the 'conqueror is dismay'd' and runs away. He is 'O'erparted', for he cannot provide the emotional or physical performance required by his words; he fails to express an adequate subtext. Moth has no words as the infant Hercules and so his performance is not open to challenge in the same way. Holofernes describes what the boy presents quite fluently, but when he ceases to be the schoolmaster-chorus and speaks as Judas Maccabaeus he cannot find the spirit to complete more than one line of his part—despite the fact that he probably wrote it himself. Armado as Hector, however, does not speak so much as a line before criticism begins: his leg is thought 'too big for Hector's' and his 'faces' are not acceptable. Costard, as Pompey, is the only one to speak out his part, but he probably did not attempt too 'great' a verbal performance; he had earlier explained:

> It pleased them to think me worthy of Pompey the Great; for mine own part, I know not the degree of the Worthy; but I am to stand for him.
>
> (V. ii. 504–6)

In this display Shakespeare has obviously used varying discrepancies between text and subtext, between attempted and achieved performance, for comic effect: as the Princess says, 'Their form confounded makes most form in mirth'.

At the end of *A Midsummer Night's Dream*, in the play of *Pyramus and Thisbe*, the device is repeated in a more elaborate way, and, in

[6] See chapter II, p. 34 above.

preparation, Theseus explains that he values subtext above text, tongue-tied 'modesty of fearful duty' above 'saucy and audacious eloquence':

> Where I have come, great clerks have purposed
> To greet me with premeditated welcomes;
> Where I have seen them shiver and look pale,
> Make periods in the midst of sentences,
> Throttle their practis'd accent in their fears,
> And, in conclusion, dumbly have broke off,
> Not paying me a welcome. Trust me sweet,
> Out of this silence yet I pick'd a welcome;
> And in the modesty of fearful duty
> I read as much as from the rattling tongue
> Of saucy and audacious eloquence.
> Love, therefore, and tongue-tied simplicity
> In least speak most to my capacity. (V. i. 93–105)

Clearly Shakespeare was aware of more than comic implications of a failure to sustain a part by an appropriate impression of emotional and physical truth. Some of his earliest major characters are portrayed as actors of varying achievement. Richard of Gloucester is confident of a successful performance:

> Why, I can smile, and murder whiles I smile,
> And cry 'Content!' to that which grieves my heart.
> (*III, Henry VI,* III. ii. 182–3)

But in contrast, when Richard II has seen his own face in a glass, he knows that his words have been less powerful than his silent feelings:

> My grief lies all within;
> And these external manner[s] of lamen[t]
> Are merely shadows to the unseen grief
> That swells with silence in the tortur'd soul.
> There lies the substance.
> (*Richard II,* IV. i. 295–9)

Later, in solitary confinement, he recognizes that he has 'play[ed] in one person many people, and none contented' (V. iv. 31–32). In *Julius Caesar*, Brutus counsels the conspirators to hide their true feelings:

> Let not our looks put on our purposes,
> But bear it as our Roman actors do,
> With untir'd spirits and formal constancy. (II. i. 225–7)

and Casca is said to put on a 'tardy form' of speech in order to disguise the 'quick mettle' of his wit which might be dangerous if spoken openly (I. ii. 294–301). In these instances Shakespeare requires, specifically, that an actor in his play should represent a man whose subtextual reality is different from what his words imply: more murderous, more cunning or more pained.

Hamlet's first long speech to his mother is perhaps the most comprehensive account of this, but here the imperfect performance is mostly in action and appearance:

> 'Tis not alone my inky cloak, good mother,
> Nor customary suits of solemn black,
> Nor windy suspiration of forc'd breath,
> No, nor the fruitful river in the eye,
> Nor the dejected haviour of the visage,
> Together with all forms, moods, shapes of grief,
> That can denote me truly. These, indeed, seem;
> For they are actions that a man might play;
> But I have that within which passes show—
> These but the trappings and the suits of woe.
>
> (I. ii. 77–86)

The actor of Hamlet must represent a man who says his behaviour is like an imperfect actor's performance, that what he does is not fully true to his inward and hidden nature; yet he, himself, does not know at this stage in the play what actions could 'denote him truly'. By such theatrical metaphors, and by the failure of 'overparted' actors in the pageant of the Worthies and *Pyramus and Thisbe*, we know that Shakespeare distinguished verbal, or outward, performances from true, or 'inward', performances, and that he sometimes required his actors to sustain a subtextual reality beneath a false or imperfect textual performance.

By the use of conscious disguise—Shakespeare also devised situations in which inward emotion or thought is opposed to the words spoken, denying the meaning of speech or extending its reference. This is clearest in comedies like *Twelfth Night* or *As You Like It*. When Orsino asks his page, Cesario, 'How dost thou like this tune?', the reply is

> It gives a very echo to the seat
> Where Love is thron'd.
>
> (*Twelfth Night,* II. iv. 19–21

Through these stilted words Viola's subtextual affection for Orsino is expressed, so that the seeming boy is said to speak 'masterly'. Later in the same scene, when Orsino talks about his love for Olivia and Cesario—or rather the disguised Viola—interrupts with, 'Ay, but I know . . . ', the Duke suddenly stops his own line of thought to ask 'What dost thou know?' (ll. 102–3). This is an incomplete verse-line, probably indicating a pause while Viola remembers that she is Cesario; she then continues in a vein a little more like the boy's: 'Too well what love women to men may owe'. But as her hidden concern was not wholly disguised by her words, so she is not capable of keeping it silent; she proceeds:

> My father had a daughter lov'd a man,
> As it might be perhaps, were I a woman,
> I should your lordship.

These are not remarkable words, but their subtextual feeling completely holds Orsino's attention so that he forgets his own concerns to listen to this supposed fiction and insists on knowing her 'history'. When Viola, gaining confidence in verbal expression of her love, has told how:

> She pin'd in thought;
> And with a green and yellow melancholy
> She sat like Patience on a monument,
> Smiling at grief . . .

she reassumes her role of Cesario and it is again Orsino who presses the question, 'But died thy sister of her love, my boy?'. At last Viola can use Cesario to extricate herself from the too-revealing pathos and intimacy, and asks briskly, 'Sir, shall I to this lady?'; and only now does Orsino remember his own 'theme'. At least twice in this scene Cesario gains far more attention than his words could ever claim without a sustaining and overwhelming emotional performance; only the power of subtext could so draw Orsino's attention away from his obsession with Olivia. If the pause and sudden changes of rhythm, language and subject-matter are to be enacted in 'imitation of life', the characters' inward feelings must be expressed in contradiction to the verbal and costume disguise.

Rosalind posing as Ganymede often gets Orlando to betray his deepest feelings in supposedly fictitious words, and expresses her own love while speaking against love. But when she recovers from her swoon on seeing Orlando's bloody handkerchief and tries to act the man, she cannot convince Oliver:

> This was not counterfeit; there is too great testimony in your complexion that it was a passion of earnest.
>
> (IV. iii. 167–8)

In this instance, her inward feelings lag behind the bravery of her verbal performance so that she, in effect, denies her words even as she speaks them.

There are many disguises in Shakespeare's plays which do not use costume at all. So, in *Much Ado*, the unconscious attraction of Benedick and Beatrice to each other is concealed by their words and expressed at first only by the way in which they draw together on each entry and awaken unusually energetic antagonism. When two invented conversations are staged for their benefit, they accept the fictions as true—despite the inefficiency of Leonato who 'dries' in his role and the fantastic elaboration of both sets of performers—because their hidden feelings prompt them to believe, against almost everything they have said, that they love each other. Verbal disguise of this sort is found in every play—sometimes consciously assumed, as by Richard III or Casca; sometimes unconsciously as by Richard II or Brutus; sometimes half-intentionally, as by Hamlet.

Here, as in the two plays-within-plays, Shakespeare has forced the actors to distinguish text from subtext, and sometimes subtext becomes uppermost so that the words which conceal also reveal, directly by quibbles or allusiveness, or indirectly by the marks of subtextual tension that must be sustained in physical performance—sudden changes of subject matter, tone or tempo, broken syntax or metre, apparently disproportionate or surprising reactions.

* * *

When he was defining subtext, Stanislavski said that it 'flows uninterruptedly beneath the words of the text', and this continuity (as contrasted with intermittence of verbal performance) is an important source of its effectiveness. Often Shakespeare's strategy is to start impressing the inner nature of a character by merest hints in the text, or other outward activity, and to reveal only one part of the subtextual basis at a time until a complex interplay of conscious and unconscious motivation has been built up through a continuous series of impressions.

Then the ground has been prepared and subtextual reality is at last directly expressed in the text as well. Benedick and Beatrice are obvious examples, declaring their mutual love in words only at the end of the very last scene; by that time, what was earlier *said* to be impossible, has become inevitable and is acknowledged fully in the text.

Claudius, in the first Acts of *Hamlet*, is an example of a character whose deep sense of guilt is progressively revealed and also a contrary, and conscious, subtextual effort to suppress it. In Act III, Scene i, some moralising from Polonius releases a long aside that gives textual definition to the insecurity of his disguise as a confident and powerful king up to that moment:

> O, 'tis too true!
> How smart a lash that speech doth give my conscience!
> The harlot's cheek, beautied with plast'ring art,
> Is not more ugly to the thing that helps it
> Than is my deed to my most painted word.
> O heavy burden!
>
> (III. i. 49–54)

In a reading of the play this aside may seem like a brash intrusion of obsolete stagecraft that falls too pat after Hamlet's talk of the 'conscience of the King' in the last line of the previous scene. But in performance it seems necessary because it gives textual expression to an inner consciousness which has already been suggested in a sequence of subtextual revelations.

Claudius does not enter until immediately after the Ghost has provoked curiosity and concern, so the audience will attend closely and perhaps sense a purposeful evasion when his public speech begins by showing most art where its matter is most strange: discretion 'fighting' with nature, 'mirth in funeral', 'our sometime sister, now our queen', and so forth. Power, ease and astuteness are dominating textual impressions, but his reliance on embellishing art—or 'most painted word'—can serve the actor as occasion for expressing a need to 'cover up'. Contrasted with his talk of haste and immediate business, Claudius' words of dismissal:

> Take thy fair hour, Laertes; time be thine,
> And thy best graces spend it at thy will!
>
> (I. ii. 62–63)

can go beyond their obvious meaning and sound like a regret for his own strict concerns, especially if the syntactical separation and metrical strength of 'time be thine' are given full value. Answering Hamlet's scorn with continuing urbanity, Claudius can turn talk of love and gentleness into a show of force. When he twice breaks in between Hamlet and his mother, his speech, movement and bearing can seem motivated by fear of some unnamed consequence. All this is before the Ghost has told his story; after that the audience will be more ready to notice a cloaked forcefulness in Claudius' smooth words and to observe his uneasy movements. Shakespeare now used other characters to emphasise what Claudius does *not* say: the uncertainty of Rosencrantz in reply to entreaties where he had expected 'commands', or the way in which Polonius is allowed to run on in expounding Hamlet's love for Ophelia so that Claudius seems lost in thoughts he will not, or cannot, express. The King's silence here also contrasts with Gertrude's impatience; his replies are short and infrequent, and (when state affairs have just established him as prompt and careful in detailed planning) he leaves practical suggestions to Polonius. Judged over three Acts and in relation to other characters, the inner tensions of Claudius are not expressed in one sudden and blunt aside, but are manifested progressively on his every appearance.

It is often necessary to look backwards over a role in order to appreciate the opportunities for subtextual expression. At the beginning of *The Winter's Tale*, Leontes' silence as he holds centre-stage and the terseness of his speech can be seen as expressions of his insecure and self-regarding nature, once we have read on and come to his jealous outbursts. Similarly Henry IV's early appearances must be revalued after studying his death-bed scene in *Part II*: guilt, loneliness and weariness had been his deepest reactions while he gave commands and appeared as the crowned King of England among his nobles. Henry V's prayer before Agincourt:

> More will I do;
> Though all that I can do is nothing worth,
> Since that my penitence comes after all,
> Imploring pardon.
>
> (IV. iii. 298–300)

leads an actor to reassess the King's anger at the French Ambassador, his demands for absolute proof of his right in France, his response to the traitors as to 'Another fall of man' (II. ii. 142), his ruthlessness before Harfleur, and so on. Beneath his verbal assurance there is a fear, that can be expressed subtextually until Henry acknowledges it textually, just before the crucial battle.

In *Macbeth* the hero's non-textual response is obvious and large from the very beginning, but still Shakespeare has made the audience wait until the close of the first scene before beginning to identify it textually: so Macbeth's instinctive responses seem more deep-seated and his power to conceal more impressive. Here again the other characters on stage have important parts to play in marking silent reactions. When he enters, marching to a drum, his first words seem unmotivated—'So foul and fair a day I have not seen' (I. iii. 38)—unless we suppose that he instinctively senses the Witches' presence before he sees or hears them; such an unwilled response is implied by the fact that he echoes the Witches' words from the play's first scene (l. 10). Certainly Banquo's reply—'How far is't call'd to Forres?'—because no true response to what was *said*, can suggest that this companion is unable to enter Macbeth's thoughts. When the Witches become visible, Macbeth says nothing although their interest is centred on him: now some subtextual response holds him silent; Banquo interrogates, until Macbeth asks curtly, 'Speak, if you can. What are you?' So Banquo has again helped to present Macbeth, for his speculation suggests by contrast that his leader accepts the strange creatures in his silence, and expects a message. When Macbeth has been greeted three times with three hopeful prophecies, he is again silent and Banquo describes his reaction: and it is a surprising reaction, neither incredulity, nor hope, nor pleasure, but 'fear':

> Good sir, why do you start, and seem to fear
> Things that do sound so fair?

In whatever style the actor performs Macbeth, he must show a total response through gesture, bearing and movement, through his physical performance; it must be a response large enough to include thought and conscious reaction and yet be stronger than all these because uncontrolled by them—the valiant Macbeth would not intend to reveal fear. Held by his secret feelings, he does not respond to Banquo's question. From his later words we know that he listens, but he takes no part in the continuing interrogation. Then as the Witches 'Hail' him together with Banquo, he speaks directly to them ignoring his partner; his questions are now concerned with himself, and are clear, precise and astute. This transition restores the earlier impression of decisiveness;

his powers have been increased, not diminished, by the chiefly inward excitement of the encounter. To deliver this kind of dialogue and to hold the centre of the complicated scene, the actor must make silence as real, complex and forceful as words, and show, in a continuous and integrated performance, how an instinctive reaction over-masters, and then is controlled by, conscious intention.

When the Witches vanish, it is again Banquo who speaks first, but Macbeth now responds and his contrasting speech, by accounting for the disappearance of the Witches as a matter of fact, reveals how much further they have taken hold of his imagination than of the still speculative Banquo's. Then he adds 'Would they had stay'd'; there is little logical progression of thought here, so the words will seem motivated subtextually by thoughts and feelings drawing his mind away from Banquo's. It must be spoken in a manner that prevents reply, for Banquo continues to wonder about the nature of the Witches. The next time Macbeth speaks he ignores Banquo's direct question to elicit a response about the prophecies themselves: 'Your children shall be kings!' Since it is made clear later, in soliloquy, that he has been considering his own 'imperial theme', the actor must again give an impression of words disguising thoughts. This time Banquo seems to catch the subtextual implications:

MACBETH. Your children shall be kings.
BANQUO. You shall be King.
MACBETH. And Thane of Cawdor too; went it not so?

Banquo's straight reply contrasts and therefore underlines the indirection of Macbeth: why had he spoken of Banquo rather than himself? and why does he then pass by the immediate challenge of his own royal hope to speak of secondary matters? He is both disguising his inner thoughts and seeking confirmation of them; he wants to be sure of the prophecies and he wants to hide their true effect on himself. He is so engaged in what pretends to be casual talk that only Banquo hears approaching footsteps. And it is when Ross and Angus have hailed him as Thane of Cawdor that Macbeth is at last given an aside to make his unspoken consciousness more explicit. Shakespeare resorts to this device only when the instinctive, emotional and physical reactions have already been established, and the conscious attempt to conceal them. Yet still there are reserves, to show that Macbeth cannot name 'that suggestion Whose horrid image doth unfix my hair', even to himself;

for nowhere does he name the man his thought would murder. Besides the astonishing fear, that could come only from immediate and guilty thoughts of murder, there is also a half-spoken sensitivity to guilt or to the suffering of others. At the end of the scene he speaks aside to Banquo, with disguising easiness and assurance, of a 'free heart'. Since he is later to suffer for the loss of 'troops of friends' (V. iii. 25), it might be appropriate for the actor to suggest a desire, stronger than his words, for a life of trust and affection—even when considering murder. He rejoins the others with a brief 'Come friends', which is certainly a verbal disguise of his fears and intentions, but perhaps, also, a yearning for what he is about to destroy.

* * *

Of course, subtext is not so easily 'read' as the text. The first task is to discover where it must be impressed in order to carry the words, and where gestures, stage-business or emotional performance necessarily take over from words. But then its precise nature and strength, at any moment, must be defined in relation to the text of the complete play.

In practice, the subtextual implications of any one role in performance will depend considerably on what the individual actor can do, on his temperament and physical talents which are the medium for its enactment. Each actor is like a unique coloured filter, that emphasises certain aspects of a part and is incapable of transmitting others.

The last words of Malvolio in *Twelfth Night* show what freedom an actor has in interpretation—or, to put this another way, how much depends on his gifts and decisions. The words 'I'll be reveng'd on the whole pack of you' (V. i. 364) *read* like a quick conclusion to a practical joke with allusions to revenge which are unusual in a comedy. But in performance Malvolio speaks the line after a long silence in which he has heard how the trick was played on him and has refused to respond either to a plea to be reasonable, or to sympathy. The management of the scene focuses attention on his silence, so that his reactions to all he sees and hears will be noticed. When at last he speaks, his total performance will seem to express previously hidden thoughts.[7] The audience will be made to realise that Malvolio is isolated and incapable of being helped; but the actor can choose what emotion or thought is

[7] Compare Shylock's brief speeches on his exit from the Trial Scene; Chapter VI, pp. 88–89, below.

the cause of this: humourless self-concern, pride, stoicism, contempt, bewilderment, suffering, fantastic daydreaming. When an actor tries to portray any of these motivations, he is not attempting to express 'more than is set down for him,' but giving a substance and clarity to the brief words made obligatory by the long silence. Shakespeare has also given him an exit with which to enforce his response with protracted physical movement (there were long distances to be crossed on Elizabethan stages), and he has marked a hiatus following his departure by Olivia's 'He hath been most notoriously abus'd' and Orsino's 'Pursue him, and entreat him to a peace.' Moreover this expression of inward feeling is placed at the latest point in the play, a position of great importance after the affairs of Viola, Orsino, Olivia, Sebastian, Sir Toby and others have been concluded; there follows only a concluding speech by Orsino that has no narrative or character development, and then the riddling song of Feste.

Even when there is a great deal of text for the actor to speak the choice of subtext can be difficult and bold decisions must be taken, preferably after experimentation in rehearsal. For example, it might be argued that Hamlet's 'To be, or not to be—that is the question. . . .' should be acted so that the subtext implies 'To be, or not to be—that is *not* the question. . . .' (I know that this is practicable for at least one actor of the role.) The textual argument of the soliloquy draws together in:

> Thus conscience does make cowards of us all; . . .
> And enterprises of great pitch and moment,
> With this regard, their currents turn awry
> And lose the name of action.

The spoken words throughout are concerned, as the famous first line says, with the task of making up one's mind to act. But then Hamlet sees Ophelia, and there is a surprising verbal transition:

> Soft you now!
> The fair Ophelia.—Nymph, in thy orisons
> Be all my sins rememb'red.

After the conscious deliberation of the soliloquy there is an unexpected call on Hamlet's emotions, but his reaction to this disturbance is not disturbed; his words are *not* ill-formed or obviously unprepared. The tempo changes, the mood, tone and phrasing, but smoothly so. From his tough, practical considerations he can move *easily* to peace, softness, woman and guilt ('all *my* sins'), as if these thoughts had lain, ready for expression, under the earlier soliloquy. Noticing this transition, we should revalue the earlier text; the incidental colour of its images and the changes in direction of its argument seem more important than they did at first. What the earlier words had only hinted may have been Hamlet's deepest, unexplicit concerns, and capable of subtextual expression: the pain in *slings and arrows, heartache, natural shocks, rub, whips and scorns, spurns*; and the desire for a natural peace in *sleep, consummation, devoutly, quietus, bourn*. 'To be or not to be' is quite certainly not the only question; under the apparent concern of these words must be another, at first merely suggested but then wholly expressed to Ophelia; and it must prove, finally, to be the stronger. This is not the Hamlet of indecision and attempted resolution towards 'enterprises of great pitch and moment', but the Hamlet who at the end of the play will allow his mother to wipe his brow, the Hamlet who looks for felicity beyond death and accepts silence.

Shakespeare wrote poetic drama of great verbal power; but the words are not all. Always the text is accompanied by continuous physical performance which can transform the effect of spoken words; it is sometimes necessary for mere intelligibility. Silence and gesture are also important. And the text often lies.

V

Shakespearian Actors

*

> Behind the dialogue of Greek drama we are always conscious of a concrete visual actuality, and behind that of a specific emotional actuality. Behind the drama of words is the drama of action, the timbre of voice and voice, the uplifted hand or tense muscle, and the particular emotion. The spoken play, the words which we read, are symbols, a shorthand, and often, as in the best of Shakespeare, a very abbreviated shorthand indeed, for the acted and felt play, which is always the real thing. The phrase, beautiful as it may be, stands for a greater beauty still.

THESE words by T. S. Eliot, in an essay on *Seneca in Elizabethan Translation* (1927), sharply delineate the central difficulty in understanding plays in theatrical terms. For Shakespeare, as they suggest, the literary text is a particularly abbreviated account because of the scope for physical and emotional performance that his dialogue gives to actors. Granville-Barker judged that a play of any quality is 'like the iceberg, floating one-ninth above water and eight-ninths submerged';[1] the 'literary record' is the one-ninth we can see.

Granville-Barker went on to say that 'Ideally, everything should be implicit in the record . . .: set the play in motion and all the hidden things *should* come to light and life.' It follows that, first of all, we must learn to set the play in motion for ourselves, in the theatre of our mind. We can learn to hear the words as we read, to recreate changes of tempo and rhythm, deduce the places where gesture and stage-business are important and look for opportunities for subtextual impressions and for the progressive clarification of that physical and emotional reality which lies beneath the observed text.

The main difficulty is that the theatre of the mind is intangible. When we only *imagine* that a play is in performance, the actual physical facts can slip out of mind, and we can find our attention engrossed by one interesting detail. We can forget, too, the temporal control and

[1] *On Dramatic Method* (ed. 1956), p. 22.

sequence of performance, and that sense of scale which comes by witnessing a whole play without a break. Our imaginary enactment is too indulgent of our own interests, and of course it is severely limited by our own particular talents and experience.

The other recourse is to actual performances. These are tangible, and in them almost the whole play can be heard and seen, and studied. Moreover the text has been studied before performance by the men for whom Shakespeare wrote, individual actors. They are not Elizabethan actors, of course, but in many of their instincts and skills are more like Elizabethan actors than most readers and students of Shakespeare. Moreover an actor's interpretation must be one that is convincing to himself as a performer, and it must make consistent sense—physically, emotionally and, in some degree, intellectually—to his audiences. The evidence of performance is of crucial importance.

But actual performances are also of limited use for learning about Shakespeare's plays. Productions are created under difficulties of casting and organisation; there's too little time and too little money to provide satisfactory conditions, to take sufficient risks, develop imaginative acting, learn enough about the demands of the text or appropriate ways of staging. They are limited, too, by the talents of the performers, and obscured by the additions and alterations which no creative artist seems able to resist making to Shakespeare's text. And we as spectators are also unsatisfactory, especially limited in our response to effects which are new to our experience.

Both the theatre of the mind and actual performances need to be supplemented by reading accounts of earlier productions. Here we shall find approaches to the text that are now out of fashion but of proved validity for audiences, and the effects appropriate to different theatres and styles of performance some of which may be closer to Elizabethan conditions than any known today. Moreover only the greatly gifted actors have left sufficient evidence behind to be usefully studied and so through theatre history we can share imaginative and appropriately ambitious readings of the texts. We do not respond here to actual performances, but we can study the wide range of descriptions, sympathetic and hostile, that these earlier interpretations have provoked; sometimes the records illustrate the development of a performance during ten or twenty years of repertory playing.[2]

[2] See, for example, my forthcoming *Henry Irving's Shakespeare: the actor's interpretation of plays and characters.*

Present and past productions are, then, essential stimulants and guides in our pursuit of a theatrical understanding of Shakespeare's plays. History proves that, among the great quantity of dross in theatre productions, the riches of Shakespeare's dramatic invention are constantly rediscovered. Each age, each decade, has its own way of performing and producing, and every one reveals some new elements that have been hidden in the text until the moment when an actor, with a particular style and experience, has been able to effect the surprise. On the first performance, a famous Shylock was praised in rapid doggerel:

> This is the Jew
> That Shakespeare drew,

and every year reviews speak of 'revelation', 'originality' and Shakespeare's play being 'given' new value or coherence.

For example, a detailed report from *The Examiner* of 5 June 1814, shows how Edmund Kean sought a deep consistency and unusual psychological truth in his roles, and so developed the contrasts implicit in situations. It concerns his Iago:

> The actors of this part in general . . . stab Roderigo, and then walk away with perfect east and satisfaction. Mr. Kean . . . gives and repeats the atrocious thrust, till it may be supposed no life remains; but he feels this to be a matter too important to be left in doubt. He therefore, though he at the same time converses coolly with those about him, throws his eye perpetually towards the prostrate body . . .: sometimes he walked by it carelessly, and surveyed it with a glance too rapid to be observed; sometimes he deliberately approached it, and looked at it with his candle . . .: and thus he continued to hover over and watch it till he leaves the stage.

If the tension created by this business seems like an intrusion upon the text, we should remember that the usual playing of this incident on the modern stage often evokes laughter from the audience at Iago's and, possibly, the play's expense. Perhaps Kean discovered the secret of how to play this dispersed, short-phrased and oddly cloak-and-dagger scene. Certainly few Iagos have been so admired.

When a study of performances goes intimately with a renewed study of the theatrical detail of the texts, it will lead us closer to the acted and felt play that lies hidden behind the printed words. If we find more possible interpretations than certain ones, that may be a sign that we begin to respond to the full wealth and demands of Shakespeare's imagination. We should always be willing to test the value of an actor's discovery by reference to the text, to the character as a whole and the play as a whole. We should, as it were, keep the plays in constant rehearsal in the theatre of our mind.

Michel Saint-Denis has a description of an actor's approach to a part that suggests an appropriate encounter with Shakespeare, always remembering that we have to consider the wider dramatic effects as well as individual roles. It is a stern and exciting direction:

> In a classical play [and, specifically, he includes Shakespeare's in this class] the actor must not hurry or jump upon the character. You must not enslave the text by premature conception or feeling of the character. You should not hurry to get on the stage and try to act, physically and emotionally, too soon. Psychological and emotional understanding of a character should come through familiarity with the text, not from outside it. You must know how to wait, how to refuse, so as to remain free. You must be like a glove, open and flexible, but flat, and remaining flat at the beginning. Then by degrees the text, the imagination, the associations roused by the text penetrate you and bring you to life. Ways are prepared for the character to creep in slowly and animate the glove, the glove which is you, with your blood, with your nerves, with your breathing system, your voice, with the light of your own lucid control switching on and off. The whole complex machinery is at work; it has been put into action by the text. . . .[3]

[3] *Theatre: the Rediscovery of Style* (1960), pp. 68–69.

VI

Creating a Role: Shylock

★

EVER since 14 February 1741, when Charles Macklin persuaded the management of Drury Lane to restore Shakespeare's text in place of George Granville's adaptation and to allow him to play Shylock, *The Merchant of Venice* has nearly always been revived for the same purpose—to give some actor the chance of playing the lead. For that is what Shylock is: although he appears in but five of its twenty scenes and not at all in the last Act, he can dominate every other impression and display the powers of many kinds of actor. He often takes the final curtain-call, without Portia or Bassanio, without Antonio, the merchant of Venice. This tradition is so strong that it is easy to forget how strange it is: how odd that a villain—the one who threatens the happiness of the others—should so run away with a play that is a comedy by other signs, and that makes only a passing, unconcerned allusion to him at its conclusion. But the records are unequivocal.[1] In the theatre it is his play. Fortunately the records are also unusually detailed, so that we are able to reconstruct the different ways in which Shylock has been given life and observe the qualities in Shakespeare's text which make this a star part. And from this inquiry, other questions arise: have ambitious actors misrepresented Shakespeare's play? is one interpretation, one reading of the actor's opportunities, more faithful than another? is a fully realised Shylock incompatible with a well proportioned *Merchant of Venice*, one that is satisfactorily concluded?

★ ★ ★

[1] Records quoted in this chapter are taken chiefly from: F. Gentleman, *Dramatic Censor* (1770); J. T. Kirkman, *Memoirs of Macklin* (1799); *Memoirs of Charles Macklin* (1804); G. H. Lewes, *On Actors and the Art of Acting* (1875); F. W. Hawkins, *Life of Kean* (1869); J. Doran, *Their Majesties Servants* (ed. 1897); H. H. Hillebrand, *Edmund Kean* (1933); W. Winter, *Shakespeare on the Stage* (1912); L. Irving, *Henry Irving* (1951); and A. C. Sprague, *Shakespeare and the Actors* (1944).

At first the part seemed to have been written especially for Macklin, as Kemble's *Memoirs* (1825) affirm:

> His acting was essentially manly—there was nothing of trick about it. His delivery was more level than modern speaking, but certainly more weighty, direct and emphatic. His features were rigid, his eye cold and colourless; yet the earnestness of his manner, and the sterling sense of his address, produced an effect in Shylock, that has remained to the present hour unrivalled. (i. 440)

It was thought that Shakespeare had drawn Shylock 'all shade, not a gleam of light; subtle, selfish, fawning, irascible, and tyrannic', and that Macklin's voice was:

> most happily suited to that sententious gloominess of expression the author intended; which, with a sullen solemnity of deportment, marks the character strongly; in his malevolence, there is a forcible and terrifying ferocity. (Gentleman, i. 291)

He cast his performance between two extremes, sullen and malevolent, and the two were linked by weight and power in his deportment and his eyes:

> There was, beside his judgment which went to the study of every line of it, such an iron-visaged look, such a relentless, savage cast of manners, that the audience seemed to shrink from the character.
> (*Memoirs*, pp. 405–6)

His performance began sullenly:

> when Shylock and Bassanio entered, . . . there was an awful, a solemn silence. . . . He approached with Bassanio. . . . Still not a whisper could be heard in the house. Upon the entrance of Anthonio, the Jew makes the audience acquainted with his motives of antipathy against the Merchant. Mr. Macklin had no sooner delivered this speech, than the audience suddenly burst out into a thunder of applause, and in proportion as he afterwards proceeded to exhibit and mark the malevolence, the villainy, and the diabolical atrocity of the character, so in proportion did the admiring and delighted audience testify their approbation. . . .
> (Kirkman, i. 258–9)

Macklin himself spoke of the first scenes as 'rather tame and level' but:

> I knew where I should have the pull, which was in the third act, and reserved myself accordingly. At this period I threw out all my fire;

> . . . the contrasted passions of joy for the Merchant's losses, and grief for the elopement of Jessica, open a fine field for an actor's powers, . . . (*Memoirs*, p. 93)

For this scene with Salerio and Solanio, and then with Tubal, he 'broke the tones of utterance' and ensured that his 'transitions were strictly natural' (Kirkman, i. 264). But for the trial he reverted to what he called 'a silent yet forcible impression' (*Memoirs*, p. 93):

> Macklin . . . 'stood like a TOWER,' as Milton has it. He was 'not bound to *please*' any body by his pleading; he claimed a right, grounded upon LAW, and thought himself as firm as the Rialto.[2]

The kind of detail that impressed an audience can be judged from this account in a letter by a German visitor, Georg Lichtenberg, who saw Macklin in 1775:

> Shylock is not one of those mean, plausible cheats who could expatiate for an hour on the virtues of a gold watch-chain of pinchbeck; he is heavy, and silent in his unfathomable cunning, and, when the law is on his side, just to the point of malice. Imagine a rather stout man with a coarse yellow face and a nose generously fashioned in all three dimensions, a long double chin, and a mouth so carved by nature that the knife appears to have slit him right up to the ears, on one side at least, I thought. He wears a long black gown, long wide trousers, and a red tricorne, after the fashion of Italian Jews, I suppose. The first words he utters, when he comes on to the stage, are slowly and impressively spoken: 'Three thousand ducats.' The double 'th', which Macklin lisps as lickerishly as if he were savouring the ducats and all that they would buy, make so deep an impression in the man's favour that nothing can destroy it. Three such words uttered thus at the outset give the keynote of his whole character. In the scene where he first misses his daughter, he comes on hatless, with disordered hair, some locks a finger long standing on end, as if raised by a breath of wind from the gallows, so distracted was his demeanour. Both his hands are clenched, and his movements abrupt and convulsive. To see a deceiver, who is usually calm and resolute, in such a state of agitation, is terrible.[3]

Macklin's imitators cheapened this portrait, presenting a Shylock 'bent with age and ugly with mental deformity, . . . sullen, morose,

[2] J. Boaden, *Memoirs of J. P. Kemble* (1825), i. 440.

[3] *Lichtenberg's Visits to England*, tr. Margaret L. Mare and W. H. Quarrell (1938), p. 40.

gloomy, inflexible, brooding over one idea, that of his hatred, and fixed on one unalterable purpose, that of his revenge'.[4] If this mood was relieved it was by laughter at Shylock's expense, especially in the Tubal scene which often excited 'a mixture of mirth and indignation'.[5] But then, on 26 January 1814, Edmund Kean played the Jew at Drury Lane with 'terrible energy'; like Macklin he established a reputation overnight and founded a new tradition.

His Shylock was not so easy to imitate, for it depended on most unusual gifts. His voice had a range 'from F below the line to F above it', its natural key being that of B♭. His hard guttural tone upon G was said to be 'as piercing as the third string of a violon-cello', and his mezzo and pianissimo expressions as 'soft as from the voice of a woman'. This instrument he learned to control so that it gave sudden and thrilling effects: he could give 'the yell and choaked utterance of a savage':

At times he gave 'a torrent of words in a breath', yet with 'all the advantages of deliberation'. His pauses could give a 'grandeur', speaking 'more than the words themselves':[6]

Kean was fond of 'abrupt transitions . . . mingling strong lights and shadows with Caravaggio force of unreality'. He gave an irregular

[4] W. Hazlitt, *Works* (ed. 1930), iv. 320–4.
[5] R. Hole, *Essays by a Society of Gentlemen, at Exeter* (1796), p. 559.
[6] W. Gardiner, *The Music of Nature* (1832), pp. 48–49.

performance, always seeking 'points' for passion and power. This might have degenerated into trickery, but he 'vigilantly and patiently rehearsed every detail' until his artistic sense was satisfied; and he acted with his whole being, watching the after-effects of passion as well as its sudden expression:

> a strong emotion, after discharging itself in one massive current, continues for a time expressing itself in feebler currents. . . . In watching Kean's quivering muscles and altered tones you felt the subsidence of passion. The voice might be calm, but there was a tremor in it; the face might be quiet, but there were vanishing traces of recent agitation.
>
> (Lewes, pp. 2–8)

His arms, hands and large black eyes were, with his voice, eloquent of intelligence, spirit and power.

Kean's first scene as Shylock started, as Macklin's did, slowly, but added dignity and a crushing, sardonic humour:

> From the first moment that he appeared and leant upon his stick to listen gravely while moneys are requested of him, he impressed the audience, . . . 'like a chapter of Genesis'. [Then followed] the overpowering remonstrant sarcasm of his address to Antonio, and the sardonic mirth of his proposition about the 'merry bond' . . .
>
> (Lewes, p. 11)

As he spoke of Laban and his flock (I. iii. 72–91), he seemed 'borne back to the olden time':

> Shylock is in Venice with his money-bags, his daughter, and his injuries; but his thoughts take wing to the east; his voice swells and deepens at the mention of his sacred tribe and ancient law, . . .

But he can change rapidly:

> The audience is then stirred to enthusiasm by the epigrammatic point and distinctness with which he gives the lines:
>
> Hath a *dog* money? Is it possible
> A *cur* can lend three thousand ducats?
>
> (Hawkins, i. 129)

In Shylock's second scene, taking leave of Jessica, Kean revealed yet another facet of his powers, for in his calling 'Why, Jessica! I say' there was a 'charm, as of music' (Doran, pp. 429–30). But his chief triumph was, like Macklin's, in III. i. This became the crucial test for all succeeding Shylocks; Squire Bancroft, discussing one particular failure at the end of the century, noted that:

> The fact of rushing on the stage in a white-heat frenzy, with nothing to lead up to its passion, I take it, is the main difficulty.

He had seen only Kean's son, Charles, assay it satisfactorily, and he closely reproduced his father:

> Apropos of which, Mr. Wilton often spoke to me; he having once, when quite a young actor, played Tubal to the Shylock of Edmund Kean. The great actor did not appear at rehearsal, but sent word that 'he should like to see the gentleman who was to be the Tubal at his hotel'. Mr. Wilton obeyed the summons, and spoke always of the kindness with which Kean instructed him, after saying, 'We'll run through the scene, Mr. Wilton, because I'm told that if you don't know what I'm going to do I might frighten you!' Mr. Wilton described the performance as *stupendous!* and said that, although prepared beforehand, at night Kean really frightened him.[7]

For this scene Kean could use his flashing transitions; he showed, with alternate force:

> Shylock's anguish at his daughter's flight; his wrath at the two Christians who make sport of his anguish; his hatred of all Christians, generally, and of Antonio in particular; and then his alternations of rage, grief, and ecstasy, as Tubal relates the losses incurred. (Doran, p. 430)

In the speech beginning 'He hath disgraced me, and hindered me half a million; . . .'

> He hurried you on through the catalogue of Antonio's atrocities and unprovoked injuries to him, enforcing them with a strong accentuation, and a high pitch of voice; and when he had reached the *climax*, he came down by a sudden transition to a gentle, suffering tone of simple representation of his oppressor's manifest un-reason and injustice, on the words
>
> 'I am a *Jew*![8]

In the trial scene was noted:

[7] S. B. and Marie E. Bancroft, *Mr. and Mrs. Bancroft* (8th ed., 1891), p. 212.
[8] Vandenhoff; quoted by Hillebrand, p. 346.

> His calm demeanor at first; his confident appeal to justice; his deafness, when appeal is made to him for mercy; his steady joyousness, when the young lawyer recognizes the validity of the bond; his burst of exultation, when his right is confessed; his fiendish eagerness, when whetting the knife;—and then, the sudden collapse of disappointment and terror, with the words,—'Is *that*—the LAW?' . . .
>
> Then, his trembling anxiety to recover what he had before refused: his sordid abjectness, as he finds himself foiled, at every turn; his subdued fury; and, at the last, (and it was always the crowning glory of his acting in this play), the withering sneer, hardly concealing the crushed heart, with which he replied to the jibes of Gratiano, as he left the court.
>
> (Doran, pp. 430–1)

To this account must be added the return of his sardonic humour, in lines like:

> An oath, an oath! I have an oath in heaven.
> Shall I lay perjury upon my soul?
>
> (IV. i. 223–4)

or in, 'I cannot find it; 'tis not in the bond' (l. 245), which, according to *The Examiner*, was accompanied with a 'transported chuckle'. There was in Kean's performance, as the same journal noted, a 'union of great powers with a fine sensibility': for Macklin's malevolence he had given sardonic intellect and fiery spirit, for his sullen strength, family love and racial pride, both being subjected to suffering and pain; all impressed by a series of instantaneous, forceful effects. So he reversed a tradition and, for Hazlitt, Kean's Jew was:

> more than half a Christian. Certainly, our sympathies are much oftener with him than with his enemies. He is honest in his vices; they are hypocrites in their virtues.[9]

Irving's Shylock at the Lyceum on 1 November 1879 was the next to be generally accepted as an original reading. He accentuated earlier suggestions of dignity, was venerable, lonely, grieved, austere: he moved with pride and grace; his humour was coldly cynical, rather than sardonic; his thought was meditative, not sullen, and his anger was white and tense; in defeat he called forth pity and awe. When he first played the role he bent all his effort toward gaining sympathy, but later he allowed his Shylock to become more 'hard, merciless, inexorable,

[9] *The Chronicle* (6 April 1816).

terrible' (Winter, pp. 175 and 178). Irving's elevated tone was established in that early, 'tame and level' scene: his first lines were spoken half-turned away from Bassanio, in a subdued monotone, and the whole was played more deliberately than was customary, even in the sneers and expressions of anger. In III. i, to Salerio and Solanio, he spoke wildly at first, but then with the 'calm tone of desperate resolve' (Irving, p. 341). He eliminated the 'almost incessant movement [and] explosive vociferation' that was customary, but gave a 'lightning flash' at 'To bait fish withal' (l. 45); and, after a pause of suspense, 'there ensued the torrid invective . . . uttered at first in an almost suffocated voice, . . . but presently in the fluent tones of completely liberated passion' (Winter, pp. 187–9). With Tubal he played for pathos; there was a break-down after 'would she were hearsed at my foot. . . .' (ll. 77ff.), and the speech finished ('no tears but o' my shedding') with sobs; on 'I will have the heart of him, if he forfeit', he tore open his robe, repeatedly striking his breast.

But unlike other Shylocks, Irving made his strongest effects in the beginning of the Trial Scene. Here his dignity had full scope: he entered in dead calm, as 'a priest going to the altar', or as 'a figure of Fate—pitiless, majestic, implacable'.[10] Yet he was also a 'lethal monster, sure of his prey, because bulwarked behind the pretence of religion and law' (Winter, p. 196); there was a:

> momentary flashing out of a passionate delight, where Portia's words to Antonio, 'You must prepare your bosom for his knife,' seem to put within his grasp the object of his hate.

And both these impressions contrasted finely and surprisingly with:

> the total collapse of mind and body, when at a glance the full significance of the words—'This bond doth give thee here no jot of blood' (l. 301)—burst upon his keen intellect. In these words, and what follows, he seems to receive his death-blow. . . . We feel the prop is in effect gone 'that doth sustain his life'. But he keeps a firm front to the last, and has a fine curl of withering scorn upon his lip for Gratiano, as he walks away to die in silence and alone.[11]

Yet this was not all: he moved away slowly and with difficulty, as if

[10] *The Theatre* (1879), p. 294.
[11] *Blackwood's Magazine* (Dec. 1879).

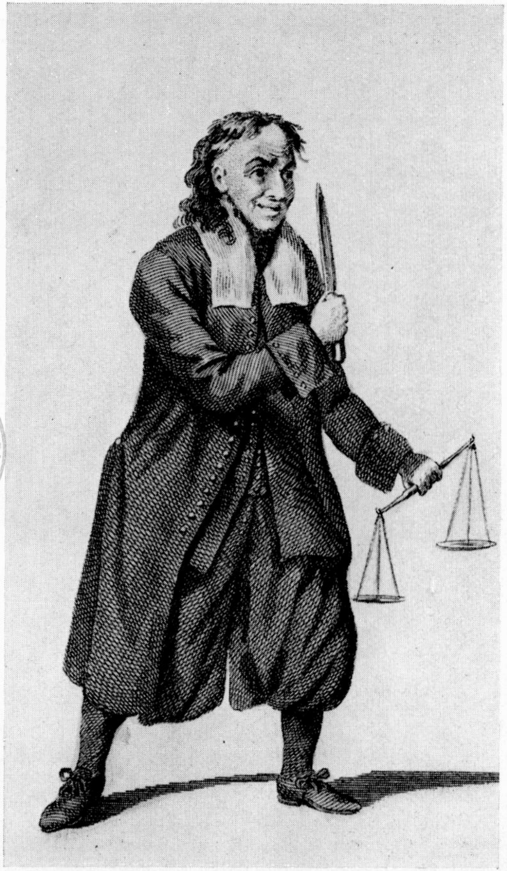

I (left) Macklin as Shylock: IV.i. 'Most learned judge! a sentence; come, prepare.' (from *Bell's Shakespeare*)

II (above) Edmund Kean as Shylock (H. Meyer, after W. H. Watts; 1814)

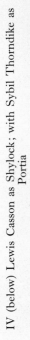

III (left) Henry Irving as Shylock: I.iii. 'How like a fawning publican he looks!'

IV (below) Lewis Casson as Shylock; with Sybil Thorndike as Portia

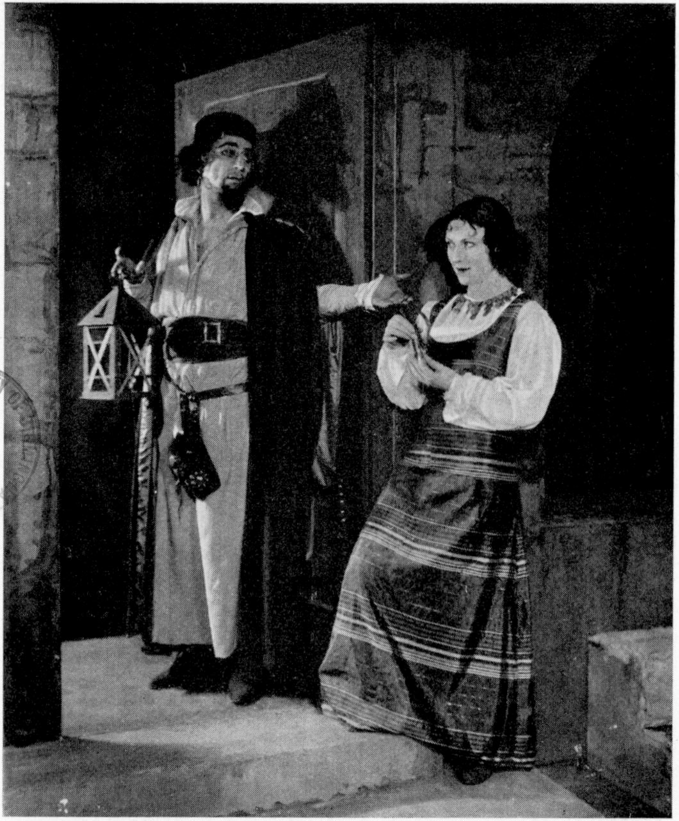

V Ernest Milton as Shylock; with Lydia Sherwood as Jessica

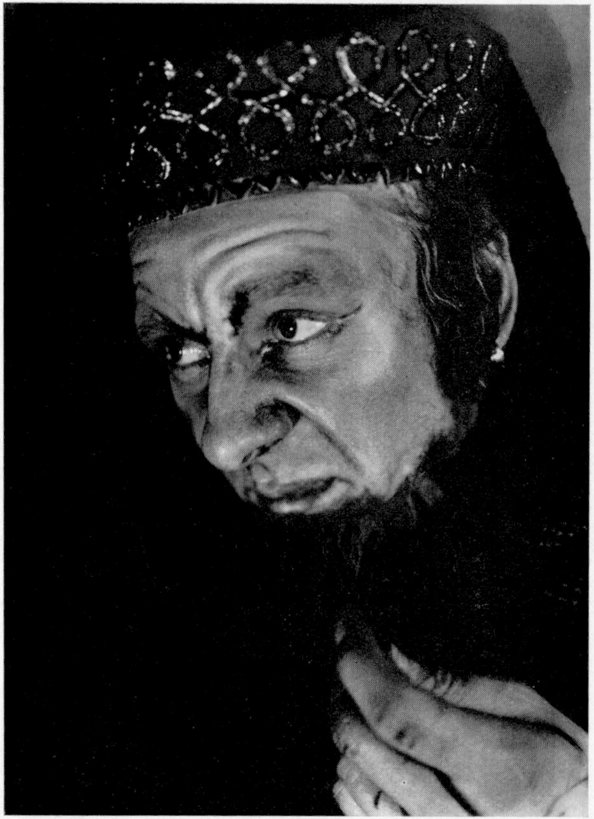

VI John Gielgud as Shylock

VII William Burton as Autolycus: IV.iii. 'See'st thou not the air of the court in these enfoldings?' (Published by Johnson, Fry; 1859)

opposing a fatal weakness by an act of will; at the door he nearly fell, to recover and 'with a long, heavy sigh' to disappear (Winter, p. 195).

After Macklin, Kean and Irving, no one has so completely captured the public's imagination with an original Shylock. Most actors have moved somewhere within the earlier limits while frankly comic interpretations, or a woman in the role, have been short-lived eccentricities; occasionally there have been clear failures. Lewis Casson, Ernest Milton and John Gielgud have probably been the most assured and independent. Casson, performing with the Old Vic Company in 1927, stripped Shylock of romance, dignity and moral stature; this gave a 'new comic quality in his lighter scenes', and in the trial held attention without relying on purely 'theatrical effects'.[12] St. John Ervine in *The Observer* complained that this Shylock lacked the 'magnificence of baffled rage and the courageous abandon of a man whose life is filled with despair'. But to this Casson replied that he could find neither of these qualities in Shakespeare's text: instead of dying for his religion and his oath or remaining scornful to the end, Shylock replies, 'I am content,' and to Casson that was 'contemptible' conduct.[13] He acted within an everyday and even petty idiom: his first scene was the 'ordinary bluff of commerce, common to all tired businessmen'; he dined with Antonio, against his religious scruples, to satisfy mere 'spite'. Casson believed that what is mean, malicious, cunning, cruel and cowardly—traits found in almost every man—draws Shylock on to his 'abominable acts', and this process he tried to portray. The performance was continuously interesting (especially to experienced playgoers), but not compelling; and it did not establish a tradition.

Ernest Milton, five years later, likewise avoided easy theatricality; he played the opening scenes lightly, but with a studied Jewishness, and then, on discovering that Jessica has fled, 'the lamp he is carrying falls from his hand and fate suddenly and savagely transforms him'.[14] From this point he showed more power, but without spectacular strokes, and the final prolonged moment before he leaves the court, as he looks round and 'shows his teeth in a snarl of impotent but silent hatred',[15] was one that could be successfully attempted only by an actor who had played with consistent and minute truth, and with progressive tension.

[12] *Daily Telegraph* (18 Oct. 1927).
[13] *The Observer* (23 Oct. and 24 Dec. 1927).
[14] *The Times* (29 April 1932).
[15] *Daily Telegraph* (29 April 1932).

John Gielgud came to the role in 1938, influenced by a highly acclaimed Chekhov season. He thus saw his problem as that of acting 'in style', appropriate to Shakespeare's language and period, while still acting 'in character'; and as he rehearsed he came to believe that Shakespeare himself had 'obviously calculated' on this attempt, and given full scope for it.[16] As with Casson's, some critics complained that his Shylock fell 'rather from the pavement to the gutter, than from the mountain to the abyss',[17] but Gielgud had added intensity, throughout. He provoked *The New Statesman* to give a detailed account:

> Mr. Gielgud is riveting as the Jew, . . . most careful not to sentimentalise the part. . . . When he is on the stage you can feel the whole house motionless under the painful weight of his realism. In the trial scene he obliged us to suspend disbelief in the impossible story, and when he stropped his knife upon his shoe, we were appalled, not by fear for Antonio, but by the sight of hatred turned to madness. His appearance throughout was extraordinary—gummy, blinking eyes, that suggested some nasty creature of the dark, and loquacious hands with as many inflections as his voice. 'But stop my house's ears,' 'I had it of Leah when I was a bachelor,' 'I am not well'—the intensity with which he delivered such phrases lingers in the memory.

Shylock could sustain Chekhovian attention to subtext, and could evoke pathos without sentimentality, intensity without theatricality.

* * *

Literary critics might complain that these various Shylocks tell more about the 'pitiful ambition' of the actors who invented them than about Shakespeare's play. They could cite, in evidence, the 'No, no, no!' which Kean added after his '. . . would she were hearsed at my foot, and the ducats in her coffin!', or Irving's interpolated scene of Shylock's return at night after Jessica's escape, to knock at his closed door and wait as the curtain fell.[18] But as surely as such additions alter Shakespeare's play, so surely did the interpretations they serve arise from that play: all these Shylocks, despite their contradictions, exist only in and through *The Merchant of Venice*; nothing else could inspire them. The

[16] Cf. an interview in *The Observer* (3 April 1938).
[17] *The Saturday Review* (30 April 1938).
[18] Cf. A. C. Sprague, pp. 24 and 22.

text itself shows how they exploit opportunities given to the actor by Shakespeare.

Shylock's entry is delayed until I. iii, when the audience has already seen Antonio, Bassanio and Portia. The heroine leaves the stage with tripping rhyme:

> Come Nerissa. Sirrah, go before.
> Whiles we shut the gate upon one wooer, another knocks at the door.

and Shylock enters with Bassanio, or, rather Bassanio with Shylock, for the Jew but echoes him:

> SHYLOCK. Three thousand ducats—well.
> BASSANIO. Ay, sir, for three months.
> SHYLOCK. For three months—well.
> BASSANIO. For the which, as I told you, Antonio shall be bound.
> SHYLOCK. Antonio shall become bound—well.
> BASSANIO. May you stead me? Will you pleasure me? Shall I know your answer?
> SHYLOCK. Three thousand ducats for three months, and Antonio bound.
> BASSANIO. Your answer to that.

Shylock's words are pedestrian on the printed page, but they are not so when acted. Of course, repetition without variation would deflate the 'strongest' scene; but no actor would be guilty of that in this situation. Shylock's slow movement and speech at first contrasts with the gay departure of Portia and Nerissa; thus a distinct impression is made at once and the very flatness of the words arouses curiosity. Then as Bassanio becomes more impatient—'Ay, sir, . . .' and 'as I told you' —Shylock's repetitions, in his own tempo and intonation, assure the audience that this man has his own time and his own thoughts; he neglects the three urgent questions to repeat earlier points yet again. And in distinguishing his delivery from Bassanio's, the actor can find many suggestions from the text. As Lewis Casson played him, he is a canny business man, by flat repetitions drawing his client out to show how much he needs the money. For Macklin, the echoing would be sullen and heavy, a slow savouring of 'it now appears you need my help' (l. 109). With Kean the repetitions would show a sharper satisfaction with the twice repeated 'Antonio bound', supported by 'I will feed fat the ancient grudge I bear him' (l. 42), and:

Fast bind, fast find—
A proverb never stale in thrifty mind.

(II. v. 53–54)

The repetitions need a subtext, or 'under-meaning', in order to sustain the introduction of the new character. Probably the stronger they are, the closer they will be to Shakespeare's intention. The ambiguous 'well's' (variously printed as exclamations or questions by editors) can allow two under-meanings to each speech: Shylock's repetition of Bassanio's words can thus be so private with hatred that the 'well' is a necessary declension towards conversation; or the repetition could be falsely bland and the 'well' spoken aside, voicing a private satisfaction. In any case the effect of thus introducing Shylock with thoughts and feelings not directly expressed in the words themselves is to awaken a precise curiosity, induce an intense focus, as the audience watches for explicit statement.

If so far only the privacy of Shylock's thoughts has been fully established, the duologue at once proceeds to further complication:

SHYLOCK. Antonio is a good man.
BASSANIO. Have you heard any imputation to the contrary?
SHYLOCK. Ho, no, no, no, no: . . .

The emphatic reply suggests that the Jew is surprised at being misunderstood, or pretends to be, and it can be used to add to the impression of guile which may already be implicit in the way in which he made Bassanio talk. At once he explains patiently:

. . . no, no; my meaning in saying he is a good man is to have you understand me that he is sufficient. . . .

Shylock's intellectual superiority is nicely established by this elaboration, and by the ironic tone of 'good' and 'sufficient'. And the impression is strengthened by the ease with which he proceeds to make the rich merchant seem a bad security, by his precise and humorous enumeration of risks, his parenthetic explanation of 'water-rats', and his final show of modesty—'I think I may take his bond'. Bassanio's short-phrased and, perhaps short-tempered reply—'Be assur'd you may'—enhances Shylock's control by contrast; and the repetitive rejoinder,—'I will be assur'd I may'—gives opportunity for re-impressing the ominous subtext of the opening.

So far the dramatic issues have been most strongly expressed through contrasts and a controlled manner of speaking, but then Shylock is stung by a chance word of Bassanio's:

> SHYLOCK. . . . May I speak with Antonio?
> BASSANIO. If it please you to dine with us.

Possibly the invitation is diffident, for it implies a show of familiarity with someone the speaker despises; but, however it is spoken, Shylock's reply has contrast enough in its forceful vocabulary and phrasing, and in the sudden particular scorn of 'Yes, to smell pork, to eat. . . .' The projected bargain is forgotten, apparently by a stronger impulse:

> . . . to eat of the habitation which your prophet, the Nazarite, conjured the devil into! I will buy with you, sell with you, talk with you, walk with you, and so following; but I will not eat with you, drink with you, nor pray with you. What news on the Rialto?

The sharp, piled-up phrases culminate in his first allusion to religious observances in 'pray with you'; then, as if by an enforced recall to immediate concerns, there is the sudden anti-climax of 'What news on the Rialto?' and, quickly, the feigned ignorance of 'Who is he comes here?' The *power* of Shylock is first shown in this sudden gust of utterance so firmly subdued for some subtextual reason; and its cause is not money or personal animosity, but race and religion. As Bassanio briefly identifies Antonio and joins him, Shylock is left alone for a soliloquy which, at last, expresses directly what has hitherto been suggested under the lines, by 'sheer acting'; and Shakespeare has prepared for this moment the audience's curiosity and expectation.

Yet as Shylock speaks now with the greater control of verse, all is not made plain. His hatred, avarice and cunning become unequivocal, but there is confusion about the relative importance of two grounds of hatred. The first statement is quick, as if unstudied:

> I hate him for he is a Christian.

But the second, while claiming to be more important, has a show of reason which makes it sound considered rather than passionate:

> But more for that in low simplicity
> He lends out money gratis, and brings down
> The rate of usance here with us in Venice.

His next phrase, 'If I can catch him once upon the hip', is both an everyday idiom and a possible allusion to Jacob's wrestling with the angel (Gen. xxxii); certainly it is no casual thought, for it awakens, in 'I will feed fat the ancient grudge I bear him', the physical idea of devouring as a beast, linked with the solemn connotations of 'ancient'. Then racial consciousness is uppermost again with 'He hates our sacred nation'; and, as this new intensity echoes in tempo and words the first rush of feeling, so it also is followed more reasonably, with explanation and enumeration:

> . . . and he rails
> Even there where merchants most do congregate,
> On me, my bargains and my well-won thrift,
> Which he calls interest.

The soliloquy concludes sharply:

> Cursed be my tribe,
> If I forgive him!

The actors were all, in their partial interpretations, responding to the opportunities of the text: the Shylock who confronts Antonio has had opportunities for inviting an intense and precise scrutiny, for suggesting cunning, avarice, deliberation, power and control—and a hatred that is private and considered, and then irrational and uncontrolled. And in all this he towers—in force, intellectual finesse and quick sensation—over Bassanio, the romantic hero.

With Antonio present Shylock still dominates the scene and calls the tune. As Bassanio recalls him from soliloquy he makes a sudden transition to blandly assumed simplicity and forgetfulness. He taunts Antonio by reminding him that he breaks his principles in asking for money on interest. He tests the importance of the loan by making Antonio listen to a detailed story of Laban and Jacob, his ancestors, and at the same time shows his isolation by being himself absorbed in it. When Antonio turns aside to talk to Bassanio, he can draw him back, simply by mentioning 'Three thousand ducats'. Moreover he shows that he has a keener awareness of the situation than Antonio: the Christian's assumed and brief courtesy—'shall we be beholding to you?'—is answered with sharp parody and a scornful reminder that he has been kicked and spat upon; he even imitates the fawning reply which Antonio seems, somewhat naïvely, to expect. The Christian deals shortly with Shylock to good purpose, because he hates his avarice and cruelty and because he is thinking of his friend, but little is said or done to draw the audience's attention to this; the handling of the scene makes the audience follow Shylock, for he most fully, consecutively and immediately responds to the situation.

Antonio now drops his pretence to Shylock and, dilating on truly generous friendship as his love for Bassanio allows him to do, asks for the loan 'as to thine enemy'. The two men are irreconcilable, but, whereas Antonio sounds annoyed, Shylock is self-possessed and knows that, in 'a merry sport', he can now propose his bond for the forfeit of a pound of flesh if the debt is not repaid in three months. He seems to have arranged the impasse purposely: the audience will have been reminded by his mockery that he seeks to catch Antonio 'on the hip' and will now intently watch his hypocritical finesse and relish:

> Why, look you, how you storm!
> I would be friends with you and have your love.

The ploy works and, after more mockery, he leaves the stage, ostentatiously busy with mundane considerations. He has given a new direction and uncertainty to the action, and the brief comments that follow his subtextually triumphant exit only accentuate the danger by suggesting that Antonio and Bassanio underestimate the inflexible hatred and the cunning management of this man.

Shylock is allowed to grow in the audience's knowledge independently of the other major characters, for while he is often spoken of during the next two Acts, he is seen only with minor characters until just before the trial. With Launcelot and Jessica he appears in a new setting, his own household. He easily dominates this scene (II. v), still isolated ('Who bids thee call?'), sarcastic at Antonio's expense (expecting his 'reproach'), concerned with his race ('By Jacob's staff, I swear'); and, in short time, much is added to his realisation on the stage—chiefly his concern and affection for his daughter. Characteristically there are no long speeches of explicit feeling, but the lines require subtextual feeling to support them. Hatred of the Christian is expressed by his willingness to 'eat pork' to further it and by an allusion to fabulous tales of Jews eating Christian flesh:

> I am not bid for love; they flatter me:
> But yet I'll go in hate, to feed upon
> The prodigal Christian.

From this build-up of hatred there is a sudden transition:

Jessica, my girl,
Look to my house.

Its rapid contrast, the simplicity of 'my girl' at the line-ending, the suspicion implied in 'Look to my house', show Shylock exposed, touched, in need, for the first time. This must be the right reading, for now he can express fear:

I am right loath to go:
There is some ill a-brewing towards my rest,
For I did dream of money-bags to-night.

The 'money-bags' turns the subject to one in which the audience may laugh at Shylock as a mere miser, but only after the sudden transition to tenderness and fear has brought them more close to him than before. Macklin's solemnity, the musical 'charm' of Kean's voice and Irving's dignity, all found scope here. The scene proceeds to show Shylock concerned that Jessica shall not hear the music of the masque nor 'gaze at Christian fools with varnish'd faces', and watchful for his 'sober house'. And during this the audience is made aware at least twice that his daughter is about to rob him and escape from the home she calls a 'hell'. So now the audience sees that Shylock is limited in knowledge, ignorant about the affection for which he has shown his need. After this disclosure, challenging and therefore reawaking earlier ones, the plot interest quickens and Shylock leaves intent on 'Fast bind, fast find'. No other character in the play holds comparable interest for the audience in his own development, as distinct from that of the action and interplay of characters; Shylock alone has such surprising and developing responses.

The opportunities for the actor in the scene (III. i) with Salerio and Solanio, and then Tubal, are well displayed in accounts of performances, but the points of emphasis need to be distinguished. Shylock's first entry, in grief and anger, is an overwhelming visual contrast to his early control. His immediate and direct reproach to the gossiping young men and their freedom to quip and jest at his expense represent loss of cunning and command. His outright self-exposure:

> My own flesh and blood to rebel! . . . I say my daughter is my flesh and my blood.

shows him impervious to mockery and shame. However much he later laments his loss of money and jewels, all these unguarded, unpremeditated moments show the centre of his grief: his family, home, authority, race. And thus his heart is alarmingly exposed. The two young men turn the talk to Antonio and this provokes the first of the great 'transitions' of the scene, used to such powerful effect by Macklin and Kean; the change is to vivid and personal scorn of Antonio, but this develops to a hope of revenge, and his scorn then returns. Now he openly lists Antonio's deeds which he counts injuries, and this halts only for the second, and greater, transition:

> . . . cooled my friends, heated mine enemies. And what's his reason? I am a Jew.

Then through the rest of the speech—remarkable for its range of sensation, from laughter to tears and thoughts of death, for its sarcasm and its pleas for acceptance as a human being (his reasoning in this respect is much like Henry the Fifth's before Agincourt[19])—he draws away from this fact to a still more sustained threat of villainy and revenge. The mere release of energy, of crowded and baffling impressions, make this unanswerable; the young men go without replying, quickly responding to a message from Antonio. Shylock stands now, silent, alone, unapproachable; the actor can, and must, hold the whole theatre silent.

Tubal, a fellow Jew, enters and with him Shylock, still unexhausted, has a series of transitions between grief (for the loss of his daughter and his ducats) and pleasure (in the 'good news' of Antonio's losses). He concludes it after Tubal's account of Jessica's exchange of a ring for a monkey. This must be the climax of the scene, not only by its position but also because here alone Shylock remembers a freer past ('I had it of Leah when I was a bachelor') and sees the difference between himself and his daughter: 'I would not have given it for a wilderness of monkeys'. The last phrase may be a wry or helpless jest; certainly 'wilderness' seems to release from his unspoken thoughts a sense of desolation.[20] The overwhelming effect of these feelings upon him is shown in his reaction to Tubal's next piece of news about Antonio: this time, instead of exulting, he makes deliberate and practical plans to 'have the heart of him'. Shylock is now so alone, intemperate, in-

[19] Cf. *H5*, IV. i. 99–108.

[20] At the time of writing *The Merchant of Venice*, the connotations of this word for Shakespeare appear to have been desolation and savagery: cf. *2 H6*, III. ii. 360; *Tit.*, III. i. 54 and 94; *2 H4*, IV. iv. 137; and *Lucr.*, 544.

human and assured, that the scene, if acted slackly, would be ludicrous and muddled. With absurd, painful, powerful earnestness, he twice appoints Tubal to meet him 'at our synagogue'—again words which touch his deepest feelings—and he does not wait for an answer. For this central manifestation—a moment of clarity and powerful utterance, an opportunity for Irving's pathos and Kean's terror—Shakespeare has contrived the impression that Shylock is driven by feelings too deep to be resisted or fully uttered. The Jew at once dominates the play and makes it appear unable to contain him; the emotions which drive and threaten him cannot be made fully articulate in sustained speech.

Before the trial, a short scene (III. iii) shows that the manacled Antonio confronting Shylock is resigned to death, if only Bassanio will return. However, this is already known from his letter, and a more important development is the return of Shylock's sardonic humour in this scene, and the emphasis it gives to his inflexible intention to 'have his bond'.

By this means, when Shylock enters the Trial Scene (IV. i), silent and alone, to listen to the Duke's last plea, and when he makes his politely and solemnly phrased reply, the audience can at once recognise the deadly inhumanity underneath his 'performance'. So his long taunting speeches and sharp rejoinders alike show confidence and composure without concealing his savage, fixed intent. Shylock's stature is maintained to the last possible moment (here Irving's dignity had strong effect) and, in contrast, Bassanio's most generous sentiment is lightly mocked by Portia and considered a trifle by Shylock. Antonio is not belittled, but this is through lofty resignation, the acceptance of himself as the 'tainted wether of the flock, Meetest for death'; he seems to live outside the issues of the court-room. In her disguise, of course, Portia withstands Shylock, and her plea for mercy—more solemn and sustained than any of his speeches—brings before him the antithesis of his hatred: but he is unmoved and, once more, demands the forfeit. His defeat, therefore, comes very suddenly, by a verbal quibble, as he is about to kill the silent Antonio; the surprise is instantaneous and as thrillingly dramatic as Claudius' 'Give me some light', or Hal's 'I know thee not'. Portia and Shylock are opposed and, as it were, spot-lit.

It may at first seem strange that Shylock should be denied any words with which to express his immediate reaction to the reversal in full measure; yet this is the very means by which Shakespeare has, once more, drawn almost all of the audience's interest to him. He collapses physically as Portia elaborates the case against him and then, after Gratiano has had time to taunt him, there is probably a moment of total silence (the break of the verse-line suggests this) before he speaks, incredulously: 'Is that the law?' On the other side they now speak in turn, but he alone faces them and they must wait for his answers; there are more pauses, in some of which Gratiano mocks him or Portia questions. Except for the garrulous Gratiano, his opponents do not speak of their joy in victory, and so Shylock holds the dramatic focus until he leaves the stage. As the audience waits on his words to satisfy their interest, they will watch closely and see that he is struggling inwardly to understand and come to terms: rapidly he tries two bolt-holes and then a plea for death. But there is no escape and he must listen to his full sentence and the 'utmost' mercy of his enemies, which is a life of poverty and the outward acceptance of his daughter's husband and his enemies' religion. The verbal conclusion of his role is:

> I am content

and

> I pray you, give me leave to go from hence;
> I am not well; send the deed after me
> And I will sign it.

The speeches are brief and must be sustained by subtextual feelings; so they can express renewed control—a dignity (especially in the assurance of fulfilling his word), or a new, hidden purpose (as of suicide or revenge), or an accepted hopelessness. And there is yet the silence in which Shylock leaves, hearing the Duke's curt command and Gratiano's jibe: this cannot fail to impress the audience, at least with his physical weakness as he moves slowly and with difficulty, and probably with his restraint and isolation in saying nothing more; and if he turns towards Gratiano for a moment only, there will be an impression of rekindled scorn for such Christians, or of now-impotent hatred. The slow, silent exit is an unmistakable invitation for the actor to reinforce at the conclusion the salient traits of his characterisation; and it was surely meant to be powerfully affecting, for Shakespeare immediately changed the subject, providing a contrast in relieved inquiries about dinner-engagements.[21]

[21] Cf. Menenius' attempt at a similar change of subject; *Coriol.*, IV. ii. 49.

By many devices Shakespeare has ensured that in performance Shylock is the dominating character of the play; none other has such emotional range, such continual development, such stature, force, subtlety, vitality, variety; above all, none other has his intensity, isolation, and apparent depth of motivation. The various interpretations that have become famous do not overgo the intended impressions.

VII

Playing for Laughs: the Last Plays

★

SHAKESPEARE'S company, in common with other Elizabethan acting groups, would have been quick to find how to get laughs from his plays. Each company had good comics—enough to play Malvolio, Sir Toby, and Sir Andrew as well as Feste, or to bring Jonson's *Bartholomew Fair* to its abundant life—and the chief clown[1] was often its most important member. Richard Tarlton of Queen Elizabeth's Men, who died in 1588, was the first of a line of comedians who could claim to be the funniest men in England. The succession passed to the Chamberlain's Men and then to the King's in the clowns William Kempe and John Armin. In notoriety these men surpassed the heroic and romantic actors like Alleyn, Burbage, and Perkins. Professor Nungezer, who has collected eye-witness accounts in his *Dictionary of Actors . . . in England before 1642*, found that:

> No other Elizabethan actor has been the object of so many notices in contemporary and later writing as Tarlton, or has been remembered with such various and practical tokens of esteem. (p. 355)

His face was instantly recognisable and inns were named after him; as Joseph Hall satirically announced:

> O honour, far beyond a brazen shrine,
> To sit with Tarlton on an ale-post's sign!
> (*Satires* (1599), vi; l. 204)

The great clowns were star actors, capable of thriving on their own verbal wit or their own projected personalities. Tarlton was famous for solo 'jigs' (or song-and-dance routines) and for extemporising verses

[1] In this chapter 'clown' indicates a kind of actor; a star, 'personality' comic. This corresponds to Elizabethan and Jacobean usage; for example, Feste, the professional fool in *Twelfth Night*, is designated 'Clown' in the speech-prefixes of the Folio text.

on themes proposed by members of his audience. Kempe left the Chamberlain's Men about 1599 to exploit his individual talents, as by dancing from London to Norwich and writing a book about it. Armin, who was known as a writer before succeeding Kempe, wrote a play, *The Two Maids of More-Clack* (1609), in which he could act himself—taking three distinct parts, not counting the occasion when in his second role he pretended to be in his first. These clowns were prepared to succeed without much help from the literary art of others. If we merely read the roles they accepted we shall get a dull and unvaried impression: as in low comedy at all times, falls, blows, knavery, mimicry, stupidity, and surprise provided constantly recurring jokes. There was, indeed, good reason for clowns to say and do more than was set down for them; they needed new ways of sustaining old routines; they had to be individual and original to succeed. In a crazy, exaggerated, and energetic art, Tarlton, Kempe, and Armin established themselves—themselves rather than their authors or their roles.

Certainly the individual art of the chief clowns helped to sustain the ubiquitous comedy in the plays of the time; and Shakespeare was well aware of the talents of his company's clowns. In four of the plays originally printed from his autograph manuscript, or a good copy of it, the names of actors found their way into the speech-prefixes or stage-directions, usurping the characters they were meant to sustain. Twice it was the thin man of the company, John Sincklo, who in *Henry IV, Part II* played the Beadle described as an 'anatomy' or skeleton, and could not have been replaced easily; but twice the actors named were clowns. In *Much Ado About Nothing*, Kempe appears in IV. ii instead of '*Dogberry*' or '*Constable*', and Cowley for '*Verges*', '*Headborough*' or '*Con. 2*'. In *Romeo and Juliet*, IV. v, the direction '*Enter Will Kemp*' appears instead of '*Enter Peter*'. In each case the actor seems to have been more formative in Shakespeare's creating mind than the character he had invented; none of the straight actors of the company ever took over a role to similar effect.

Shakespeare, whose Hamlet could reprove clowns for speaking more than was set down for them, used clowns for important roles in almost all his plays; his respect for the single judicious auditor did not banish fools, fights, and merry bawdy incidents from his plays. From the slapstick incidents of *The Comedy of Errors* and *The Taming of the Shrew* to the subtle and elaborate foolery in *Twelfth Night*, or from the crazed and cruel humour of *Titus Andronicus* and *Henry VI* to the intensities of Lear's Fool and his own madness, there is an obvious refinement and deepening of comedy; but that should not be allowed to obscure the prat-falls and absurdities of his neatest comedies—Maria promises that Sir Toby shall 'laugh himself into stitches'—or the tripping-up and abuse of Oswald by Kent in *King Lear*. If *Henry VIII* is wholly by Shakespeare he there introduced two comic porters with a pushing crowd in despite of the play's prologue that scorned both 'fool and fight': here are blows enough, and the usual bawdy jokes about 'the Indian with the great tool', about women, honour, and cuckoldom—and all this by way of preparation for a great prophetic concluding scene.

If we wish to understand Shakespeare's plays in performance, we must learn to notice the cues he has provided for these clowns to get their laughs. First there are opportunities for impressing a dominant personality. Often a role will begin with a solo entry, without much reference to the existing dramatic situation and often without reference to any other character. This is varied by immediately providing the chief comedian with an obvious foil or 'feed'. Often the textual provision is most detailed at this point, as if Shakespeare felt the need to insist on the clown taking some colour from his author's conception on the all-important first impression. Verbally the comic parts tend to peter out when a sufficient head of dramatic energy has been established; at the end of a successful low comedy performance the actor's hold over an audience ensures that a very little material will go a sufficiently long way.

Whatever the demands of plot or theme the clown had to be able to use his traditional business, and Shakespeare must have known that his words would stand more chance of being respected if they invited this usual co-operation. Any reference to an ugly face, for example (or, ironically, its opposite good looks) would be taken up at once, for clowns, then as now, exploited out-of-the-ordinary features. Henry Peacham used the effect of this as an almost mythological simile:

> As Tarlton when his head was only seen,
> The tirehouse door and tapestry between,
> Set all the multitude in such a laughter
> They could not hold for scarse an hour after . . .
>
> *Thalia's Banquet* (1620)

Other clowns used a 'scurvy face' as a circus clown uses exaggerated make-up. Grimaces were invented and grotesque gestures. Thomas Goffe wrote in the Praeludium to his *Careless Shepherdess* (1618–29):

> I've laughed
> Until I cried again to see what faces
> The rogue will make. O it does me good
> To see him hold out's chin, hang down his hands,
> And twirl his bauble. There is nere a part
> About him but breaks jest . . .

Silent by-play was often accompanied by trite words. In the 'bad' Quarto of *Hamlet*, the prince takes his complaint of clowns a step further than in the authoritative text:

> And then you have some again, that keep one suit
> Of jests, as a man is known by one suit of
> Apparel, and gentlemen quote his jests down
> In their tables before they come to the play, as thus:
> 'Cannot you stay till I eat my porridge?' and 'You owe me
> A quarter's wages', and 'My coat wants a cullison',
> And 'Your beer is sour'; and blabbering with his lips
> And thus keeping in the cinquepace of jests,
> When, God knows, the warm clown cannot make a jest
> Unless by chance, as the blind man catcheth a hare.
>
> (Sig. F2f.)

Many authors, including Shakespeare, provided running gags of this sort for their clowns, as popular radio or television programmes today have their marks in 'Don't forget the diver', or 'Hullo . . . Eth!', or 'Yeah! Yeah! Yeah!'

The clowns also had more normal skills and these had to be provided for. They could play on tabor and pipe. They were active and nimble, Tarlton being a fencing master and Kempe a notorious dancer. They were skilled, too, in mimicry, becoming sad or gay on demand, and were often given speeches which allowed them to imitate different kinds of behaviour within a short compass, as in Touchstone's party-piece on the various degrees of quarrelling. In this way they could show their imitative skill and project shrewd and compendious social comment. When the Clown enters in Thomas Heywood's *Rape of Lucrece* (1609) and is asked for news, he offers court-news, camp-news, city-news, country-news, and news-at-home, and is asked for them all ($C2^v$–3). The Porter in *Macbeth* was probably meant to mimic the walk and talk of the farmer, equivocator, and tailor whom he imagined at the castle gate; so played the scene is still continuously funny today.

One of the greatest strengths of the clowns was their ability to call forth abnormal responses, to make pathos, villainy, wisdom, or cowardice both funny and acceptable. As Launcelot Gobbo is given opportunity to mock his blind and mistaken father in *The Merchant of Venice*, so the servant-clown in *The Miseries of Enforced Marriage* (1607) mocks his mistress's misery:

> From London am I come, though not with pipe and drum,
> Yet I bring matter, in this poor paper,
> Will make my young mistress, delighting in kisses,
> Do as all maidens will hearing of such an ill,
> As to have lost the thing they wish'd most—
> A husband, a husband, a pretty sweet husband—
> Cry: 'Oh, oh, oh,' and 'Alas!' and at last 'Ho, ho, ho!'
> as I do. (Sig. C3)

Thieving is a common occasion for enjoying the clown's skill: Mouse, the clown in the long-popular romance *Mucedorus*, steals a pot of ale and a stage-direction follows to describe his subsequent engagement with the ale-wife:

> *She searcheth him, and he drinketh over her head, and casts down the pot. She stumbleth at it, then they fall together by the ears; she takes her pot and goes out.*

Often these escapades were mixed with an element of cowardice, as when Cuckedemoy in Marston's *Dutch Courtezan* (1603–4) picks the pocket of Malheureux as he is going to execution. Sometimes two divergent responses were called forth together, notably bawdy enjoyment with some piece of social criticism or a mocking imitation of some unamorous activity; the school lessons in *The Taming of the Shrew* are opportunities for this, and the clown's tilt at pedantry in his disavowal of any intention to flirt with Lucrece's maid in Heywood's play:

> If ever I knew what belongs to these cases, or yet know what they mean; if ever I used any plain dealing or were ever worth such a jewel, would I might die like a beggar; if ever I were so far read in my grammar as to know what an interjection is, or a conjunction copulative . . . why do you think, madam, I have no more care of

> myself, being but a strippling, than to go to it at these years; flesh and blood cannot endure it. I shall even spoil one of the best faces in Rome with crying at your unkindness . . .
>
> (D4f.)

Here too is the obvious lie, superlative overstatement, mock weeping, and ugly face. And here is the clown's deliberate and two-faced concern with sexual virility: so, in *As You Like It*, Touchstone complains that Corin brought the 'ewes and rams together' and betrayed a 'she-lamb of a twelve-month to a crooked-pated, old, cuckoldly ram', and then justifies his attachment to Audrey in that as 'horns are odious, they are necessary'. Launcelot Gobbo is allowed to complain that Lorenzo 'raised the price of hogs' by making more Christians and then boast of the dishonesty of the Moor whom he, himself, has got 'with child' (III. iv. 16–37).

The strangeness and licence that the clowns' humour sometimes required is well illustrated by their animal disguises. *Ram Alley* (1607–8) by Lording Barry has a clown who dresses as an ape to do lewd dances; Fletcher's *Mad Lover* has a dog-barking episode by a clown who had been in a masque of beasts. A tract called *This World's Folly: or a Warning-Piece discharged upon the Wickedness thereof* written by I. H. and published in 1615 has much to say about 'obscene and light jigs, stuff'd with loathsome and unheard-of ribaldry, suckt from the poisonous dugs of sin-swell'd theatres'. This critic singled out Greene of the Queen's Men for his 'stentor-throated bellowings, flash-choaking squibbles of absurd vanities' and his speciality of dancing as a baboon, 'metamorphosing human shape into bestial form'.

* * *

Performances of clowns and fools of Elizabethan theatres are well documented compared with those of their fellow actors, but even so our knowledge is fragmentary. But, as fooling is timeless, we can learn more from later-day comics who have left detailed memoirs. Three extracts, in place of many, can show the unchanging form of clowning and suggest something of the actors' art behind the brief facts that have survived from Shakespeare's time.

The clown's 'scurvy' face and comic dress has always been sufficient cause of laughter. *The Life of the Late Famous Comedian, Jo Haynes* (1701) tells how:

> There happen'd to be one night a play acted call'd *Catiline's Conspiracy*, wherein there was wanting a great number of senators. Now Mr. Hart, being chief of the House, wou'd oblige Jo to dress for one of these senators, altho' Jo's salary, being then 50s. per week, freed him from any such obligation. But Mr. Hart, as I said before, being sole Governor of the Playhouse and at a small variance with Jo, commands it and the other must obey. Jo, being vex'd at the slight Mr. Hart had put on him, found out this method of being reveng'd on him: he gets a Scaramouch dress, a large full ruff, makes himself whiskers, from ear to ear, puts on his head a long Merry Andrew's cap, a short pipe in his mouth, a little three legg'd stool in his hand, and in this manner follows Mr. Hart on the stage, sits himself down behind him, and begins to smoke his pipe, to laugh and point at him.
>
> (p. 23)

A century later *Oxberry's Dramatic Biography* (new series, i; 14 April 1827) gave a compendious picture of Grimaldi that illustrates how a clown can centre attention on his assumed character no matter what is happening elsewhere on the stage and can make the audience laugh at actions that would usually evoke an anxious concern:

> The hopelessness of one who knows not what to do next, he hits to a nicety—he always appeared to us to represent a grown child waking to perception but wondering at every object he beholds. Then, his exuberance of animal spirits was really miraculous; what a rich ringing laugh!—the very voice of merriment! Then, the self-approving chuckle, and the contemptuous look, half pity, half derision, that he gave to the dupe of his artifice; his incessant annoyance to *Pantaloon* and his feigned condolence for the very misfortunes of which he was the author; his amazement and awe of *Harlequin*, his amorous glances at *Columbine*, and his winks at the imbecility of the doting and the dandyism of the young lover; his braggadocia blustering, his cautious escapes from detection and his ludicrous agony during fustigation, an operation duly performed on *Clown* by all the personages of the motley drama—were all his, and HIS ALONE. He was the very *beau ideal* of thieves: robbery became a science in his hands; you forgave the larceny, for the humour with which it was perpetrated. He abstracted a leg of mutton from a butcher's tray, with such a delightful assumption of *nonchalance* (he threw such plump stupidity into his countenance, whilst the slyness of observation lurked in his half-closed eyes). He extracted a watch, or a handkerchief, with such a bewitching

> eagerness—with such a devotion to the task—and yet kept his wary eye upon the victim of his trickery. He seemed so imbued with the spirit of peculation, that you saw it in him, merely as a portion of his nature, and for which he was neither blameable or accountable. His pantomimic colloquies with the other sex, too, were inimitable—his mincing affectation, when addressing a dandizette; his broad bold style, when making love to a fisherwoman—were all true to Nature.

A clown's struggles to be funny have been disclosed in some memoirs. In *Grock, King of Clowns* (tr. 1957) the great twentieth-century circus artist has contrasted himself with a straight actor:

> Unlike an actor who has his set part to play, a clown can vary and embroider his part every night if he chooses. The chief thing is that what he does makes a hit.
>
> (p. 83)

He is free to improvise for each new audience and he is also imprisoned by the absolute need to raise a laugh. Grock tells the story of how he invented his 'piano-lid trick'. At each routine joke with the piano, his feed, Antonet, had been saying 'Do you think that was funny? . . . Do you really think that was funny?' and so had killed his effects. Grock became truly enraged and took off the piano lid to strike Antonet:

> My costume and make-up must have made my genuine rage incredibly funny. The public shrieked with laughter. I came to my senses and pursued Antonet no further.

Grock returned to the piano to put the lid on, but failed to do so:

> Something had to be done to amuse them now that I was alone in the ring. But what on earth was I to do? I rested the lid against the left-hand side of the piano, sloping to the ground from the end of the key-board. At the sight of it, the idea came to me to let my hat slide down it. No sooner thought than done. My hat tobogganed merrily to the ground. I was just going to pick it up and put it on when the great inspiration came! Why not toboggan down after my hat? I climbed up on to the piano, slid down the slope straight to my hat, which I put on and then walked proudly off. The effect was stupendous!
>
> (pp. 85–86)

Anger and a ludicrous face; obvious child-like pleasure; unexpected and disproportionate behaviour; the simple action of putting on a hat;

these can raise stupendous laughter and applause, given a clown's agility, resilience, and sense of scale and timing.

* * *

Read with the eyes of a clown Shakespeare's plays offer abundant cues for business and improvisation. *The Winter's Tale*, which E. M. W. Tillyard has called a presentation of 'the whole tragic pattern from prosperity to destruction, regeneration, and still fairer prosperity',[2] can be taken as an example.

For clowns Autolycus is the star part. He enters with a solo song, with no immediate dramatic task beyond the establishment of his assumed *persona*. The words Shakespeare has given him invite mimicry and business on the four times repeated 'With heigh!', and on the 'tirra-lirra' for lark-song and the constrasting references to thrush and jay. A brief, prose speech serves to connect the character with 'Prince Florizel' and so, vaguely, to the plot, but at the same time, makes pointed reference to his comical rags, being 'out of service' like himself, and also provides an excuse for imitating a superior person dressed in 'three-pile' velvet. At once he has another song, contrasting in mood with the first:

> But shall I go mourn for that, my dear?
> The pale moon shines by night; . . .

The imitation of the forlorn lover is quickly revalued as a prelude to mischief when a second stanza presents Autolycus again as an adventurer, this time with a reference to punishment in the 'stocks'. Even here there is a usual twist, for he will 'avouch' his account in the stocks as if formally claiming right while being punished for wrong. With his prose speech that immediately follows Autolycus is established by name and by his thieving; and as something of a coward and an indolent innocent:

> beating and hanging are terrors to me; for the life to come, I sleep out the thought of it. (ll. 29–30)

With the entry of the shepherd's son, he lets the audience share his hope of successful trickery and at once goes into a new imitative routine: this time he is a poor robbed and beaten man crying out for death.

[2] *Shakespeare's Last Plays* (1951), p. 40.

Tears will bring laughter here; and so will his dexterity in picking the young shepherd's pocket while talking of a 'charitable office'. The comic business has its surprises, for his victim offers to give him money and so threatens to discover the robbery, and Autolycus himself nearly spoils everything by talking in his assumed role about his real one and so nearly giving himself away by calling his vices virtues. Before he successfully shakes off the shepherd's son, the joke of imitation is taken a step further as he has to pretend to be a bigger coward than the coward he really is. Alone again, he raises expectation for his next appearance at the sheep-shearing—and makes the obvious word-play in hoping that the 'shearers prove sheep'. With a further glance at 'virtue' he leaves the stage with a third song which again invites imitative gestures and picks up the pace of the performance:

> Jog on, jog on, the footpath way,
> And merrily hent [jump] the stile-a; . . .

It also justifies his villainy by the merriment it brings, and gives a further opportunity for mimed action:

> A merry heart goes all the day,
> Your sad tires in a mile-a.

A master-clown would use this introductory scene to show off many of his tricks and gain the connivance of the audience.

His next entry is a further transformation. Now a pedlar he enters with yet another song, this time giving opportunity for by-play with his audience on the stage and a run of sexual innuendoes. After telling tall stories to the credulous rustics he 'bears' his part in a song for three voices:—'you must know 'tis my occupation', he says, with a clown's extra-dramatic statement about his own interests and a glancing jest at the expense of puritans whose accustomed phrase this was. He leaves the stage to follow his dupes with a brief aside to keep the audience aware of his intentions ('And you shall pay well for 'em') and with another song asking questions of 'My dainty duck, my dear-a' and, finally, telling even his victims that 'Money's a meddler'.

His second appearance in IV. iv begins with another soliloquy, as Camillo, Perdita, and Florizel talk aside. Autolycus is in full triumph after his 'sheep-shearing', but when he thinks he is overheard he has only one thought: 'hanging'. Camillo supplies a spoken stage-direction in case the actor does not see the cue for yet another transformation:

> How now, good fellow! Why shak'st thou so? Fear not, man; here's no harm intended to thee.

He is asked to exchange his poor clothes for Florizel's and when his benefactors leave him outwardly transformed to a gentleman with a 'Farewell, my friend', he is ready for his new role in 'Adieu, sir:'—comically he is only *just* ready, for he is still wearing his pedlar's false beard (cf. l. 702).

In soliloquy he congratulates himself on coping with business somewhat out of his usual line of pickpocketing. He is allowed a glance, too, at the traditional art of the clown: 'Sure, the gods do this year connive at us, and we *may do anything extempore*'; he, the clown as well as Autolycus, proclaims himself 'constant to my profession'. Then more 'matter for a hot brain' enters with the shepherd and his son; more 'work' for a 'careful man' he claims, indulging a clown's customary transference of values.

A few preparatory asides and the business of taking off a false beard and he is then ready to encounter the rustics as a full-fledged courtier. Here the clown can satirize the familiar distinctions between town and country, and would give himself away to anybody but fellow clowns by picking his teeth and wearing his clothes 'not handsomely' (ll. 738 and 742). The necessary plot-development being complete, the episode ends with Autolycus terrifying the shepherd's son with a description of tortures and at the same time assuming the role of outraged and self-secure morality. The others leave Autolycus behind for a soliloquy in which he expostulates about his embarrassment of riches:

> If I had a mind to be honest, I see Fortune would not suffer me; she drops booties in my mouth.

The last scene in which Autolycus appears (V. ii) would seem an anti-climax to any actor but a clown. He is now in Sicilia and at first he is but one of an audience for the news of Perdita's reunion with her father. But his presence from the start of the scene ensures that he can react to the new situation and allows him a soliloquy immediately before the shepherd and his son enter dressed in new finery. He is dejected:

> Now, had I not the dash of my former life in me, would preferment drop on my head . . .

His 'merry' philosophy has let him down and he is even envious:

> Here come those I have done good to against my will, and already appearing in the blossoms of their fortune.

But dejection for a clown is a new ploy, even if it appears unassumed. The actor will take advantage of the silence with which he answers the first overtures of the now irrepressible shepherds, and will give a dawning irony to his belated response: 'I know you are now, sir, a gentleman born' (l. 130). After hearing further chat he is ready to make a cumbersomely humble approach. His last words promising to 'prove' a tall fellow is no large conclusion for Autolycus, but that is provided by the last words of the shepherd's son: 'Come, follow us; we'll be thy good masters.' The crucial point is that Autolycus makes his exit after them: for a clown, this is an invitation to provide his own idiosyncratic business. He can take his choice: simple mimicry, or a renewed picking of pockets (this became a stage tradition, with words added from David Garrick's version of the play) or, more comprehensively using grimace and gesture, a rehabilitation of the clown's hopefulness, his nose catching the smell of new trickery, a dawning satisfaction at the prospect of his old comfortable discomfort, his old virtuous vices. With a good clown as Autolycus—and the part calls for one—the mere call to *follow* the others off-stage ensures that he has the last laugh. As Grock would say: 'The chief thing is that what he does makes a hit.'

Autolycus does not attract much attention from readers of *The Winter's Tale* and most literary critics pay only passing recognition. Even in performance he can fall flat. *Punch* of 1 February 1933, said of an Old Vic production:

> There was little in this dark gymnastic gipsy of Mr. Geoffrey Wincott to suggest that here was one of the great Shakespearean characters. It is not a part which plays itself . . .

Comment in other papers agreed with this, and with the *Manchester Guardian*'s judgement of 7 July 1948, that a Stratford-upon-Avon production had a 'rather too zealously grotesque Autolycus'. The part comes to life only when a clown contributes his own art and personality, and takes up most of the cues that Shakespeare has given him.

In the great age of English pantomime, Garrick's *Florizel and Perdita* held the stage instead of Shakespeare's play. Besides curtailing the action of the play this version gave considerable prominence to Autolycus and the shepherds. But a prompt-book for Kean's revival of Shakespeare's play at the Princess's Theatre in 1856 (now in the Folger Library) shows another way with Autolycus—to cut him down in the interest of stage spectacle and narrative clarity: here, for example, he makes no appearance in Act V. In the theatre Autolycus must be a clown's star performance, or nothing.

A very well-documented production is one sponsored by a famous clown at his own theatre and for his own Autolycus. A published *Collection of the Critical Opinions . . . of 'the Winter's Tale' at Burton's Theatre, New York* gives some idea how Simon Forman, a Jacobean playgoer, came to note in his diary after seeing a performance: 'Beware of trusting feigned beggars or fawning fellows.' The New York *Sunday Times* said of William Burton:

> He seems to have entered completely into the spirit of the thing; he is so jovial a vagabond, so amusing a specimen of rascality, and commits petit larcenies and small swindling transactions in such a funny, jolly sort of way, that one cannot help enjoying the entertainment he creates as a set off against his natural and unconquerable depravity. . . . The rags are worn with such a jaunty, swaggering air, and he is altogether a most magnificent specimen of the 'bummer' of antiquity. One can hardly help admiring the lazy nonchalance and consistent independence of the honest labor with which he gains a questionable livelihood. . . . In an age of large financial speculation, he would have been a great capitalist, and we admire and respect him accordingly.

The *Albion* also saw contemporary point in Burton's Autolycus—successful clowning is timeless and therefore free to mirror the concerns of any particular age:

> He is the embodiment of the vulgar idea of success and the sharpest satire on the worship of the almighty dollar. His 'revenue is the silly cheat.' O, Wall Street, behold thy King! 'Hanging and beating are terrors to him; for the life to come, he sleeps out the thought of it!' Comfortable nodder, in the deep wall pew, behold thy ancestor!

The *Sunday Despatch* described the effect of this Autolycus on the play as a whole:

> Our only regret is that Master William Shakespere does not send that rogue Autolycus upon the stage before the fourth act, when, in reality, that life which alone can give general popularity to the play only begins. Burton is grand, rich, unctuous, racy, roguish, and funny all at one and the same time in the part. . . .

Burton had much the same creative qualifications for the role as an Elizabethan clown. Like Tarlton and Armin, he had published his *Waggeries and Vagaries*; and he wrote several farces. 'Mirth', it was said, 'came from him in exhalations', and 'the resources of by-play, grimace, and mimetic effect, were his at command' (W. Keese, *Actors and Actresses*, iii (1886), p. 224).

> The secret of Burton's power did not lie in any single gift; it was not only his mirth-provoking face, his ability to infuse character and comicality together into his countenance, though doubtless this was the most peculiar of his talents; he had others. . . . Burton had a creative faculty. He did more for many of the characters he played than the author of the piece. His *Toodle* and *Sleek* were absolute creations, and indicated an ability quite akin to that of a great dramatist. . . . He could play with success scenes of great pathos, and would often have brought tears to the eyes of his auditors were it not for their recollections of his more familiar comic scenes.
>
> (*Sunday Times*, New York, 12 Feb. 1860)

A full clown's performance in *The Winter's Tale* importantly affects the theatrical life of the play. In a story that moves from prosperity through destruction to regeneration, from separation to reconciliation, the clown presents a character who is both a failure and a success. In an intensely felt narrative he evokes from the audience laughter, connivance and appreciation, relaxation and admiration. In a drama about the influences of time, he provides a timeless artistry and remains unchanged at the conclusion. He brings topicality to a fantastic tale, an escape from the consequences of knavery to a moral confrontation, and a grotesque embodiment of irresponsible fears and aggressions, of vigorous and sexual activity, to a shapely and often refined romance.

The relevance of his role can be gauged partly through particular verbal contact with the rest of the play: Florizel calls Perdita a gooddess, as Autolycus sings his wares 'as they were gods and godesses'; Polixenes calls her a 'knack', the word he used for Autolycus' pedlar's wares; Perdita's 'blood looks out' at Florizel's whisperings, after Autolycus had hailed 'red blood' that reigns in 'winter's pale'; and Florizel had disappeared from court, as Autolycus' ballad promises:

> Get you hence, for I must go
> Where it fits not you to know.

So the clown's disguise, trickery, thieving and easy excitement of 'summer songs. . . . While we lie tumbling in the hay' are shown to be relevant to the affairs of the main plot. Later the very clothes for disguising Florizel are taken from Autolycus' disguise, and the fearful trembling of this clown is a reminder of the dangers the King's son is risking.

But Autolycus' contribution to the play is greatest at its most general. His heightening of the 'mirth of the feast'—the licence of instinctive and irresponsible enjoyment—enables Shakespeare to present Florizel and Perdita without stiffness and yet with contrasting carefulness; it also enables the dance of the wild 'men of hair' to make its contrast with the earlier decorous dance with immediate acceptance as another divertissement. The last exit for Autolycus in Act V, with its climactic and possibly silent humour, is an important device to relax the critical attention of the audience immediately before Hermione is revealed as a painted statue. Grock used to play Verdi on a diminutive concertina at the end of his act, and it always seemed powerfully seductive to the audience; and so here, the audience's contentment at the invincible humour and roguery of Autolycus disposes it to accept the strange, severe and sweetened (cf. l. 76) theatricality of the concluding scene. Laughter and dreams alike release our fantasies from the restrictive control of our censoring minds; so, having joined everyman's laughter at the undeserved and unfounded resilience of Autolycus, the audience will more readily accept the dreamlike conditions of the final scene, the living statue that

> Excels whatever yet you look'd upon
> Or hand of man hath done.
>
> (ll. 16–17)

Laughter has contrived the relaxed and uncritical condition suitable for the acceptance of a further and solemn fantasy.

'Dreams are toys' argues Antigonus in III. iii, and at the end of *A Midsummer Night's Dream* Puck asks that the whole comedy should be accepted as an idle dream. So much Shakespeare certainly knew about the connections between fantasy and humour, and his contemporaries accepted it too. The total solemnity of much criticism of the last plays that is current today would strike Elizabethans and Jacobeans as pompous and restrictive. Romance, for them, spelt wonder, delight, *and* mirth. The prologue to the romantic comedy *Mucedorus* expresses this directly:

Mirth drown your bosom, fair Delight your mind,
And may our pastime your contentment find.

And *The Winter's Tale* has more 'pastime' than Autolycus. The two shepherds are traditional rustic comics, with muddled meetings and muddled speeches; they mix comedy and pathos in discovering the disastrous end of Antigonus; they mistake meanings, labour slowly in witticisms, attempt mimicry, and, like Autolycus, leave the play with more troubles obviously to come. There is comedy, too, in the earlier scenes of the main plot, especially in the contrasts between the forthright Paulina and the timid jailor and courtiers, and the two husbands, Antigonus and Leontes. All the comedy contributes to the final effect of the play, by its fantasy and freedom, obviously; but also by the individuality, topicality and robust vitality that are required to perform the more comic roles.

* * *

Shakespeare understood the acting talents of clowns and gave them scope—but always appropriately to his main design. The other romances use clowns' performances in various ways, according to their narratives and themes. *Pericles,* that is probably not wholly by Shakespeare, has least comedy. In the last three Acts, where the authorship is less disputed, humour is concentrated in the brothel scenes, allowing a kind of ease or 'delight' to incidents out of tone with the thrusting and evocative narrative of the rest of those Acts. The whole incident takes some colour from Boult, notably in a short scene (IV. v) with the memorably exaggerated line, 'Come, I am for no more bawdy-houses. Shall's go hear the vestals sing?', with which an anonymous Gentleman suggests a zany impracticability in sudden conversion. Boult remains unchanged when he leaves the play, but subdued to Marina's purposes and having voiced, in unusually solemn tones, the clown's usual defence of his misdeeds—that is, that the fault lies in the world, or with 'others':

What would you have me do? Go to the wars, would you, where a man may serve seven years for the loss of a leg, and have not money enough in the end to buy him a wooden one?

(IV. vi. 168–70)

In *Cymbeline*, Shakespeare uses a tighter rein. The jailor is the only outright clown's part, but his clown's defence, 'I would we were all of one mind, and one mind good' (V. iv. 200), is an important, verbal preparation for the Soothsayer's final:

The fingers of the pow'rs above do tune
The harmony of this peace. (V. v. 464–5)

Cloten looks at first to be a loutish clown, amusingly and coarsely interrupting the courtly scenes and then becoming the foolish wild-man of the woods who ineffectually tries to ravish Imogen and kill Posthumus. But in his two soliloquies, 'I love and hate her' and 'Meet thee at Milford Haven!' (III. v. 70 ff. and 131 ff.), he is presented with too strong an impression of pent-up and self-conflicting feelings to remain either a clown or a comic villain. His end is funny, like a typical braggart's combat, but Belarius reminds the audience of the risks he has so far taken:

not frenzy, not
Absolute madness could so far have rav'd
To bring him here alone. (IV. ii. 135–7)

and he differs from other braggarts in actually taking the initiative in the last engagement—'Yield, rustic mountaineer'—and actually, though off-stage, dying.

In *Cymbeline* the humour is dispersed throughout the action; but the relaxed enjoyment of comedy is seldom unalloyed: the Queen, Posthumus, Iachimo, Pisanio, Belario, Guiderius, Arviragus, Cymbeline himself perhaps, and certainly Imogen, all raise laughter at times, as does the contrivance of the plot, and yet all these characters, at times, command the audience's closest and directest sympathy. When Imogen mistakes Cloten's headless body as Posthumus', laughter and tears are brought together most sharply. For Imogen the experience is specifically like a 'dream'. The apparent reality as expressed here:

Pisanio might have kill'd thee at the heart,
And left this head on.

is so absurd that very few actresses have dared to use all the words provided. Bernard Shaw recognised that Shakespeare had successfully created the 'dim, half-asleep funny state of consciousness' but he nevertheless advised Ellen Terry to cut 'A headless man' from her performance:

> This is what I cannot understand; and I believe it is an overlooked relic of some earlier arrangement of the business.[3]

[3] *Ellen Terry and Bernard Shaw; a Correspondence*, ed. C. St. John (1949), pp. 45–46. See also, Chapter XII, p. 189, below.

The whole soliloquy so mixes abrupt comedy with deepest feeling that, temporarily, the comedy is entirely subdued, becoming part of the terror of Imogen's nightmare-dream. Only out of dramatic context, without the passion and uncertainty of the 'felt' situation, are the lines at all funny; trust the mixture of absurdity and fantasy and the scene becomes wholly affecting.

In the last scene the persistent mingling of comedy and affecting dramatic narrative is smoothly resolved. The characters file off-stage together, no one drawing all sentiment to himself but all moving at the bidding and with the reassurance of the Soothsayer, Philarmonus. All are 'o'erjoy'd' (l. 401): 'joy'd' that others are what they are, and prepared to 'laud . . . the gods' and wonder at the new 'peace' (ll. 424 and 474–83). It would be wrong to cut from this last scene its hints of comedy, the laughter that can so readily be raised by Posthumus' 'Shall's have a play of this?', Cymbeline's 'Does the world go round?', the Doctor's 'I left out one thing . . .', Belarius' 'My boys, There was our error' and 'Not too hot . . . I am too blunt and saucy', and the sudden reappearance of the Doctor for the ludicrously neat 'By the Queen's dram she swallow'd'. At these and other points the contrivance of the play's conclusion can appear hilariously complicated; and the laughter that will undoubtedly come during rehearsals must be prized and its occasions carefully retained and possibly augmented in order to help present the delight and fantasy of the happy ending. This romantic play uses clowns and comic dialogue as an entry and support for fantasy, and so gains moments of feeling that are all the sharper for contrast; and it arrives at a conclusion that in performance can seem sublime because it is not always perfectly serious and so not always obviously impossible.

The conclusion of *The Tempest* is the most grave and considered of all. But in this play, too, the importance of the clowns' roles can be under-estimated. The last arrivals when Prospero stands revealed as the rightful Duke of Milan are a drunken jester and butler, and a 'thing of darkness': such emphatic placing alone requires respect. Obviously Trinculo and Stephano seeking shelter or profit from Caliban is a normal clown's trick, like the disguises and trickery of Autolycus. The songs 'Freedom' and 'Scout 'em and flout 'em', and the falling-out about the finery Prospero sets as a trap, invite comic team work and embellishment. Caliban himself as a strange 'monster' is partly a clown's role; even his attempted rape of Miranda and attack on

Prospero, together with his care for the island's beauties, are in the comic tradition. Bremo, the wild-man in *Mucedorus*, tries to woo Amadine by offering, like Caliban to Stephano:

> If thou wilt love me thou shalt be my queen;
> I'll crown thee with a chaplet made of ivory,
> And make the rose and lily wait on thee.
> I'll rend the burly branches from the oak,
> To shadow thee from burning sun,
> The trees shall spread themselves where thou dost go,
> And as they spread, I'll trace along with thee . . .
>
> (IV. iii)

and much more. The clown, William Burton, played Caliban in his own theatre, along with Autolycus, Bottom, Belch, Falstaff, and a host of his farcical creations:

> The most superb performance of Burton's which I remember was his *Caliban*. A wild creature on all fours sprang upon the stage, with claws on his hands, and some weird animal arrangement about the head partly like a snail. It was an immense conception. Not the great God Pan himself was more the link between the man and beast than this thing. It was a creature of the woods, one of nature's spawns; it breathed of nuts and herbs, and rubbed itself against the back of trees.
>
> (*New York Times*, 20 June 1875)

To give Caliban to a clown does not mean underplaying the obvious pathos and power of feeling in the role:

> His Caliban we have tried to forget rather than remember; [wrote W. L. Keese in his memoir of Burton] it terrified us and made us dream bad dreams; but for all that, we know that it was a surprising impersonation. (p. 175)

There are, in fact, changes in Shakespeare's use of his comics: from the beginning of this play their characters carry a more than usual burden of immediate and inescapable feeling. They are closer to Cloten than to Autolycus or the shepherds. Trinculo and Stephano are afraid of the storm, the monster, the island and strange noises, but are denied the compensating resilience of other clowns; they are saved by mutual recognition (II. ii. 92–3) and later by Caliban's 'Be not afeard. The isle is full of noises . . .' (III. ii. 130 ff.). The coward revealed under

Trinculo's jesting and the bully under Stephano's good cheer are displayed at last without the usual chance of laughing away the consequences. The last appearance of the trio raises an obvious laugh from the callow Sebastian, but their ludicrous debacle produces a muddled exhortation that is more surprising than the jailor's or Boult's last resort, less obviously hypocritical than that of Autolycus:

> Every man shift for all the rest, and let no man take care for himself; for all is but fortune.
>
> (V. i. 256–7)

In the confrontation that follows, the severe moral tone of Prospero's judgement quenches the irresponsibility of fooling:

> TRINCULO. I have been in such a pickle since I saw you last that, I fear me, will never out of my bones. I shall not fear fly-blowing.
> SEBASTIAN. Why, how now, Stephano!
> STEPHANO. O touch me not; I am not Stephano, but a cramp.
> PROSPERO. You'd be king 'o the isle, sirrah?
> STEPHANO. I should have been a sore one, then.
> ALONSO [*pointing to Caliban*]. This is as strange a thing as e'er I look'd on.
> PROSPERO. He is as disproportioned in his manners
> As in his shape. Go, sirrah, to my cell;
> Take with you your companions; as you look
> To have my pardon, trim it handsomely.
> CALIBAN. Ay, that I will; and I'll be wise hereafter,
> And seek for grace. What a thrice-double ass
> Was I to take this drunkard for a god,
> And worship this dull fool!

Each of the trio makes a forced jest at his own expense; but not as a comic escape route. The despatching words do not suggest a funny *exeunt*:

> PROSPERO. Go to; away!
> ALONSO. Hence, and bestow your luggage where you found it.
> SEBASTIAN. Or stole it, rather.

They do not have the usual chance to encourage sympathy. Laughter has been aroused by the earlier meetings and conspiracy, but, remembering them, Prospero had been so disturbed that his daughter had never seen him 'touch'd with anger so distemper'd' (IV. i. 144–5).

Shakespeare has tightly reined all other laughter in this deliberately judicial play. Miranda's first encounters with Ferdinand cause her to 'prattle something too wildly', to ask outright 'Do you love me?', to announce unbidden 'I am your wife'. Prospero's comment when he finds them together suggests the incipient comedy—'Poor worm, thou art infected! This visitation shows it'—but within forty lines he is caught by a very different response:

> Fair encounter
> Of two most rare affections! Heavens rain grace
> On that which breeds between 'em!
>
> (III. i. 32–76)

In the last scene too, Miranda's 'Sweet lord, you play me false' and

> How beauteous mankind is! O brave new world
> That has such people in't!
>
> (V. i. 172–84)

may well bring laughter for their ironical innocence; but, even more quickly than at the end of *Cymbeline,* this comedy is lost in wonder and in the joy of reconciliation.

So Antonio and Sebastian's jests with Gonzalo turn awry as 'Widow Dido' is introduced and Alonso is forced to think anew of his lost son and daughter. When the lords mock the idealism of Gonzalo's utopian discourse, the jesting gives place to a conspiracy to kill Alonso.

Ariel has some flashes of irresponsible, Puck-like humour, as in:

> The King's son have I landed by himself,
> Whom I left cooling of the air with sighs
> In an odd angle of the isle, and sitting,
> His arms in this sad knot— (I. ii. 221–4)

He imitates the grief-stricken prince, to raise laughter as any clown might do, and he seems to relish joining the clownish quarrels of Trinculo and Stephano. But Ariel is also, from the first, a 'moody spirit', and one who is busy in order to win freedom from contact with everyone in the play. Once he does sing '. . . merrily. Merrily, merrily . . .', but that is only when his own freedom is in sight. He does not answer Prospero's 'I shall miss thee' (V. i. 95) and he is almost silent on his last errands. Dismissed in the very last speech of the play he has no words of farewell to Prospero—perhaps he should laugh 'merrily' after he has left the stage, 'delighted' and free.

Shakespeare depended on comic performances, giving laughter to all his romances, mixing mirth with delight and dreaming. But the clowns must observe the implied limits; in the play which ends with a solitary man wanting:

> Spirits to enforce, art to enchant;
> And my ending is despair
> Unless I be reliev'd by prayer, . . .

he banished laughter before its conclusion; it is lost in punishment, in wonder and joy, in conspiracy and treachery, and in the escape of Ariel.

PART TWO

Action and the Stage

VIII

Narrative and Focus: Richard II

★

So far I have considered the actor's contribution to performance, but relationships between performances, shifts of interest from one character to another, the effects of movement and changing modes of illusion have already drawn our attention. Now the stage-picture must come to the forefront. As a play is performed, a dramatist is controlling the audience's view of its action, now towards a single character, now a group, now a dead body, or an empty throne, or nothing.

An audience is aware of the physical objects displayed before it, as well as the words it hears. Shape, size, colour; contrasts, numbers, distance; movement, organisation and lack of organisation are all influencing the audience's response. There are moments when a number of figures seem to stand within a realistic perspective in calculated relationship to each other, and moments when they form a two-dimensional frieze (no figure more important than another), or when a small eccentric detail dominates the whole, or when an empty space is more impressive than the rest of a crowded stage. We need to speak of the changing picture on the stage as of a composition, as we might speak of the formal characteristics of a painting. This deployment is part of the performed play and strongly affects what it does to an audience; it is part of the theatrical language which Shakespeare developed during the course of his career.

Two warnings are needed. First it will not be sufficient to list the contents of the stage-picture and their relationships. We must try to describe how the audience perceives that picture. In a picture gallery we recognise that there is an appropriate way of looking at any picture. It would be absurd to stand all the time within a foot or two of a French impressionist painting, a Monet or a Degas. That would be appropriate only if we were considering the painter's technique. In order to see the effect that his picture is able to transmit, we would automatically step back a few paces and so become aware of the relationship of the brush-strokes to each other, of the whole effect of light, colour, movement and space. The picture is made for such a wide focus. Other pictures—some Dutch realists for example—invite, and require, a minute scrutiny: one needs to step up close to the canvas. So it is in the theatre: the right focus, be it wide or intense, is necessary for seeing the masterpiece. Without this adaptation we may see only what appears to be incompetent brush-work, or an inability to give distinction or emphasis.

In watching a play in a theatre—any play, in any theatre—we sometimes sit forward in our chair, head forward and eyes intent on one particular point in the arena or picture which is the stage; this kind of dramatic focus is intense, concentrated. We observe or watch for the minutest action or word; we often see only one particular person or hear only one particular sound, even though the stage may be crowded or noisy, or disorderly. The opposite extreme is a wide dramatic focus. Instead of sitting forward we are sometimes relaxed, sitting back, and responsive to the whole picture. At such a time no one person or sound, or action dominates the impression we receive; we are sitting back and 'taking it all in'; we are conscious of the overall effect, of the interweaving of pattern and the range of colour. It is a wide focus. We can become aware of a changing dramatic focus by marking these two extremes.

We must also remember constantly that the play exists in time; the stage picture is always developing from one form to another and at varying speeds. One momentary grouping may gain emphasis or meaning because it echoes an earlier grouping, in a different setting or with another dominating figure. A single figure may be more eloquent of loneliness because just before the stage had been crowded and animated. The changing visual impressions are also modified by narrative. So a sudden liveliness may appear to be little more than a meaningless disturbance, because the audience is wholly unprepared for it and so it shocks rather than elucidates. When narrative expectation is thwarted by a movement to some other part of the fable, an apparently static, formal scene may lose its impression of stability, or a brief descriptive scene take on an unusual air of deliberation. The stage picture is always changing and the audience's reaction to it can be controlled by dramatic narrative and response to character and situation.

The stage picture cannot be assessed easily; but if we do not discover the appropriate focus for each moment we may misread the dramatic text—and that is done all too easily.

* * *

I shall consider first, *Richard II*: an early play, written, for the most part, in a particularly lucid style.

It begins with the stage set formally. Richard is enthroned and surrounded, as the Quarto edition of 1597 says, with '*nobles and attendants*'. Richard commands the centre of the stage, but he is seen as a king in relationship to his subjects, rather than as a person interesting in his own right. He speaks in set fashion to his uncle, John of Gaunt, and requires precise, official answer. When Gaunt's son, Henry Bolingbroke, and Thomas Mowbray, Duke of Norfolk, are called to the King's presence, they bitterly accuse each other of treason. Richard fails to reconcile their demands of honour and appoints a day for trial by combat at Coventry. The whole stage empties at once, and on the outcome of that future event the audience's attention will wait.

So the first scene would appear if it were played on its own merits, with each word spoken as simply as possible. But if the audience has some previous knowledge of Richard's history, or if the actors try to give consistent portrayals of their roles, there will be further and conflicting impressions. Richard's formal protestation of impartiality, his 'Forget, forgive; conclude and be agreed', and his comments on 'bold' Bolingbroke, may carry subtextual impressions of irony, apprehension or antagonism. Bolingbroke's accusations may seem aimed at the King rather than Mowbray, and Mowbray's confidence to stem from royal support rather than his own innocence. But even if these impressions are missed, the audience will be made to question the scene's textual and visual impressions by the simple duologue of the next scene. Mowbray has been accused of murdering Thomas, Duke of Gloucester, a son of Edward III and so Bolingbroke's uncle and the King's, but now, in contrast to the visual elaboration of the first formal picture, a quiet, still, intimate scene shows Thomas' widowed Duchess appealing for revenge, and his brother, John of Gaunt refusing because:

> correction lieth in those hands
> Which made the fault.

The King and judge of the first scene had been responsible for Mowbray murdering Gloucester, a fact to which no overt allusion has hitherto been made. Now the audience must question the earlier picture in retrospect, or find their unease strengthened. The new information is given unemphatically, for Gaunt does not have to persuade his hearer of its truth, but just before the audience's interest is redirected to the lists at Coventry, the Duchess is shown alone, believing that she goes to die.

For the third scene, at Coventry, the full stage is again 'set' (as the Quarto has it) formally. The King enters in procession to the sound of trumpets, and personal feelings are subdued within the larger gestures and more fluent responses of public ceremonial. But now the focus is changed, for the audience will watch both sides closely, and 'God's substitute' also, as he stands as judge on a higher level of the stage. The excitement of the duel itself is quenched before it begins, when Richard, with a simple movement of his hand, stops proceedings. This is unexpected and so draws all the alerted attention to the King who holds attention by wise words about civil strife and his own duties, and then pronounces the judgement which he and his council have agreed upon: Bolingbroke is to be banished for ten years and Mowbray for life. But this is not all: the newly watchful audience may discern a brief sign of complicity or shame as Richard with 'some unwillingness' passes sentence on Mowbray, and a covert accusation as the banished man claims a 'dearer merit': a single hesitation can now sharpen the audience's perception of signs of subtextual motivation. Bolingbroke's submission with:

> Your will be done. This must my comfort be,
> That sun that warms you here, shall shine on me. . . .

may seem to veil a rivalry with the King himself. Richard dominates the stage as he gives judgement, but at the close of the scene Bolingbroke is left alone with his friends and, as he fails to acknowledge their farewells, the course of the drama waits upon the expression of his personal and private feelings. So a newly clarified interest is balanced between Richard and Bolingbroke.

To sum up the visual effects so far, we can say that Shakespeare has introduced the action with a wide focus so that the audience is made aware of the patterns of the King's relationship to nobles and officials, and of father to son and fatherless nephew. But a more intimate focus is then induced with a short scene which adds notably, but quietly, to the exposition, and so when the next crowded, formal scene follows there are momentary intensifications of focus; but these never lead to direct narrative statement. Sometimes the audience's curiosity is aroused by some action or speech after it has been completed; or one character, by his words, provokes a closer scrutiny of another, or of relationships between several other characters. So the moments of close interest are sporadic and always lead back to a comprehensive view of the stage, or to a quick review of the preceeding action. The audience's intense interest is not engaged for any single character or event, and yet, since the wider issues have been resolved in judgement and banishment, it is these insights which arouse most of the audience's expectation of further development. We can say that the stage-picture is at once comprehensive and subtle, that the focus is potentially intense over a wide design.

More informal scenes follow which complicate the audience's view, extending their interest and knowledge without co-ordinating individual impressions. While the splendours and proprieties are still alive in the memory, Richard is seen disrobed and at ease with his intimates. Now he is sarcastic about 'High Hereford' and answers the national threat of rebellion in Ireland by deciding to lease his royal estates and exact subscriptions from wealthy subjects. When news comes that Gaunt is sick, Richard wishes his uncle were dead so that he might seize his possessions, and then goes to visit him: 'Pray God we may make haste, and come too late', he says, and 'Amen' respond his companions. In all this the pious and responsible solemnities of the first regal scenes are mocked: is this erratic informality a truer picture of Richard and of his country?

In a solemn, static scene that follows, the dying Gaunt speaks of the 'scepter'd isle' of England with a reiterative eloquence that lends fire to patriotic commonplaces and has made the speech famous out of its context: this is a self-contained, largely verbal episode. Next Richard enters, and Gaunt denounces his husbandry and openly accuses him of the murder of Gloucester. Gaunt leaves the royal presence and, as York tries to placate the king, his death is announced. Immediately Richard confiscates Gaunt's possessions and York is no longer patient but denounces Richard like Gaunt had done: his remonstrance is breathless, not so imposing but more pitiful than Gaunt's, yet the King does not listen; rather, with surprising decision, he makes York governor in England during his own absence in Ireland, and then again hurries from the scene. As Gaunt and York have taken the centre of the stage in denunciation, Shakespeare has ensured that the King prevents a prolonged close focus by jests and rapid decisions and movements. Verbally the situation is clearer, but the focus is still predominantly wide; it has only become more insecure, more uncertain and more frequently disturbed by momentary clarifications and intensities.

As soon as Richard has left the stage, the Earl of Northumberland and the lords, Ross and Willoughby, agree together that the King 'is not himself' but transformed by his flatterers, and then they hasten to join Bolingbroke newly returned at the head of an army to redress all wrongs. Here is a simpler, stronger interest in the narrative development, but before the audience is allowed to follow it, there is a quiet moment in which the Queen mourns the absence of her 'sweet Richard' —an entirely new reaction to this baffling figure. When she hears of Bolingbroke's arrival she despairs and York is unable to reassure her: 'Comfort's in heaven', he warns, 'and we are on the earth'. He has little confidence in his resources or decisions: and, as he leaves with the Queen, the audience sees Richard's lesser friends count their chances and promptly decide to save their own skins, two fleeing to Bristol and one to Ireland. So from this gentle and then hesitating and shifting scene, the audience will turn with relief to Bolingbroke who now appears confident in arms and attended by Northumberland. They are joined by other nobles and all speak courteously, as if in homage to the new central figure. Bolingbroke's speeches are both strong and relaxed, so that the stage picture is at last ordered and assured (as it had *seemed* to be at the beginning), and the action steadily developing. York enters to denounce the rebel, but then declares himself neutral. There is a brief scene recounting the dispersal of the King's Welsh army on hearing rumours of his death, and then the action moves to Bristol where Bolingbroke, now accompanied by York as well, condemns to death Bushy and Green, Richard's cowardly friends. He takes charge of the realm as if he were the king of it, and holds the centre of the stage; again echoing the first 'set' scene.

The narrative encourages the audience to expect the uneasy focus to settle on the opposition of two main figures, two potential centres of the stage. But when Richard returns as from Ireland with Aumerle and the Bishop of Carlisle, after being absent for some four hundred and sixty lines (over one sixth of the whole play), he does not meet Bolingbroke at once. The scene of his return (III. ii) is antithetical to that of Bolingbroke's: Richard is joined by other friends, as his rival had been, but they bring bad news and not an easy courtesy; and, whereas the rebel's course was clear, the King's is makeshift. Yet from this point to his death the dramatic focus grows more and more intent upon Richard for his own sake, whenever he appears; the audience sees progressively deeper into his consciousness. Sometimes the more stable Bolingbroke is a potential rival for attention in the centre of a crowded stage, but after his opponent has surrendered he says very little: he assumes the crown, but never mentions his intention to do so; he deposes Richard, but leaves most of the business and persuasion to Northumberland and York. The audience is continually aware of Bolingbroke's presence, but he seems to stand further away from them than Richard, or than he himself had done formerly. Such is the cunning perspective of the stage picture.

The focus is intensified on Richard by huge transitions of thought and feeling, and by silences. He easily dominates the stage on his return because all the ill-tidings are known to the audience before they are told to him, and so there is no competitive narrative interest. Moreover he is eloquent and the other characters dependent upon him. But the focus is so narrowly intense because of his silences: it seems as if the extremes of his spoken despair and hope are impelled by some unexpressed fear, some knowledge or state of being which he cannot escape and cannot fully meet. He tries many ways to hope or despair, to some stable and 'true' reaction: at first plain fantasy, then affirmation of trust in God, then meditation on the oblivion of death, then renunciation of his duties. But his friends on stage cannot believe or join in any of them, and silence always follows—as if none of his words were valid the moment after they have been spoken. Richard himself is aware of this ineffectiveness and directs attention to it verbally: he thinks he will be mocked for 'senseless conjuration' and that he has been 'mistaken all this while'.

At the end of the scene he discharges his army and hurries off-stage, 'From Richard's night, to Bolingbroke's fair day' and forbids anyone to speak further. He seems to know that it is from the expression of his own thoughts that he tries to escape at the end, rather than from physical or political danger. Between the rhetoric and the silences, the audience's attention is drawn towards Richard at the centre of the stage and towards the unexpressed insecurity and suffering at the centre of his being.

The scene in which Richard confronts Bolingbroke's army provides a wide stage-picture organised, for the first time, on two opposing centres. As Richard speaks and looks royally, claiming the power of 'God omnipotent' and prophesying war as the result of Bolingbroke's treason, he seems once more to justify his position on the upper level of the stage at the centre of the picture. Yet when Northumberland promises that the rebel claims only his own inheritance, Richard suddenly changes and agrees to meet his demands: it is as if the focal point of the composition suddenly lost its substance. As his message is carried back, Richard acknowledges:

> O that I were as great
> As is my grief, or lesser than my name!
> Or that I could forget what I have been!
> Or not remember what I must be now!
>
> (III. iii. 136–9)

Then again his insecurity is made apparent by the extremity and variety of his reactions: he speaks openly and fluently of future defeat, a life of pious poverty and an obscure death. As Aumerle weeps, Richard retreats still further into the fantasy of 'two kinsmen' digging 'their graves with weeping eyes'. Mildly he submits to Northumberland's request that he should meet Bolingbroke in the base court; but before he descends from his dominating position in the picture, his mind flashes to his former power and glory:

> Down, down I come, like glis'tring Phaethon,
> Wanting the manage of unruly jades.

To his enemies it seems that:

> Sorrow and grief of heart
> Makes him speak fondly [foolishly], like a frantic [mad] man;
> Yet he is come.

The visual submission is criticised, as it were, by Richard's words, which he can not wholly control. He cuts short all argument by placing himself in the enemy's power before that is demanded of him; and, as before, he hurries to conclude the scene. From now on, the picture will tend to be dominated by Bolingbroke and his agents, but the focus is still intent upon Richard whenever he speaks or moves. Borrowing phrases from the criticism of paintings, we may say that the whole composition is static, at rest; but it is disturbed by the figure of Richard which is mobile and restless.

A wholly static interlude follows, of wide focus. It is set in a garden where Richard's Queen overhears two gardeners talk of affairs of state. They speak solemnly and pityingly of the 'wasteful king' who has not 'trimm'd and dress'd his land' as they their garden, and repeat the news that he is to be deposed. They are not Shakespeare's usual comic characters impressing their own personalities or points of view. Their quaint, slow-moving dialogue acts as a fixed point of reference like Gaunt's talk of a 'sceptred isle', an unequivocal statement of the widest dramatic issues from outside Richard's personal dilemma.

Then the action moves to London, with Bolingbroke in full control. The Bishop of Carlisle boldly denounces the rebel and prophesies 'Disorder, horror, fear, and mutiny' to future generations. He is arrested by Northumberland and at this tense moment Richard is brought on to the stage. He has already decided to resign the crown—Shakespeare does not use this incident to argue about political issues—and now gives effect to his decision step by step, as if obeying instructions or as if seeking to re-create the ceremonial solemnity of the early scenes. But he is now aware that his words and actions do not reflect his inward nature, neither his 'regal thoughts' nor his deep sorrow. And his audience, both on stage and in the auditorium, is made aware of this disparity. When he cries 'God save the king', no one dares respond 'Amen', and when he calls Bolingbroke to stand opposite him with one hand on the crown he is forced to protest that he cannot resign his cares with the resignation of his office. As he tries to speak of this, his words have a new authority: they do not express conflicting extremes and do not issue from nervous silences. The man who submits now dominates the scene: he draws all attention to himself and, within the pattern of ordained events, he controls the nature of the action and denounces his enemies. Yet this new strength derives from weakness: he speaks more firmly and steadily because he now knows he *cannot* speak of his own crimes nor alleviate his grief; he cannot tell 'what name to call himself'. It is at this point that Shakespeare introduced an incident for which his sources gave not the slightest suggestion: Richard calls for a looking glass and when he sees few signs of his suffering in it, he dashes it to pieces. The true image of Richard is not in his appearance, nor his words. Again the scene is quickly finished: he asks for leave to go and is conveyed to the Tower. Shakespeare has at once presented a wide picture and led the audience's interest intently towards a single figure standing to one side of the composition; and as the focus intensifies the drama becomes abruptly disturbed by subtextual realities and the whole wide picture is disturbed and rapidly dissolved.

There is a brief scene as the Queen greets her husband on his way to prison, not recognising the royal lion in his meek submission. There is no nervous alternation of mood now, nor anxious silence. They exchange short rhymed speeches, and then part with a kiss, in accepted silence. But the audience whose interest has been so intensified upon Richard may see the very fluency of the scene as a deliberately external manner of valediction; Richard communicates his inward grief by trying to conceal it, and in performance the dialogue can sound tender and precarious, as well as controlled. Richard yet again hurries from the stage, lest they 'make woe wanton with this fond delay': he is still afraid of what he might say; for all the verbal formalism of this scene, the centre of the picture is still mysterious, still lacking a defined and static quality.

The audience hears of further indignities that Richard is made to suffer, but it has to wait through two bustling, half-comic scenes before he is presented again. Then—and this is for the first time in the play—he appears alone. In soliloquy the audience's attention is drawn wholly to him. The focus is now undeniably intense, and yet Shakespeare introduces a considered, reflective, almost literary tone:

> I have been studying how I may compare
> This prison where I live unto the world. . . .
>
> (V. v. 1–2)

In due order Richard now describes his disordered thoughts—religious, ambitious, flattering—and acknowledges that he is content in none of them. As music is played off-stage, he speaks of 'wasting' his 'time', and of his recompense in being 'wasted' by time and being forced to 'mark the time' of Bolingbroke's progress. Grief, folly, faults, defeat and insecurity are all acknowledged; he no longer tries to escape from such thoughts but seeks to tame them by expressing them thoughtfully. The tone is almost unvaried and the pace almost steady: not quite, for still the balance is not easy. The change has left him helpless, expecting that:

> Nor I, nor any man that but man is,
> With nothing shall be pleas'd till he be eas'd
> With being nothing.

Yet music, played out of time, threatens this composure. Only when he remembers that it is meant for his comfort and is a sign of love, can he bear that too, and the scene is once more composed. Then comes a quickening of interest in an unexpected entry: he is hailed as 'royal Prince!', and Richard answers the visitor quickly with a sharply ironic 'Thanks, noble peer!' He is a groom of his stable, and tells Richard of his horse, the roan Barbary, and of this creature's pride in bearing Bolingbroke in triumph. Richard curses the horse, but then stops to consider: because the animal was 'created to be aw'd by man' he begs its forgiveness, and remembers that he himself has been forced to bear a burden and submit as if he were an animal. Immediately a warder enters with food and orders the groom away; the focus is sharpened by the unknown, and by an attendant sense of immediate danger. Richard, however, thinks of his servant—'If thou love me, 'tis time thou wert away'—and a silence can be held in performance, despite the excitement, by an undefined and unexpressed sympathy between master and groom. The latter replies: 'What my tongue dares not, that my heart shall say'. Such a silence does not require utterance; momentarily there is intimacy and understanding, and even perhaps, a deep peace.

After this intensely focused moment, Shakespeare returned to his primary sources with the warder's harsh words asking Richard to eat. The warder refuses to taste the food to guard against poison, saying that Bolingbroke's order forbids this, and then Richard leaps at him with:

> The devil take Henry of Lancaster and thee!
> Patience is stale, and I am weary of it.

There are cries for help and Exton and his assistants rush in. Action is violent and general: Richard kills two men, and then is overpowered by numbers and struck down. Suddenly the stage is fully alive with his anger, authority and physical strength, with a struggle and then defeat—all in an instant. The deep, necessarily static focus has been broken, and then when the violence is past—violence can sustain interest in the theatre only for comparatively short times—Richard speaks his last, presumably faint, words (again wholly Shakespeare's invention) that are all the more impressive by contrast with the tumult:

> Mount, mount, my soul! thy seat is up on high;
> Whilst my gross flesh sinks downward, here to die.

Richard had often longed for death because it would bring oblivion and perhaps pity, but as he faces assassination he finds new aspiration:

royal anger and, then, hope in a world beyond death and change, spring from his deepest being.

Shakespeare's Richard talks a great deal about himself—some critics have called him a poet rather than a king—but an understanding of his part in the play cannot be found by simply analysing what he says, weighing the word against the word; his stage reality depends also on subtext, and on the changing picture as it directs the audience's attention progressively towards the thoughts behind the words and the thoughts of silence, and towards his last unthinking, physical reactions. By simple quotation it can be shown that Richard is a man who talks 'too idly', one 'who wastes time' and is then 'wasted by it'; or that he is a king who must uncrown himself and yet cannot escape the cares that 'tend the crown'. But such formulae do not embrace the whole experience the play provides in a theatre.

* * *

In a tragedy, after death there is always more to say. If only the eyes are closed and pious ceremonies performed in silence, the audience is shown that death affects other people besides the protagonist. A hushed drum, a bowed head, or a moment without sound or motion is enough to establish death as a fact for others' comprehension; the hero may have unpacked his heart with words but this must still be presented, his death must have this consequence. Many dramatists have made the further communication explicitly, in a chorus which tells the men and women of Thebes that no one can be called happy until he has died in peace, that there is always an end to tears, that wisdom is taught by suffering. Some authors, more busily, have recounted death's manifold implications through a group of women tidying their thoughts aloud; others have announced a long-kept secret through the mouth of some wise, experienced man—how he who has died had been true to his heritage, or had been struck down by some hidden guilt. Authors who prefer to maintain a full dramatic illusion have presented retaliation or submission, praise or blame, in continued action, or have concluded with a prayer that begs some god to appease man's misery and remorse. In Shakespeare's day the standard procedure was explicit comment, a statement of the play's meaning or significance. Elizabethan tragedy usually drew a firm line after the death of the hero, and then totalled up good deeds and bad. In this play, Shakespeare's method is to give another scene, another picture with different figures: after the death of Richard, when the focus has been more intense than ever before, Shakespeare transferred attention to Bolingbroke seated in Richard's throne; a formal 'set' scene, with a predominantly wide focus.

The transference is, however, long prepared for: the wide focus of the early scenes had not been invoked needlessly. The first stage-pictures with Richard as judge of Mowbray and Bolingbroke, were repeated half-way through when Bolingbroke stood as judge of Bushy and Green, and then of Aumerle and Surrey against the charges of Bagot, Fitzwater and others. In his second judgement Bolingbroke dealt with the same offence as had concerned Richard: the murder of Thomas, Duke of Gloucester. But there were significant differences: the contestants were more numerous and more quick-tempered; the judge said far less than his predecessor, his most arresting contributions being his silence, his repeal of Mowbray and then, on hearing of this old enemy's death after fighting in the crusades, his praise and prayer for him. All these scenes are echoed in the last formal scene, and so strengthen it; once the momentary surprise has passed, it seems the inevitable close to the play as a whole.

Again, between Richard's farewell to his Queen and his last appearance, Shakespeare elaborated on accounts in his sources by introducing two scenes showing the Duke of York's discovery that his son, Aumerle, is engaged in conspiracy against Bolingbroke. The audience need not know these events in order to follow Richard's story—indeed, almost invariably the scenes are cut from modern productions—so Shakespeare must have had other reasons for inventing them. Firstly they demonstrate the effects of revolution; and, secondly, their comic details of calling for boots to a loquacious wife, provide a release from the tension of following Richard's story. And they also affect the dramatic focus. By introducing these scenes Bolingbroke is again seated as judge. At first he seems well able to manage the danger to his person, reducing the stature of both Aumerle and his mother with an ironic: 'My dangerous cousin, let your mother in' (V. iii. 81). But, as the Duchess kneels in supplication and refuses to obey Bolingbroke's thrice repeated 'Rise up, good aunt' until he has promised, and doubly promised, pardon for her son's life, the audience is shown both the new king's power and his subject's tendency to doubt the effect of his commanding words of friendship and forgiveness. The irony touches Bolingbroke closely, for as the suppliant rises she cries (and this is all she says): 'A God on earth thou art'—the rebel, the silent king, has to hear himself called a god by those he favours. To this salutation he answers nothing: but his tone changes and, ignoring the agonised and flustered woman, he speaks directly of tracking down other conspirators and swears that all of them shall die. The episode ends when the Duchess leaves with her pardoned son and places such revolutions of fortune in another perspective: 'Come my old son; I pray God make thee new'.

I have dwelt so long on this scene because the final scene of the play is again, for the fourth time, Bolingbroke enthroned as king and judge. The picture including its central figure is now quite familiar, so that despite its wide focus the audience may give particular attention to small points of difference, or imprecision. York, Northumberland and Fitzwater bring news that his enemies are defeated and slain; only the Bishop of Carlisle is brought a prisoner before him, and he—strangely perhaps—is pardoned because Bolingbroke has seen 'sparks of honour' in this implacable enemy. Then there follows another, more impressive entry into the royal presence: Sir Pierce of Exton with Richard's body in a coffin. At least four men are needed to bear this burden on to the stage, and they must move more slowly and ceremonially than the eager messengers who have preceded them. Bolingbroke does not speak, but as the coffin is deliberately placed before him, Exton announces:

> Great King, within this coffin I present
> Thy buried fear.

The answer is:

> Exton, I thank thee not; for thou hast wrought
> A deed of slander with thy fatal hand
> Upon my head and all this famous land.
> . . . Though I did wish him dead,
> I hate the murderer, love him murdered.
> The guilt of conscience take thou for thy labour,
> But neither my good word nor princely favour;
> With Cain go wander thorough shades of night,
> And never show thy head by day nor light.

He turns from Exton, to address his silent, watching noblemen:

> Lords, I protest my soul is full of woe
> That blood should sprinkle me to make me grow.

And the play ends with self-assumed penance:

> Come, mourn with me for what I do lament,
> And put on sullen black incontinent:
> I'll make a voyage to the Holy Land,
> To wash this blood off from my guilty hand.

A reader of the play might claim that Bolingbroke's last words are prompted by his practised political intelligence: to dash Exton's hopes, or to announce new business to employ the energies of fractious nobles (following such counsel as, in *Henry IV*, Shakespeare was to put in Bolingbroke's own mouth). But in performance such interpretations are not fully satisfying, for the picture, the visual impression, qualifies the words. On the crowded stage all are silent and intent upon their king, so that if he attempted dissimulation he would scarcely be content with the continued silence which is the only response to his words (compare Prince John and the Lord Chief Justice talking together after Henry V has made a similar announcement of foreign wars at the end of *II, Henry IV*). Moreover this moral note has been heard before where it could serve no political purpose: as Bolingbroke prayed for Mowbray, as he spoke of his son's irresponsibility hanging like a plague over him, and perhaps as he pardoned Aumerle 'as God shall pardon me', and as he pardoned the Bishop of Carlisle. Possibly Bolingbroke's silence when he heard his subjects accuse each other of treason and when he heard the Bishop denounce his assumption of the throne, should be viewed as earlier attempts to conceal a subtextual guilt. These moments passed quickly and without emphasis, but the repetition of the picture of a king crowned and surrounded by his nobles directs the audience attention progressively upon variations and movement: slight tensions beneath formal poses can thus become impressive.

As at the end of a sonnet, the last line can send the reader back to the first, till the experience which the sonnet gives is viewed whole and complete, contained and understood, so at the end of this tragedy, the audience's visual sense will retravel to its beginning, to a group of ambitious, striving, related and insecure human-beings. To ensure this response the awakening of a new Richard in his death-scene has been presented so briefly; Bolingbroke has been held un-communicative within the wide picture of the drama while the intense focus was directed more and more upon Richard; and the early scenes were allowed no single dominant interest. Instead of concentrating the drama upon a hero's story, Shakespeare has presented a man in isolation and defeat who overcomes fear and learns to recognise guilt, responsibility and courage in himself; and has off-set this with a man who knows little of fear and recognises guilt only when he assumes the responsibility he has continually sought. The last scene presents Bolingbroke in a new way, verbally: and Richard is there in his coffin, eloquent of his own story, visually.

Both Bolingbroke's and Richard's last words are about their souls, and of Heaven or the Holy Land; and this also completes a series of scenes, still moments when an isolated figure appeals to a state of being outside the world of the stage. In the second scene, the Duchess of Gloucester is told to 'complain' to 'God, the widow's champion and defence', and this resource is again invoked by the unexpected report of the banished Mowbray fighting in the crusades, by York reminding the distressed Queen that 'Comfort's in heaven, and we are on the earth', and his warning to Bolingbroke:

> Take not, good cousin, further than you should,
> Lest you mistake. The heavens are over our heads.

The last scene, in a moment of piety, lightly draws these moments together too.

The surest and most comprehensive effects of the conclusion are carried by the stage picture: viewing the wide picture the audience may see deeply into the characters and the society portrayed, and even into a timeless perspective associated with traditional religion. This visual and formal language is not so precise as words, but it can affect the audience subtlely and without its conscious knowledge; it can suggest vast implications and sensitive psychological reactions; it can awaken a response without limiting it by definition, declaration or propaganda.

IX

Setting, Grouping, Movement and Tempo: Hamlet

★

NO Elizabethan would have thought of constructing a series of stage sets to imitate or suggest the appropriate locale and mood for each scene. Nevertheless, the setting for a Shakespeare play was important then as now. Perhaps the main difference was that Elizabethan actors could never forget it, never construct an ingenious piece of scenery and then perform in front of it with no further regard for its mood or form. Setting and acting were necessarily in accord, because the most common means of changing the stage-picture were the actors' costumes, properties, bearing and behaviour. In addition, there were a few larger properties and sound effects that could be used, and music. But actors, by their very presence, could completely change the picture, its mood, line, colour, form. Many effects were obviously beyond them —the suggestion of a particular house or a particular landscape—but we should not underestimate the range or effectiveness of their method of setting a play.

Consider the change from an interior to the open air. Fine clothes would be cloaked as for a journey, or light clothes exchanged for more durable ones. Distances would seem to be greater, as the actors call instead of speak, or crowd together to hear a confidence that could be exchanged at ease within doors. In the open they would perhaps look farther off, and leave the stage with a greater sense of resolution and purpose. If this change took place during winter or at night, all these effects would be greatly accentuated; the relaxed behaviour of a sheltered interior would contrast with the quick movements and huddled forms appropriate to the cold air, the apparent openness of a well-lit interior with difficult recognitions in the dark. The fact that snow was not represented on the stage, nor darkness, great height or distance, would serve only to accentuate the means whereby the 'scene' was suggested: long, heavy and dull-coloured cloaks, close groupings, the alternating stillness and rapidity, whispers, sudden calls. Some changes of setting were even more impressive: from a court scene with costly, crowded costumes and formal groupings to the low-pitched colours and relaxation of servants' quarters, or the countryside; from a public room to a private, from a domestic scene to a military, or to a religious. These are some of the settings which Shakespeare used in *Hamlet* and which any staging of the play should try to represent, no matter how complicated or simple the scenery may be.

To consider these changes in due order is to view an element of the play which Shakespeare controlled with care:

> It begins high up in the open during a bitterly cold night, with only a few cloaked figures and a silent, questing ghost: and the ghost alone does not feel the cold nor, until the end, move with any neglect of formal majesty.
>
> Then, with a great and unheralded change, there is a crowded interior, ample in words and gesture, formal and colourful for a royal celebration. Soon the stage almost empties, but remains an interior until a return to the battlements, night and the ghost.
>
> Then it is the court again, and will remain so for more than two consecutive Acts. But now there is less formality and much coming and going, hearing and overhearing; and Hamlet is for a time alone, and for at least a few moments, silent and defeated. Within the interior, the action moves forward but the stage twice empties completely, once after Hamlet's new resolve to watch the King and once after Claudius' to watch Hamlet; and then it fills steadily towards a second formal scene, the crowded play-scene. This time there is a double formality, that of Elsinore and that of the play within the play. It ends suddenly in disorder and, as lights are called for off-stage, with a new impression of darkness, the more alert for being indoors where entrances can be made in an instant. Short, broken episodes follow, still in the interior and at night, with one long emotional scene played intimately as in the Queen's private chamber; and there the ghost reappears to be seen only by Hamlet. It is still night when, after a brief pursuit, Hamlet appears guarded before Claudius, and is ordered to leave the court under escort.
>
> Then, after this long sequence in the interior, the stage is again the open air, the change accentuated by the introduction of the new marching figures of Fortinbras and his army; they belong to a different nation, as well as introducing a full military setting. Just as they are going, Hamlet enters attended and dressed for travel. He

is soon alone again but now as if in a vast stretch of open country; and then he walks off-stage.

The release to the wider, relaxed setting was brief, for at once the scene returns to an interior for further action at court. But Hamlet is no longer there, and no more than three or four people are on the stage at any one time; and they repeatedly move apart from each other. A wider setting is, however, suggested by the freedom of Ophelia's madness which disregards court and domestic proprieties, by the entry of a sailor and, most strongly, by the noise and shouts of an angry crowd twice heard off-stage when Laertes returns from France.

Then there is a fourth move to the open, for the gravedigger, Hamlet's return to Denmark and the funeral of Ophelia. This ceremony, with procession, bell and priest, is the only elaborate religious setting in the play, but in the presence of the mourning King and Queen it echoes the formalities of Elsinore. And, like the large court scenes, this also breaks into disorder as Hamlet and Laertes have to be parted from each other by force. Then the stage rapidly empties.

The scene is once more the interior with Hamlet and Horatio alone, and twice visited by single messengers. The stage fills for the duel, and this new formality, with the King and Queen enthroned, leads, like the previous two, to an uproar; but this time the disorder leads not to hurried partings and an empty stage, but to the stillness and quietness of death. At once drums are heard in the distance and Fortinbras enters the scene, its splendour now in ruin at his feet. He is attended by his soldiers and dressed as for his earlier appearance outside Elsinore in the country, and he is accompanied by the English Ambassadors, entirely new figures who also come as from a journey. This entry from the world outside effects a last formality, so that in procession the bodies of Hamlet, the King, the Queen and Laertes are taken out of sight, borne aloft to be placed 'high on a stage' in view of the 'yet unknowing world'.

If we borrow terms from the criticism of the visual arts, we may say of the changing impression of the 'scene' that the stage-picture is alternately an 'open' and a 'closed' composition: sometimes it is a self-contained whole, bounded by apparent limits; at other times it is limitless and flowing, suggesting continuations beyond the bounds of the stage. And in these changes, the picture is eloquent: the court is a prison from which escape can be made, an established pattern that is broken, an arrangement, with a clear centre and interdependent elements, which gives place to one isolated figure within its emptied frame, and later to disorder and forced actions at night, and finally to carnage and a new central authority. Or in its open form, with distant views obscured at first by darkness, it is a place free for visitations and for movement.

This contrast between open and closed compositions was accentuated by the form of Elizabethan playhouses—a fact that performances in an auditorium of the same shape and size will quickly reveal. If an actor stood close to the tiring-house façade he was viewed by all the audience in relation to an architectural background with regular, centralised form and decoration: this would give a closed dramatic composition. (See Figs. i and ii.)

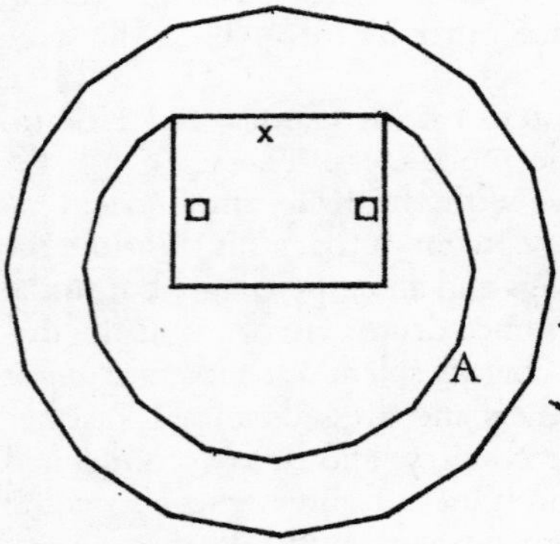

Fig. i

Fig. ii

But if he stood near the outermost edge of the platform-stage a large portion of the audience, including those in the most expensive seats, would see no background to his figure except the anonymous audience at the other side of the theatre, backed by the continuous, horizontal lines of the galleries in which they sat or stood: this would give an open dramatic composition. (See Figs. iii and iv.)

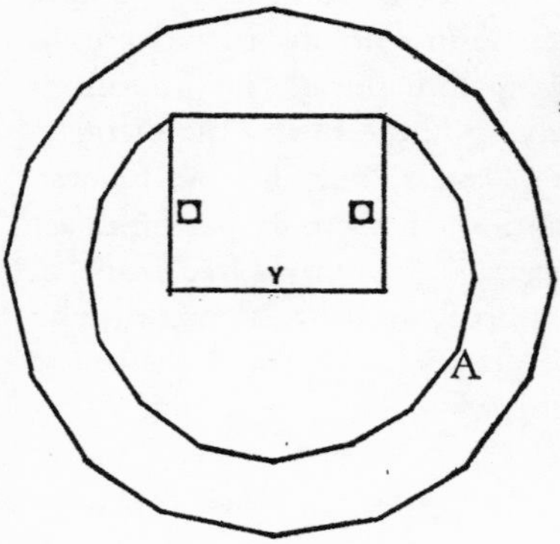

Fig. iii

Fig. iv

These two extremes were modified in many ways, particularly when a crowd of actors or, perhaps, large properties were introduced to remove the sense of isolation natural to the extreme forward edge of the stage; but the eloquent contrast between them is the reason why so many Elizabethan plays, besides *Hamlet*, involve an alternation between interiors and open country so frequently and so confidently. *Macbeth* and *King Lear* offer clear examples of its use.

The *dramatis personae* are meaningful as soon as they appear in these varied settings, before they have spoken a single word. Hamlet himself starts with a long silence in a formal set scene, watched and watching; he is drawn into the pattern and then moves apart and is left alone; he leaves on talk of the ghost, and subsequently waits for the ghost on the battlements, and then follows it; returning to the interior, he plans his own formal scene and then in darkness and rapid movement seeks his mother; he is pursued and escapes to the open; he is absent from the court to return, at first unrecognised, for the funeral; then after some preparation he takes another formal position stripping himself of his doublet and signs of rank for the duel; in the last rapid and extended disorder he assumes control and dies in silence; and then his body is honoured as it is carried off-stage.

Or for example, Laertes: dutifully taking his time and place in the formal picture and then dressed and ready for a journey from court; returning to an emptier court with an insurgent, disordered crowd off-stage; the King and Queen following him outside in mourning; taking part in the duel and helplessly dying in the final static picture.

Or, Claudius and Gertrude: leaving Elsinore only for the funeral. Or, Ophelia: moving circumspectly, until she is the only person to act within the court as if she were anywhere, or nowhere, free from all restraint. Or Horatio who goes to the court from the battlements, who greets the sailor and then appears at the graveyard: never at the centre of a formal grouping until at the end when he is with the dying Hamlet.

The story, or sequence of events, also gains relevance from the settings. This is chiefly effected by the device of repetition, so that each return to Elsinore catches reflections of its earlier manifestations and is given significance by them. The last formal grouping, for instance, contains memories of earlier ones: the first when Claudius expressed his purposes unopposed, until disturbed by the black figure of Hamlet; the second when the court watched an acted intimacy and then an acted murder; the third when the court honoured Ophelia's corpse; the fourth which is to witness a duel.[1] 'Atmospheric' effects are repeated too: the impression of darkness in Elsinore after the Play Scene recalls that of the battlements, so that the ghost's return may be almost expected. Such repetitions also tie the various elements of the action together and, in the last scene, give a clear sense of completion, a strength very necessary for such an episodic narrative with ambiguous characterisation and almost continual verbal elaboration. When Hamlet finally controls the disordered formality the audience will sense through the setting that a new pattern has been established from the old: the very thrones used in the first scene are now empty, probably in the same place, and the same courtiers are merely 'mutes and audience' to a frightening act. This may be the most powerful impression of the last scene, for it is visual and, therefore, rapid, complete and unquestioned. And, when Fortinbras and the Ambassador enter from without and in foreign costumes, the audience will know that Elsinore is no

[1] See Gordon Craig's illustrations of Act I, Scene ii and Act III, Scene ii: plates ix and x.

longer a restricted and threatened enclosure; the scene is open, if not freed.

The changing setting is a valuable means of expressing story, themes and characters, and of giving coherence to many elements. Its impressions are conveyed visually, by objects and behaviour, and affect an audience without it realising what is happening, and swiftly and largely; in performance they can carry and shape the play.

* * *

For all its broad effectiveness, the setting contributes to the subtlety of the play in performance, by the interaction of closed and open stage-pictures, and by repetitions. And subtleties, together with robust eloquence, are also communicated by the movement of the figures within the scene.

Here, the most unquestioned effect is the dominance and unusual independence of the hero. Sir Tyrone Guthrie has said that:

> *Hamlet*, oddly enough, is a play which can be rehearsed very quickly. . . . If the producer and the actor who plays Hamlet are well prepared and in full agreement, the production can, in my opinion, be put together in two weeks. The reason for this is that none of Hamlet's scenes demand a very close *rapport* between the participants. Most of the psychological material is conveyed in soliloquy; to a unique degree the *rapport* is not between actor and actor, but between Hamlet and the audience.[2]

Hamlet is alone for his soliloquies of course, and throughout the play he voices thoughts which are almost soliloquies within the dialogue; he first speaks in an aside; he watches and is watched. He repeatedly moves apart from the other figures and they must '*seek* my Lord Hamlet': the ghost, Horatio and the soldiers, Rosencrantz and Guildenstern, Polonius, the 'tragedians of the city', Claudius, Laertes, Osric and the second messenger who follows him; all these, on separate occasions, seek out Hamlet, and force an encounter. Once Claudius and Gertrude avoid an encounter with him, but Ophelia is 'loosed' to him and later his 'mother stays' for him. Hamlet does not need to seek others, but Horatio, the actors, the musicians and the Norwegian Captain come when he calls. Only the gravedigger, the memory of Yorick and

[2] *A Life in the Theatre* (1960), pp. 58–59.

Ophelia's funeral procession are encountered by Hamlet without being summoned or seeming to wait for him.

Many scenes conclude with movements directing attention towards Hamlet: the stage first empties so that Horatio may seek him and, despite many new characters and interests, it does not empty again until Hamlet is shown alone preparing to see his father's spirit. Every one of his exits arouses strong expectation for his subsequent action: he has to follow the ghost, return to court with a new and compelling duty, prepare *The Mousetrap*, fight apparent madness, confront his mother, the King, treacherous friends, his own apparent lack of resolution. In the last scene but one, after a general climax, he walks off-stage before its conclusion; but here he goes in defiance and afterwards there is a marked hiatus in dramatic development in which Claudius briefly reorganises the stage-picture before a general exeunt. Even on this occasion, when he leaves the stage for no expressed purpose, the groupings are disturbed and rapidly displaced.

Hamlet dominates so obviously that the figures among whom he appears can be underestimated, not least by those who have to produce and perform the play without sufficient time or patience to discover the qualities inherent in the text. This hero Shakespeare has placed among characters who are subtly strong, and subtly related to each other. And this achievement is not fully revealed until the play is allowed to grow and establish itself in production on the stage. First, there is a concerted effect, the impression of Elsinore as a dangerous and involved society. In both court and family, sudden arrivals are discovered to be fore-known; even casual re-entries are often expected. Other figures, besides Hamlet, are watched or shadowed—Ophelia, Laertes, the players, Claudius, Gertrude. Public occasions and general celebrations have private implications; what seems leisurely is truly hurried, and sudden orders have been long deliberated. At the very beginning, a spirit visits Elsinore who is unconfined by darkness and bitter cold, and who fades on the 'crowing of the cock' and the tender light of matin. And throughout the play there are moments, without movement, when characters remember 'our Saviour's birth', 'the burning eyes of heaven' or 'heavenly powers'; when Claudius begs help of 'angels'. The figures on stage move carefully, with hidden urgency or reluctance, with an awareness of each other and of another, spiritual reality.

Secondly, the strength of individual movement or gestures cannot be judged from the text alone; their eloquence is often achieved without words or where words seem unimportant. Here indeed is their unique contribution, for movements speak in association with words to represent reactions which are consciously hidden or beyond the conscious grasp of the characters. This may be seen in Claudius and Gertrude.

Their first appearance together with a public celebration of marriage is a large and simple visual effect, and Gertrude's close concern for her son suggests a simple, and perhaps unremarkable modification. The only movement which is obviously strange here is the speed with which Claudius leads her off to celebrate a reconciliation with Hamlet and at the same time leaves him, apparently unnoticed behind. From this point until after the Play Scene, Claudius and Gertrude always enter together, and remain together except when the King wishes to spy on Hamlet. Their movements seem to represent a comparatively single-minded relationship. But Claudius enters without Gertrude for his 'Prayer Scene' (III. iii) and, for the first time, Gertrude enters without him for the Closet Scene (III. iv) and is left alone, again for the first time, when Polonius hides behind the arras. Thereafter earlier accord is revalued by an increasing separation, often poignantly silent, and unexpected. When Claudius calls Gertrude to leave with him after Hamlet has dragged off Polonius' body, she makes no reply; twice more he urges her and she is still silent. But he does not remonstrate or question; rather he speaks of his own immediate concerns and, far from supporting her with assurances, becomes more aware of his own fears:

O, come away!
My soul is full of discord and dismay.

(IV. i. 44–45)

Emotion has been so heightened that it is remarkable that they leave together without further words. The audience has been made aware of a new distance between Gertrude and Claudius, of her immobility and silence, and of his self-concern, haste and insistence.

From this moment onwards their movements on leaving the stage become increasingly eloquent. When Claudius has set a watch on Ophelia, he appeals to Gertrude for sympathy, telling what he can of the dangers that threaten; but she says nothing and, if Claudius pauses, she will draw attention away from him to her physical withdrawal. When Laertes enters, supported by insurgents, Gertrude instinctively tries to hold him back and protect Claudius; but he, in contrast, faces

Laertes' sword, assumes command, and after curt assurances, forgets his Queen in immediate concerns. At the end of the scene, after Ophelia's second appearance, Gertrude has to leave the stage without a word from Claudius or to him. Danger had brought them together for a moment, but the spectacle of Ophelia's suffering separates them further than before: this is the first time that the Queen must leave entirely alone. The visual point will not be lost in performance, for as the King moves with urgent purpose, she will leave slowly with silent grief and helplessness; there will be a contrast of tempo, and quite simply, her exit will take much longer to complete, so that she must be seen alone on the empty stage. (An actress will be tempted to wait and then make a separate exit expressing her own unappeased grief.)

When Claudius returns with Laertes, he momentarily departs from duologue for a kind of soliloquy:

> Not that I think you did not love your father;
> But that I know love is begun by time,
> And that I see, in passages of proof,
> Time qualifies the spark and fire of it.
> *There lives within the very flame of love*
> *A kind of wick or snuff that will abate it;*
> *And nothing is at a like goodness still . . .*
>
> (IV. vii. 110ff.)

His new isolation from Gertrude supplies a motive for this digression from immediate and dangerous concerns; and will strengthen its effect. If Claudius moves apart, or merely breaks his contact with Laertes, the stage picture will lose definite focus with the absence of explicit motive, and the audience's sense of time, relevance and perspective may become insecure. It may hear echoes of the Player King:

> What to ourselves in passion we propose,
> The passion ending, doth the purpose lose. . . .
> This world is not for aye; nor 'tis not strange
> That even our loves should with our fortunes change . . .
>
> (III. ii. 189ff.)

and even of the ghost himself:

> O Hamlet, what a falling off was there,
> . . . to decline
> Upon a wretch whose natural gifts were poor
> To those of mine! (I. v. 47ff.)

These are refinements which may not be realised in performance, but because of the movements of the figures in the later passages of the play, Claudius can at least seem far removed from the immediate context of persuading Laertes, and appear to consider, momentarily, his new isolation. The audience will note an effort as he recalls himself with 'But, to the quick of the ulcer', and once more seeks 'desperate appliance.'

Nothing stops the physical and emotional separation of King and Queen and some movements express it more sharply. After Gertrude has told of Ophelia's death, Laertes leaves precipitously and it is of him that Claudius is thinking as he follows, not at all of Gertrude still rapt in her evocation of Ophelia's death, and her helpless admission of 'Drown'd, drown'd'. When Hamlet has left the graveyard, Gertrude is ordered in a single line to 'set some watch over her son;' now Claudius can easily dismiss her and be free to ensure an immediate attempt on Hamlet's life and take a kind of pleasure in the prospect. At no time has Shakespeare caused either of them to comment directly on their progressive separation, yet the audience's awareness of it develops; and so strongly can this be fostered in performance that it may seem at last that, in failing either to speak or to make a complete break, these characters are unable to understand all that is happening, and powerless to help themselves. The audience is encouraged to observe more deeply than either of the *dramatis personae*. Their dying cries gain ironic force and clarity from this long preparation: Gertrude calls on her 'dear' son and implicates her husband in murder; Claudius, with 'O yet defend me, friends; I am but hurt', appeals for a response he has never considered and tries a desperate lie. The audience may sense, without further information, that these few words express what has been progressively implied by movement and gesture, and that the subsequent immobility of death marks a true termination.

Shakespeare has ensured that the audience of *Hamlet* views its characters in depth. Yet this metaphor is hardly adequate; for what he has added to the stage picture is a fourth, or psychological dimension in which the hidden and subconscious reactions of each character can be presented, by movement as well as words.

Although movement should be viewed in its large impressions, its components can be identified most readily by following individual figures through the play. By making Rosencrantz and Guildenstern move together at Claudius' command, Shakespeare ensured that their minds seem mechanical and undistinguished: so much so, that theatre directors often assume that the two characters are indistinguishable.[3] Their unspoken thoughts are first clearly indicated after Hamlet's direct questions, when their mutual silence and then the whispered 'What say you?' draw close attention to their instinctive need to keep together. Their eagerness to play safe is also manifested when Hamlet dismisses them with brief courtesy on three successive occasions, for, as they murmer quick civilities, bow or exchange looks, the audience will see an unspoken embarrassment and, as they go out, a drawing together. When Claudius calls Guildenstern after the Closet Scene, *both* of them enter at once, silently. Guildenstern has the smarter mind, smoothing over awkward moments and being quick to question, with 'Prison, my lord? . . . In what, my dear lord? . . . A thing my lord?', and yet when action is needed for pursuing and guarding Hamlet it is Rosencrantz who assumes the lead without discussion. They at last drop all pretence of friendship and appear with the 'guard' as Hamlet's captors and warders: they leave that scene at one with the silent soldiers who move impersonally, under orders. Their natures are progressively revealed, one brusque and one watchful; and the consequences of having become the tools of Claudius are progressively manifested, without their choice or knowledge.

The audience's view of Horatio changes less, but deepens in the same way and widens. In the first scene, although he 'trembles and looks pale', he holds back his judgement until he can speak in an ordered way:

> Before my God, I might not this believe
> Without the sensible and true avouch
> Of mine own eyes. (I. i. 56–58)

And in the course of the play he has no sudden movement or impulse, or immediacy of speech, to draw attention to him. Yet he is often on stage silent and watchful, and ready with a brief reply when such is required by Hamlet. Before the Play Scene, he enters with an unassertive promptness when Hamlet calls. Perhaps the audience's view of him is more ambiguous when he proves unable to keep 'good watch' over Ophelia; but this is not made an issue in the dialogue nor emphasised by a return to the stage. It could be sensed only as an unspecified

[3] Cf. A. C. Sprague, *Shakespeare and the Actors* (1944), pp. 147–8.

VIII *Hamlet*, V.ii: The Duel (*at the Shakespeare Memorial Theatre, Stratford-upon-Avon*; *1961*)

IX I.ii: The first Court Scene

X III.ii: 'The Mousetrap'

Illustrations by Gordon Craig from the Cranach Press *Hamlet*

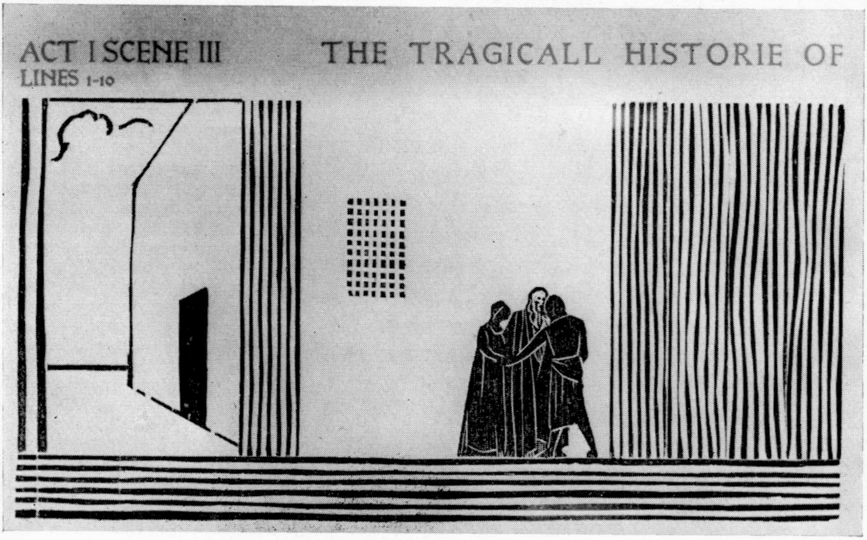

XI I.iii: Ophelia, Polonius and Laertes

XII III.i: Hamlet's soliloquy, 'To be, or not to be'

XIII The arrival of Fortinbras: V.ii. (Forbes-Robertson as Hamlet; from *Illustrated London News*)

uneasiness, and it would not prevent 'Now cracks a noble heart. Good night, sweet prince . . .' from sounding with a steady, deeply felt assurance. It is for such moments that his static and always unembarrassed physical presentation was chosen. This figure has been made remarkable and strong by the lack of movement and by silent attentiveness, as well as by brief speeches.

The comic aspects of Polonius' speech and behaviour ensure that the audience views him with a measure of detachment; yet Shakespeare has also presented him as an isolated figure and this can draw sympathy. After *The Mousetrap* has manifested something like the full danger of the situation, Polonius comes to Claudius and his busy insistence on his original plan for trapping Hamlet is neither welcomed nor heeded by his master whose thoughts are elsewhere; the eager Polonius must pause and then leave without any response commensurate with his purposes. His urgency to Gertrude meets with an almost equally slack response, as though she too has other thoughts than his. By contrasts of movement and tempo the audience will view Polonius less simply than at first: after it has been shocked by disregard for his daughter's feelings and, perhaps, has laughed at misplaced confidence in his own intelligence and petty cunning, it may recognise in hurried, surreptitious, isolated movements the limitations of a self-centred mind; there may be a quickening of sympathy for his blindness and clumsiness. His death, as he fusses helplessly in the toils of an arras, seems an unalterable conclusion.

On his return to the play in Act IV, Laertes is an important contrast with Hamlet, not only in his reckless and outspoken attitude to revenge, but also in the way that his independent action yields to movements alongside Claudius, even at his sister's funeral and between the bouts of the duel. Ophelia, on the other hand, has an effective isolation. She is presented as of key importance to Hamlet, but is not shown with him until she stands as a speechless decoy during the 'To be, or not to be' soliloquy. When she has to make a decision, her brief speeches—'no more but so? . . . I shall obey, my lord . . . My lord, I do not know . . . No, my lord . . . Ay, my lord . . . I think nothing, my lord'—cannot answer the audience's curiosity; she might evade or misrepresent; she may seem to have considered deeply, or to live only for the moment, lightly. The audience will intently view her young, untried body for some further sign: her silences and brevity of speech, contrasting with the volubility of her brother and father, and her passive waiting for Hamlet to 'affront' her, ensure that, if she speaks her lines with the studied care that their versification, syntax and vocabulary seem to suggest, she will appear to have a painfully private, uncommunicable consciousness. When she exposes herself to Hamlet's scorn ('you made me believe so, . . . I was the more deceived') and then lies to him about her father, a strong hidden conflict of sensations will be keenly felt. She sits at *The Mousetrap* taunted by Hamlet and then trying to enter the world of the play he has prepared; but he does not notice her departure and probably the audience does not either. She returns for the two mad-scenes in which both words and movements express her helpless thoughts at last, in all their range: sexual, pitiful and wilful. But her isolation is greater than before, for no one can contact her or restrain her, not even Laertes. Without her actual presence, her influence upon the play continues as Gertrude reports she died making a wreath for the dead, supported and then lost in flowing water. The movements of this slight figure express the limits of her being and so add to the impression of the effects of time and accident in the play. Most characters move towards a single-minded utterance and gesture, but the spirit of the young and beautiful Ophelia is expended wastefully and, until she has become a corpse, she is out of reach of others.

Hamlet is often seen as a hero who through uncertainty seeks to 'end his part in peace' like a perfect actor, with his cause 'rightly' known, to accept his role of 'scourge and minister', to be 'ready' for his 'end' and accept heaven's 'ordinance' in its timing and planning. But he does all this in a world which is also progressively revealed and progressively caught by processes which are not controlled by the characters' conscious thought. Hamlet's passage through the play differs most significantly in his attempt to understand this process; he has not won a 'special providence' for his particular cause but, rather, a thoughtful and difficult confidence in that providence. While his courage, affection and deliberation, his anger, pain and despair for the 'harsh world' are all revealed, the other characters move with equal certainty towards an unwilled revelation of their deepest natures. The end of *Hamlet* is the end of a world, of Elsinore as well as its prince. It is a general doom, like the last scene of *Lear*; perhaps more thoroughly, for the dead bodies must be removed by foreign captains at the command of a foreign inheritor.

The staging of the last episodes can illustrate how individual and group movements are co-ordinated. Obviously careful direction is required merely to keep the picture changing in this crowded scene. The King and Queen must enter together, with spectators and assistants for the duel; Laertes must choose the poisoned rapier so that the audience may see, but not Hamlet; a cup must be taken to Hamlet, and 'set aside'; Gertrude must be able to cross to Hamlet, give him a napkin, drink from his cup and wipe his brow, and the cup must again be put aside so that it is not spilt in the uproar that is soon to follow, and can be found quickly by the wounded Hamlet; Laertes must be able to speak aside to Claudius and then, on his return to the combat, to himself; the duel must become an 'incensed' fight; Gertrude must swoon and be attended out of reach of Claudius; Hamlet must be able, rapidly, to take command of the whole scene, order doors to be locked, kill Claudius with his rapier, reach for the cup, force him to drink from it, and put it down again so that Horatio may find it later, still with some wine in it; many voices must shout 'Treason', yet Claudius must be helpless during Laertes' eight lines of explanation. In all this, movement and positioning must be clearly fixed, or 'shaped', by the stage-director during rehearsals, so that 'rashness' and 'indiscretion' as well as considered 'plots' all work together on the crowded stage towards a certain end. The actors could not perform the scene, simulating the various passions called for by the text, without this hidden control and co-ordination. But after Hamlet's duologue with Horatio:

> There's a special providence in the fall of a sparrow. If it be now, 'tis not to come; if it be not to come, it will be now; if it be not now, yet it will come—the readiness is all . . .
>
> (V. ii. 211ff.)

we may judge that Shakespeare knew this, and calculated upon its effect. The complicated difficulties of stage-direction will mean that a plan can be sensed behind the most hurried and unconsidered movements; and this, in turn, adds to the impression in performance of fate or 'divinity' controlling the interrelated movements of the characters, an inevitability something like that of the last stage in a game of chess, without any speech to direct attention to it.[4] The attentive presence of Horatio and the precisely timed entry of Fortinbras are further movements which place Hamlet, Elsinore, Denmark and the world outside

[4] See plates viii and xiii for examples of controlled grouping in this last scene.

in a theatrical reality with a large and sweeping impression of men motivated from deep within themselves and drawn to their final positions by an unseen, unheard control or providence: a reality that reveals at last men's inward truth, through the operation of accident and intention, falsehood and truth, villainy and virtue.

* * *

The effectiveness of the changing stage picture is partly controlled by variations of tempo which are caused by both speech and movement. Anyone who has acted or directed a play will know that a change of tempo can affect mood, clarity, size, force and even meaning and character, and that an acceptable, workable tempo is often the most elusive element in a production, the one that must wait for the latest rehearsal for proper adjustment. Associated with tempo is rhythm, and both are at once general to each scene, Act and play, and particular to each incident and character. A single character may have one timing for his outward behaviour and another for his inward thoughts and feelings. Stanislavski felt the need for a conductor to give the beat to actors during a performance as if they were a complicated kind of orchestra. For some acting exercises he introduced numerous metronomes, all ticking at different but related speeds. He relegated these matters to the end of his course of instruction, because of their importance and their difficulty.[5]

Tempo, is then, a continual concern of all responsible for a performance and is capable, at all times, of affecting the audience's reaction. But to consider its large effects, that present the play forcibly to an audience, the striking contrasts, which are frequent in *Hamlet*, are the most important features.

The slowest tempos are in reflective passages, where feeling and thought are not immediately expressed in purposeful action. Among these are parts of the longer soliloquies, the disquisition on a 'sterile promontory' and 'brave o'erhanging firmament', the instructions to the players and the following talk of a man that 'is not passion's slave'. All these passages are centred on Hamlet himself and while he is absent from the stage only Gertrude's account of Ophelia's death, evoking a regard for suffering and helplessness, has anything like the same restrained tempo, or rhythms so unresponsive to other influences, so

[5] Cf. *Building a Character* (tr. 1949), Chapters XI and XII.

completely dictated by the speaker alone. Later there are passages between Hamlet and the gravedigger, allowing the prince to consider the 'noble dust' of an emperor with a curiosity which looks before and after the dramatic event. These moments sustain a slow tempo, but with them should be linked others in which this co-exists with a more urgent tempo beneath words or outward behaviour: in such passages the state of Denmark is considered deliberately while waiting for the ghost, or the formalities of Elsinore, the dumb-show, the funeral procession and preparations for the duel are presented as a cover to thoughts and inclinations which are more alert. Their main effect is the same: to encourage the audience to deliberate with Hamlet in preparation for some new action; often they insure that the audience is precisely and carefully involved with him immediately before some of the most rapid passages of the play.

Rapid tempo, as far as Hamlet is concerned, usually comes with action after some new understanding has been, far more slowly, achieved: such are his 'wild and whirling words', his strange jests and behaviour to his friends after seeing the ghost, the 'rogue and peasant slave' soliloquy as soon as he is alone after the player has wept for a 'mobled queen', his elation after *The Mousetrap* has caught the conscience of the King, his conflict with Laertes at Ophelia's grave in which he 'forgets himself' and reveals 'something . . . that is dangerous' from deep within (V. i. 256). There are a few brief passages of swift words and action when Claudius or his servants move with 'deliberate' suddenness (IV. iii. 8–9), but, as a slow tempo was mainly used to show Hamlet's deliberations, so a rapid tempo shows the flame, or as one might say 'the whirlwind' (III. ii. 7–8), of Hamlet's passion. It marks his instinctive and emotional reactions: first to his mother's marriage and Claudius' succession, then to his father, his mother, Ophelia, and, in his rapid jesting when Claudius pursues him after the killing of Polonius, to danger and gathering opposition. Slow tempo for Hamlet's deliberate involvement with himself and an ideal world; rapid for his instinctive and passionate response to the world around him: so tempo impresses an important polarity within Hamlet and within the play.

This is a simplification, a first view of the extremes. In performance large impressions may also derive from a device which brings strong and contrasting tempos into obvious conflict. This is used mainly for the presentation of Hamlet's response to women, Ophelia and Gertrude.

Other stage-techniques like the exceptional use of a sustained and simple slow tempo for the account of her death, suggest that Shakespeare was more concerned with the presentation of Ophelia than her words alone can imply, and the conflicts of tempo in Hamlet's main scene with her supports this. First, the encounter is delayed until Act III, so that the audience is particularly attentive. In soliloquy Hamlet has considered 'enterprises of great pitch and moment', but seeing Ophelia he is drawn away, simply and immediately. She acts an anonymous courtesy, and he gives a similar stumbling performance:

> OPHELIA. Good my lord,
> How does your honour for this many a day?
> HAMLET. I humbly thank you; well . . .

There is no need to suppose that Hamlet knows that Polonius and Claudius are overhearing because the tempo of this meeting is both slow *and* watchful: as he is drawn towards her, they both deceive each other, or try to do so, and, searching her eyes with 'are you honest? . . . Are you fair?', Hamlet could sense the prevarications. From this intimacy he is stung to abuse her, himself, man, woman: he loved her, and then, rapidly, he loved her not; she is fair and honest to him, yet she is no longer so; this is and is not Ophelia. His mother had left 'Hyperion' for a 'satyr' and now Ophelia becomes associated in his imagination with this betrayal; and now he is passionate in rapid denunciation. The suddenly direct 'Where's your father?' probably brings a break in the action and then comes Ophelia's lie: 'At home, my lord'. But even in his mounting anger there is conflict: as he attacks her, he leaves her; as he abuses her as whore and enemy, he repeats the one escape he can offer and, probably, again holds back to scrutinize her face:

> Get thee to a nunnery. Why wouldst thou be a breeder of sinners?

In the whirlwind of abuse he impulsively repeats 'To a nunnery, go' five times, until he rushes from the stage: in the new rapid tempo, a more deliberate, lingering reaction, the slower one of care or irony—whichever way the actor takes these words they will be slower—is still maintained as a rock among currents, an under-surface tempo emphasised by its rhythmic repetition. The existence of this stillness within the tempest is proved on Hamlet's exit, for as Claudius and Polonius hold back, Ophelia is able to speak her controlled and elaborate regret for the 'courtier's, soldier's, scholar's eye, tongue, sword; The expectancy and rose of the fair state', in a following calm.

The Closet Scene, between Hamlet and his mother, has something like the same handling of tempo and rhythm. From the first passionate interchange which makes Gertrude suppose that he will murder her, its development is strong, but there are at least three moments of contrasting calm: following the death of Polonius, on the ghost's entry and then on Gertrude's response as Hamlet drives his meaning home. At first his compulsive denunciation of his mother's 'compulsive ardour' cannot be halted by her admission of guilt and her calls for 'no more'; but when the ghost has deflected the course of the scene so that he 'temperately' proceeds (l. 140) and she forgets her own defence in concern for his apparent madness, then there is a certain calm. Now she can speak slowly and with the impression of a deep-seated truth: 'O Hamlet, thou hast cleft my heart in twain.' This is, indeed, the heart of the scene: assured in his relationship with his mother, Hamlet now looks forward and outward, seeing himself with settled deliberation as heaven's 'scourge and minister' (III. iv. 175). From this point tempo once more increases; for now he mocks the 'bloat king', his schoolfellows and politicians; he mocks at death too, and 'lugs' Polonius from the room. But in the rising tempo and more savage involvement of the end of this scene, Hamlet retains a contact with its calm centre; this is made apparent in his intimate, five-times repeated, 'Good-night' to his mother. Like Ophelia, Gertrude remains in the slower tempo. She is left alone and speechless, and when Claudius finds her, she is still rapt in silence. Twice, with Ophelia and with Gertrude, Hamlet's passionate and rapid reactions are held, or harnessed, by a fixed, slower response which is also deeply felt and instinctive.

Tempo in the last two scenes indicates a new control. When the memory of Yorick brings a flash of earlier denunciations of women, this is subdued at once. Hamlet cuts short the struggle with Laertes after his mother's final interventions, reasonably asking for understanding; but control is still precarious and Hamlet immediately leaves the stage. The last scene begins with sustained deliberation, easily rising to the rapidity and finesse of the water-fly Osric and then answering his more weighty seconder. Immediately before the court enters for the duel the tempo is slow, but with an inward excitement. Then the duel gives a new mixture of tempos, both alert and slow, and sometimes rapid; timing follows a regular pattern in the formalities and intermissions; it quickens, as one of the combatants makes a thrust, and is held back with their mutual wariness; it is circumscribed by the rules of the art of fencing and also unpredictable in its precise movements and sequences. Speed and forcefulness increase as the fight becomes 'incensed' (l. 293); and suddenly, with blood, all is still. Disorder at once follows, with sharp moments of recognition and then Hamlet with passion *and* deliberation is the central, dominating figure; and once more stillness follows, weighty with both pain and consideration. Yet, even now, the action is quickened once more by the steadier, gentler tempo of affection and responsibility, in an interchange between Hamlet and Horatio. Then, from a distance, is heard a soldiers' march and the reverberations of a 'warlike volley'. This is to be the tempo and rhythm of the conclusion: regular and impersonal.

The duel and concluding moments of Hamlet's role provide both stillness and excitement; the extremes of deliberation and passion are expressed, and the quieter impulses of affection and trust; and then there is a new and comprehensive control of tempo.

* * *

A study of the techniques of stage presentation provides an opportunity for describing the effects of the whole play. We may say, perhaps, that Shakespeare has ensured a threefold reception. First, he has presented man in society and in families and personal relationships. The settings and groupings and movements of the last scene ensure that the audience views every character on the stage, separately and together, judging their responsibilities and fulfilments, and the future of those that remain. Secondly, to a deeper view, there is the completed drama of human consciousness seen in all the characters but in Hamlet preeminently; having followed the hero through the play the audience will hear and see him as a man, not miraculously redeemed or purified, not executing an elaborately prepared revenge or process of justice, not suffering hopelessly, but acting with deliberation and passion, fully known according to his conscious, subconscious and physical being. Thirdly, there is a growing impression of inevitability and complicated control: so the play can be received as a public ritual. The hero, who has made a solitary journey through hardship and across the sea, returns to the single combat, death and acceptance; and, in all, in the final presentation of all the characters according to their inward truth, the heavens seem 'ordinant'.

One of the advantages of the theatrical view is that it can show us how the play is able to be *all* this, in the brief time of its lengthy performance, and how it involves the audience in many ways: a performance of *Hamlet* is an intellectual, sensuous, passionate, instinctive and strong experience.

PART THREE

The Play and the Audience

X

Plays in Performance

★

IN Shakespeare's own day the drama of human consciousness was the newest and most admired element in plays. Lifelike, accomplished and temperamental performances encouraged audiences to identify themselves with the 'star' actors, to wish the character portrayed, in the words of Thomas Heywood,[1] 'all prosperous performance, as if the personator were the man personated.' Robert, Earl of Huntington declares, in a play by Anthony Mundy concerning his *Downfall* (1598), that he will be a tragic actor:

> And thou shalt see me with a lofty verse
> Bewitch the hearers' ears, and tempt their eyes
> To gaze upon the action that I use.
>
> (ll. 265–7)

And here is Polymetes in Thomas May's *The Heir* (1620), a play with extensive borrowings from Shakespeare:

> Has not your lordship seen
> A player passionate Hieronimo?
> — By th' mass, 'tis true. I have seen the knave paint grief
> In such a lively colour, that for false
> And acted passion he has drawn true tears
> From the spectators. Ladies in the boxes
> Kept time with sighs and tears to his sad accents,
> As he had truly been the man he seem'd.
>
> (I. i)

Even the new form for theatre-buildings that was developed in London during the last two decades of the sixteenth century, with galleries surrounding a platform stage at two or three levels on at least three sides, would have encouraged a single point of focus. What we

[1] See Chapter II, p. 23, above.

call today the 'up-stage' position from which an actor can best control his audience would have been more nearly central to the theatre. The dramatist, John Webster, depicted an 'Excellent Actor' at the centre of a circle:

> by a full and significant action of body, he charms our attention: sit in a full theatre, and you will think you see so many lines drawn from the circumference of so many ears, whiles the Actor is the Centre.
>
> (*Characters*, 1615)

In these conditions, Shakespeare's ability to write acting parts, in which the psychological basis of character could be slowly revealed and passionate or deliberate speeches sustained by rhythm and metre, established fully the star actor's hold over his audience. Within a few decades of their first performances, *Much Ado About Nothing* was sometimes called '*Benedick and Beatrice*' and *Twelfth Night* re-christened '*Malvolio*'. And since that time, romantic actors and critics have still further established the predominance of the characters.

But Shakespeare requires more from his audience. In some plays, as *Julius Caesar* or *Coriolanus*, his theme was obviously political and social, and, as we have seen, he frequently provoked a wide focus upon the stage. His devices for ensuring this more comprehensive view are more remarkable when they are seen as counterstrokes to the newly established and creative influences that made the star actor so dominant. They are endlessly resourceful, changing from play to play to give appropriate presentation to their imagined 'worlds'.

We have seen how Exton's entry with the dead body of Richard II provokes the audience to attend more closely to Bolingbroke's words and actions, and then to observe the attendant but silent nobles. In *Romeo and Juliet*, after the death of the lovers, attention is deflected to all the 'parties of suspicion' and the families grouped on the stage; and the audience is forced, during the Friar's long explanation, to consider all the actions and motives that have led to the catastrophe.[2] In *Julius Caesar*, the minor attendant figures are not so significant but, here, two suicides follow each other so closely that the audience is encouraged to compare. Brutus says that Rome will never breed a 'fellow' to Cassius (V. iii. 101), and then Antony enters and claims that Brutus

[2] See Chapter XI, pp. 174–77, below.

was 'the noblest Roman of them all' (V. v. 68). By the side of Antony stands Octavius Caesar, who gives the last command:

> So call the field to rest, and let's away
> To part the glories of this happy day.

The contrast of this cold, efficient voice, exemplified in the phrase 'happy day', sharpens the double view of the play; the audience may remember Antony's earlier remark that 'some that smile have in their hearts, I fear, Millions of mischiefs' (IV. i. 50–51). Certainly, after twin suicides and succeeding tributes, Shakespeare's presentation of Octavius is calculated to rebuff an intense scrutiny. The audience will view the respect paid to Brutus' body as the soldiers file off stage with a concern for political consequences.

Before the end of *Richard III*, a play always performed for the opportunity it gives to a star actor, the audience's interest is widened by the Ghost Scene, in which all whom Richard has murdered move regularly across the stage cursing and then blessing: Richard is 'devil', 'butcher', 'boar', and Richmond is associated with 'good angels', 'peace', 'offspring'. But after this Richard continues to draw the closest attention, especially in the revealing and nervously intense soliloquy on awakening from his dream. In this psychological aspect of the play, Richmond is a minor contrast only, looking to the future, trusting in God, rather than to the past and present, judging and revealing *his own* life. But the contrast in presentation is an active stimulant in ensuring the widest dramatic view after the hero's role has reached its brilliantly enigmatic conclusion in blindly fighting and calling for the means to fight. Although 'A horse, a horse! My Kingdom for a horse!' has stayed longest in the memory of audiences, Richmond's long concluding speech, that announces his marriage to 'unite the white rose and the red' and the nation's purgation, invites the audience to reconsider the whole action and relate, as best they can, their experience of Richard's suffering and courage to Richmond's dismissal of him as a 'bloody dog'.

The end of *Macbeth* is a development from this technique. Malcolm also has a sustained verbal statement to offset the intensity of Macbeth's last scenes. But he has the advantage of the England Scene (IV. iii), the longest in the play, which establishes his political ability and association with Macduff, Ross, and the holy English King. He is also convincingly young, so that his less mature, less practised voice will accentuate the turning forward of dramatic interest. Moreover, Malcolm's political and military initiative is made theatrically more obvious: drums beat only for him; thanes are shown deserting Macbeth to join him; and his army carries green boughs that are emblems of renewal and a fulfilment of the last prophecy of the Witches. Old Siward's expression, and then suppression, of grief for his son's death immediately after Macbeth's last exit from the stage fighting has an intensity that is sufficiently sudden and unprecedented to draw attention for a moment to what is, in terms of narrative, a minor incident; this, too, helps to free the audience from the hold Macbeth exerts, so that it can turn more freely to the moral, political, royal and religious aspects of the tragedy that are stated by Malcolm in the conclusion.

Two plays in which the transference to a wider interest is effected by ensemble playing against the strong attraction of a single star role, are *Henry V* and *The Merchant of Venice*. In the first, the star part is restricted during the final Act, and in the second it is omitted altogether. After the audience has centred its attention on Henry in thoughtful prose speeches to the three soldiers and then the soliloquy which identifies his subtextual guilt and tensions, the battle fills the stage with various business. In the wooing episode of the last Act, Henry has to speak plainly and repeatedly in order to be understood and so the focus is narrowed; but the climax of this scene is a silent, shared kiss, and immediately the stage picture is widened as the French and English courts re-enter and take up formal positions. Henry has now comparatively little to say, being shown as one of many on whom responsibility for continued peace must rest. Queen Isabella of France is given new prominence for the penultimate speech which likens peace to a 'spousal' that can be threatened by jealousy. There is a general 'Amen' and all Henry does to conclude the play is to arrange for oaths to be taken and ask for prosperity: here, again, the audience will view the whole assembly of recent enemies and look for signs of good faith. The last moments provide a trumpet call and a silent *exeunt* of French and English together, and then the Chorus enters to remind the audience that France was subsequently lost, and England made to suffer with blood.

The conclusion to *The Merchant of Venice* is often considered a failure, for, unless stage-business is tactfully managed and the acting of the whole company well judged, the intense focus evoked by Shylock's suffering and destructive impulses will not yield to the wider issues of the last Act; the lover's behaviour can seem wantonly light, a shallow game of hide and seek. Obviously Portia has stood over against Shylock in the Trial Scene, but her wholly successful disguise and the sustained eloquence of her 'Quality of Mercy' speech did not encourage the audience to attend to her in the same way as to Shylock. (Indeed, it is hard to imagine a drama that could present two roles as deeply realised as Shylock's in one episode.) The fifth Act, which moves back to Belmont, can only satisfy the interest that has been awakened if, first, the music called for by the text provides a relaxed and dignified harmony appropriate to the associated talk of the music of the spheres, and, secondly, if the quick, glancing wit and the rapid encounters and lively spirits of the lovers are played as surface excitements covering an inner assurance of mutual love, a private and as yet untried enjoyment, that can respond to the harmonious music. In this way the formal grouping of the final *exeunt* can have a subtextual basis—as Shylock's impassioned performance and last exit must have had—and thus carry appropriate conviction. So the last Act is revalued in performance: for example, the sober willingness of Antonio to hazard, even now, his soul for his friend is heard as a brief textual expression of the usually unspoken trust, generosity and love which underly the temporary excitements and are the beginning of the only adequate answer to Shylock's remembered pleas for judgement.

* * *

Generally the comedies, by reason of their multiple plots, evenly matched roles and general liveliness of action, maintain a predominantly wide focus. Laughter depends on release from too narrow concerns—as Feste, the professional fool in *Twelfth Night,* knows when he takes Olivia's mind off the immediate cause of grief in order that she will laugh and then be able to see her own predicament in a wider context. (The man who slips on the cunningly placed banana-skin does not laugh so soon as those who set the harmless trap and so, from the first, observe the whole scene.) 'Humour', said Cazamian,

> demands the freedom of an unattached mind: . . . [and] lives in the relativity that is fair to all creatures.[3]

The very titles of Shakespeare's comedies demonstrate a broader in-

[3] L. Cazamian, *The Development of English Humour* (1952), p. 302.

terest than either the histories or tragedies. When Shakespeare adapted Thomas Lodge's novel, *Rosalynde*, he kept the heroine and her name, but called the play *As You Like It*; at its conclusion Rosalind and Orlando are only one out of four pairs of lovers and celebrate not only their journey's end but also the return of her father to his dukedom.

The Church Scene in *Much Ado* (IV. i) illustrates the dominant width of view for the comedies. It presents an incident which told simply could scarcely avoid an intensification of interest. But, first, Shakespeare ensured that the audience knows all the story, that Hero is truly faithful and her enemies already apprehended. Then he gives Hero, who suffers most, very little to say and little opportunity to provoke or hold attention. Claudio speaks with clear, strong sentiment and compelling imagery as the situation demands, but the fluent and sustained rhythm of his verse (not equalled elsewhere in the play) cannot represent passion with an impression of either immediate sensation or subtextual feeling. And, even while he holds the centre of the stage, attention is deflected by supporting speeches from Don Pedro and by three interruptions, one from Don John whose compact, cold utterance easily attracts attention by contrast. Benedick's abrupt and unnecessary comment, 'This looks not like a nuptial', may be intended as a forced joke, relaxing the tensions of the scene as well as deflecting interest. By these means, even during Claudio's powerful denunciation, the audience views the whole stage.

All the comedies end with general celebration, often involving music and grouped movements across the stage. In *Much Ado*, news comes of Don John's capture, but the *dramatis personae* take pleasure in not thinking about him—and so will the audience—as the pipers strike up for the final dance. After Mercade's entry and a more searching focus than elsewhere in the play, *Love's Labour's Lost* closes with songs which celebrate Spring and Winter, and tell of all married men, and Dick, Tom, Joan and Marian. Indeed, in the comedies, Shakespeare's cunning manipulation of the stage picture is most remarkable in providing moments of intense focus, so that his characters are progressively revealed in scenes separated by so much other lively business. The predominant focus is so broad and the dramatic material so abundant, that the plays might have become superficial and their general conclusions slick and mechanical.

Soliloquies and climactic revelations of character in extended speeches where the comic situation releases unusual and fantastic reactions are the main ways of presenting the drama of human consciousness in the widely focused comedies. For example, in *A Midsummer Night's Dream* the contrasts of wood and city, and of experienced courtiers, young courtiers, mechanicals and fairies have so influenced the dramatic structure and complicated both plot and theme that the widest aspects of the comedy have continual fascination. But the audience is also closely involved with individual characters and this depends on moments of surprisingly intense focus. Bottom, in particular, is presented before appearing at court with increasing freedom and a progressive revelation of his innermost nature. When he first enters with an ass's head on his shoulders, his fellows run away at once, like 'wild geese' frightened and 'distracted' and he is left alone in ignorance of what has happened. As he tries to be realistic and to rouse his own vanity and bravery, his words have the rhythms and progressions of actual thought and fear; the focus is intent on him:

> I see their knavery: this is to make an ass of me; to fright me, if they could. But I will not stir from this place, do what they can; I will walk up and down here, and I will sing, that they shall *hear* I am not afraid.
>
> (III. i. 109–13)

There is a still more sustained intensity when he wakens from his 'dream' (IV. i. 197ff.). Here Bottom is revealed as the actor who wishes to be glorious in great company, even if it means singing a ballad about his own unbelievable, foolish and unsubstantial dream. Shakespeare has interweaved echoes from earlier talk of rehearsing so that this soliloquy begins and ends with amateur theatricals and is thus a convincing development from the less heroic Bottom of the first Acts. These successive moments of revelation and intimacy mean that when he absurdly performs the part of Pyramus before the Duke, the audience will not laugh like the courtiers on the stage; it has thought of Bottom as he does of himself and after that, as Theseus explains, even such 'shadows' as these 'unfitted' actors may 'pass as excellent men' (V. i. 210–15).

* * *

Changes between wide and intense dramatic focus are elements in what happens when a Shakespearian play is performed. The varying focus controls, on the one hand, the social relevance of the action and, on the other, the opportunities for actors to reveal the emotional and intellectual strength of their characters, especially where a train of subtextual impressions is progressively developed and at last stated more directly. To the customary discussions of a play's language, themes, plot, situation and characters must be added a consideration of these techniques. They are not so easy to describe, being untouched by literary criticism and needing a full response to visual and temporal, as well as verbal, elements; but, along with the other theatrical devices that we have examined in this book, they can account for characteristic effects in performances of Shakespeare's plays.

In the theatre each play offers a kind of encounter, an invitation to move into a play world, to see it generally and with the eyes of particular characters; and then, perhaps, to be led to see from a different viewpoint, or with more penetration, or to be cheated of firm understanding when that had seemed to be offered. At times Shakespeare thwarts his audience, but more frequently he *seems* to allow its members absolute freedom, to imagine further or more precisely in their own terms: at moments of fullest or sharpest realisation, the dramatic facts may be left behind—the actual stage, setting, actor, even the words that are spoken. It seems to me that this is because the most deeply felt moments are not strongly textual: they rely on subtextual exposure or intensity, on changes of tempo, rhythm, texture or weight, on 'large and sweeping impressions of scene and the movement of figures', on the release of laughter or grip of expectation, or on a close, particular *view* of the whole stage of characters after sequential changes of the stage picture. The audience is encouraged to respond by less precise means than words alone, but means that have a developing strength and relevance through consecutive and complete performance, and in no other circumstance.

There are two important consequences of this dramatic strategy. First, actors and directors must learn to discover and use the opportunities Shakespeare has provided, and this will involve close textual study as well as patient, imaginative and experimental rehearsals. And, secondly, critics and students must recognise that Shakespeare's art can never be represented by the printed text of his dialogue, his intentions never explained by simple quotation. The complex and subtle setting for any speech, and the speed, rhythm, weight or body of its words, as well as their meanings and allusiveness, must also be described in terms of an actor's performance and in relation to the changing stage picture. Only so can Shakespeare's plays be considered, as he intended, as if being performed in a theatre.

To try to discover the stage life that suits the text of any one of the plays is a fascinating pursuit, and to try to describe it only less interesting than its re-creation.

PART FOUR

English Shakespeare in the 'Sixties

XI

Zeffirelli's Romeo and Juliet

★

AN editorial in *Theatre Notebook* spoke of 'revelation', *The Observer* of 'revelation, even perhaps a revolution', and *Theatre World* of excitement, 'unity of presentation', and a 'reality which lifted one inescapably back to medieval Italy.'[1] These are examples of the enthusiastic reception which kept Franco Zeffirelli's production of *Romeo and Juliet* in the repertory of a London or touring company of the Old Vic from 4 October 1960, into 1962, bringing them a greater success than they had enjoyed for more than a decade. Yet on the morning after its first night, the critic of *The Times* spoke coldly of the performances, and in *The Sunday Times* Harold Hobson described a failure: to his disenchanted view, Romeo was 'well-spoken' but 'pasty-faced and sulky', Juliet flapped 'her arms about like a demented marionette'. After its season in London these conflicting reactions seem less remarkable: it was a production of unique and consistent achievement which exchanged a number of conventional virtues for others which are not often found in our presentations of Shakespeare. And it was effected with such intelligence, sympathy and authority that we can now take stock and ask how important these unusual virtues are for this play and, perhaps, for others.

★ ★ ★

The break with custom was clearest in Zeffirelli's visual presentation of Romeo. Audiences have come to expect a dark handsomeness, reminiscent of Sir Laurence Olivier in the production of 1935 (see Plate XVI). A white shirt is usually open at the neck; a dark wig accentuates a tall, noble brow; the eyes are made-up to appear large and deep. The pose chosen for official photographs usually suggests a lonely, haughty and brooding mind. With some additional swagger from the

1 *Theatre Notebook*, xv (1961), 75; *The Observer* (9 October 1960); *Theatre World* (November 1960).

cloak Motley designed for him, Richard Johnson's Romeo at Stratford-upon-Avon in 1958 was in this tradition (see Plate XVII). Another recognisable but less common strain is the poetic—graceful, fluent, light: Michel Bernardy's Romeo for Saint-Denis's Strasbourg company in 1955 exemplified it, looking like some 'herald Mercury' (see Plate XVIII). Both these traditions Zeffirelli broke. John Stride, his Romeo, wore no velvet; he had no wig, no cloak, no ornament; his shirt did not open at the neck (see Plate XIX). One of his costumes, devised by Peter Hall (the designer, not the director), seemed to be made of tweed, and none of them imposed grandiloquent postures; they were comfortable, hard-wearing, familiar clothes in greys and greyish-blues. In them Romeo could sit, squat, run or stroll; he could run his hand through his hair, or look insignificant among a crowd. He was so little the gilded youth that it seemed odd that he should have a personal servant. Clearly, this director had paid less attention than usual to the opening words of the Prologue: 'Two households, both alike in dignity'; but in recompense he had avoided the meaningless gloss of 'fancy-dress' which many other Romeos assume with their splendid clothes. John Stride seemed to be English rather than Italianate, lively rather than sensuous; and he looked more convincingly in his teens than other actors of the part who have been equally young in fact.

To varying degrees all the young people in the play, except Paris, shared these qualities. Perhaps the Capulets were more richly dressed than the Montagues, but all the youth of Verona were at ease. Running and sauntering, they were immediately recognisable as unaffected teenagers; they ate apples and threw them, splashed each other with water, mocked, laughed, shouted; they became serious, sulked, were puzzled; they misunderstood confidently and expressed affection freely. Much of this behaviour has been seen before in Peter Hall's production of *A Midsummer Night's Dream* and *The Two Gentlemen* at Stratford-upon-Avon,[2] but besides dispensing with the magnificent clothes that sat incongruously on Hall's Lysander or Silvia, Zeffirelli did not condescend towards his young lovers and did not underestimate them. He gave prominence to a sense of wonder, gentleness, strong affection, clear emotion and, sometimes, fine sentiment, as well as to high spirits and casual behaviour. His characters were exciting and affecting as less responsive heroines and heroes could never be.

[2] I reviewed these productions in *Shakespeare Survey*, XIII (1960) and XIV (1961).

For after the first visual surprise there were others. Despite the prodigality of the director's invention, the stage-business seemed to spring from the words spoken, often lending them, in return, immediacy, zest or delicacy. So the unpompous behaviour caught the audience's interest for the characters and for the old story. In the balcony scene after Juliet (Miss Judi Dench) had been called away, there was a still silence on her return before she dared speak again or Romeo dared to come out of hiding. And by illustrating their mutual sense of awe and fear—their new-found happiness needs each other's presence to persuade them it is real—this silence brought back a memory of Romeo's words:

> I am afeard,
> Being in night, all this is but a dream,
> Too flattering-sweet to be substantial. (II. ii. 139–41)

It also helped to prepare the audience for the direction and urgency of Juliet's following speech:

> If that they bent of love be honourable,
> Thy purpose marriage, send me word to-morrow. . . .

Words and stage-business together drew the audience into the dramatic illusion. Such should be the aim of all directors of plays, but Zeffirelli has been unusual among our contemporaries in unifying Shakespeare's words with an inventive, youthful and apparently spontaneous action. Again, as the lovers leave the stage with the Friar to be married, Romeo walked backwards, so that he continued to face Juliet who was supported on the Friar's arm: Romeo was 'bewitched by the charm of looks' (II. Prol. 6) rapt in

> . . . the imagin'd happiness that both
> Receive in either by this dear encounter. (II. vi. 28–29)

So the stage-business took its cue from the words spoken, and centred Romeo's interest, without respect to absurdity or other concerns, on his delight in love. As the lovers encountered adversity and danger, phrases like 'Stand not amaz'd' (III. i. 131), ''Tis torture' (III. iii. 29), 'Blubb'ring and weeping' (III. iii. 87) were all directly and convincingly related to the action, and consequently they were far more compelling than is customary in productions which deliberately court a sumptuous setting and exotic mood.

The street 'brawls' were realised in the same way. The fight between Mercutio and Tybalt had a mixture of daring and mockery which reflected the exaggeration of the text:

> Consort! what, dost thou make us minstrels? An thou make minstrels of us, look to hear nothing but discords. Here's my fiddlestick; here's that shall make you dance. Zounds, consort!
>
> (III. i. 44–47)

Since few people in a modern audience can judge its fine points, the conventional duel usually appears either elegant and correct, or dangerous, or sometimes impassioned; it can hardly reflect the tone of this passage. Yet Zeffirelli made the fight high-spirited, like the words: Mercutio, gaining possession of both swords, used one as a whetstone for the other before handing Tybalt's back—stopping to wipe its handle with mocking ostentation. With such preparation, Romeo could respond to Mercutio's sour jests after he is wounded as casually as the text demands—'Courage, man; the hurt cannot be much'—without appearing callow; the dying man's protestations could be taken as the holding up of an elaborate jest. Enacting the mood of the text in this way did not devalue the scene: the bragging turned to earnest all the more effectively with the suddenly involved and simple words of Romeo, 'I thought all for the best' (l. 101).

The greatest innovations of this production lay in unifying words and stage-business, and in making the actors' speech as lively and fluent as their physical action. The result was that the dialogue did not appear the effect of study and care, but the natural idiom of the characters in the particular situations. It is a long time since Shakespeare's text has been so enfranchised. Juliet's 'I have forgot why I did call thee back' is often answered with rhetorical neatness, or passionate emphasis, or fanciful humour, in Romeo's 'Let me stand here till thou remember it' (II. ii. 171–2), but in this production the reply was frank and happy, appropriate to the quick sensations of the situation and suggesting a mutual response; the literary finesse of the text was not used to draw attention to itself but to give form and pressure to the dramatic moment. Or again, the interchange between the Friar and Romeo:

> FRIAR. . . . Wast thou with Rosaline?
> ROMEO. With Rosaline, my ghostly father? No;
> I have forgot that name and that name's woe.
>
> (II. iii. 44–46)

was transformed by making Romeo pause after 'no' and then blurt out 'I have forgot that name' as a sudden realisation, a thought which had, at that instant, come to him for the first time; it was still an antithesis to the Friar's expectation, as a literary analysis of the speech requires, but its sudden clarity was represented and accentuated by the manner in which it was spoken.

Some critics complained that this treatment of the dialogue destroyed the 'poetry' of the play. But it would probably be truer to say that the poetry was rendered in an unfamiliar way. Zeffirelli has directed many operas, and turning to a Shakespeare production he ensured that many speeches, even in the lively and fluent tempo, were tuned with musical exactness. Changes of tempo, pitch and volume were used to strong dramatic effect. For example, when Romeo called 'Peace, peace!' at the climax of the Queen Mab speech, Mercutio's 'True' followed quickly and flatly, and then, changing the key, 'I talk of dreams . . .' was low and quiet, rapt in mood; but all was nicely proportioned and rhythmically unified. This director knows more about musical speech than most of those working in our theatres today. There were, however, some notable lapses: Mercutio's speech and Juliet's potion soliloquy lost their cumulative effects because they were broken by too much stage-business (Juliet was made to writhe about in a red spot-light); the moments of incantatory stillness, which can have, in T. S. Eliot's words, a 'winged validity' beyond their immediate dramatic impulse, were surrendered for livelier effects; and the actors did not always delight in the 'concord of sweet sounds' when the writing was obviously euphonious. But Zeffirelli's animated style of speech was appropriate to much of the dialogue of the young characters in the play and, in its new dramatic life, the 'poetry' showed both its bravery and gentleness.

By making it sound like the natural idiom of the lovers and their companions, the director was restoring many of the original tones, the original freshness. In *Much Ado About Nothing*, Benedick says that Claudio was 'wont to speak plain and to the purpose, like an honest man and a soldier', but being turned lover he is 'turn'd orthography; his words are a very fantastical banquet, just so many strange dishes' (II. iii. 15–18). Romeo is such a lover: meeting with Mercutio after the balcony scene his verbal wit runs 'the wild-goose chase' and he is told: 'now art thou what thou art by art as well as by nature' (II. iv. 86–87). The 'art' of much of the poetry in this play was surely intended to sound like a delighted and energetic response to immediate sensations, and in regaining this impression the actors responded in an appropriate way to the conscious artifice of their text. Their speaking reflected many of its moods, mixing humour with concern (as in Juliet's 'Swear not by the moon'), mockery with envy, passion with fear and hesitation. The metrical basis of the speech was sometimes insecure and its euphony obscured, but its colour and movement were often wonderfully accurate. Individual actors and actresses have achieved this dramatic life in Shakespearian roles at the present day—Sir Laurence Olivier and Miss Dorothy Tutin are the most gifted and unfailing of them—but here the same quality was sustained through whole scenes. The director had treated wit, rhetoric and 'poetry' as an integral part of his production.

* * *

His success was chiefly with the young characters in the earlier part of the play. The first signs of merely routine handling were in the figures of authority. The Prince was given customary emphasis by two attendants with halberds, a voluminous gown and, by the standards of this production, rich accoutrements. On his first entry he stood up-centre, and his words were accompanied by a muffled, rolling drum off-stage. But he lacked dramatic life comparable with that of the figures around him: the stage devices had added only an undefined impressiveness. This might be judged appropriate for his early appearance, but on his return after the death of Tybalt, when he stood down-stage centre, he still seemed out of touch with the other characters, for these hitherto agile and fluently organised figures immediately became fixed in postures at either side (see Plate XX). In the last scene where the Prince finds himself implicated in the general sorrow and guilt ('for winking at your discords'), he stood so unmoving, and so high above the heads of everyone else on the stage, that he necessarily spoke in the earlier lifeless and formal manner. The director did attempt a more animated Friar, but here the business he invented seemed inapposite and occasionally impertinent: in the middle of his first speech a bell sounded off-stage and he stopped abruptly to kneel and cross himself; and when Juliet met Romeo at his cell he stepped between them to effect a comic collision involving all three figures—a kind of humour wholly different from the quieter kind written into the lines he speaks—and this stage-trick was repeated before the end of the short scene. In the last Act, at the tomb, the Friar had such little relevance to the dramatic situation that he did not re-enter after he had left Juliet alone with Romeo's body: his speeches and all reference to him were cut.

While Zeffirelli had created an animating style for the story of the young lovers, he had not found a means to represent the authoritative figures (which Shakespeare has made the centre of important scenes) with a comparable life-likeness. In this, the production was like many others which have been seen in England recently: Sir Tyrone Guthrie's treatment of the King of France in *All's Well*, Peter Hall's of Priam in *Troilus*, and Tony Richardson's of the Duke of Venice in *Othello*, all shown at Stratford in recent years, are examples of the same malaise. Even when it was Romeo and Juliet who assumed new dignity and authority in confronting catastrophe, this director seemed unsure. Juliet's 'Is there no pity sitting in the clouds. . . .?' (III. v. 197), was said hurriedly; she sat on the floor, as if she needed no strength of mind to frame and speak this question. (One may contrast Alan Webb's dignified and affecting delivery of the comparable, 'O heavens, can you hear a good man groan And not relent, or not compassion him?' from Peter Brook's production of *Titus Andronicus*.) Juliet's concluding line in this scene, with its authoritative and calm phrasing, 'If all else fail, myself have power to die', she spoke lightly on the point of running from the stage. Similarly, Romeo's stature in the final scene was belittled by his failing to show authority and compassion before the dead bodies of the other young men as Shakespeare's text ensures: his description of Paris as 'One writ with me in sour misfortune's book' and:

> Tybalt, liest thou there in thy bloody sheet?
> O, what more favour can I do to thee
> Than with that hand that cut thy youth in twain
> To sunder his that was thine enemy?
> Forgive me, cousin.
>
> (V. iii. 97–101)

were both excised from the text used for this production, and no such effect was attempted.

Important moments of grief also seemed underplayed. The distraction, frustration and fear of the young lovers were well enough represented with nervous intensity, although cries and groans and other physical reactions were sometimes at odds with the technical demands of long speeches with elaborate syntax and rhetoric. The more general and more considered grief seemed most hollow. The mourning for Juliet when she is discovered as if dead was staged formally like the authoritative scenes (see Plate XXI), and anonymous servants were introduced mechanically, two at a time, to extend the tableau and so attempt to create a climax. This indeed is one old-fashioned way of responding to the formal nature of the verse, and in another production it might serve: but here it was a glaring contrast with the minutely and freshly motivated stage-business of adjacent scenes. The illusion previously established was lost in this presentation of general sorrow and was replaced with something lifeless and dissimilar in all points of execution. Romeo's address to the Apothecary showed the failure to represent a more considered grief. This is a speech of peculiar difficulty, for it must manifest complex reactions. But Zeffirelli concentrated on its agitation, so that his Romeo repeatedly struck and browbeat the 'caitiff wretch'. This manner could not present consideration and compassion, responses that are implicit in:

> The world is not thy friend, nor the world's law;
> The world affords no law to make thee rich . . .
>
> There is thy gold—worse poison to men's souls,
> Doing more murder in this loathsome world
> Than these poor compounds that thou mayst not sell . . .
>
> Farewell; buy food, and get thyself in flesh.
>
> (V. i. 72–84)

And the long and detailed description of the apothecary's shop and wares issued strangely from the mind of this Romeo, given over to turbulence and spite. The scene should surely be directed in a way that can show how grief *and* resolution have entered deeply into Romeo's soul, making him precise, understanding, compassionate, sharp, subtle and even cynical: it is a complex moment, that cannot be presented by a simple pursuit of energetic expression.

The still moments of general or deliberate grief were, like the figures of authority, unsatisfactory. In the concluding scene Zeffirelli cut a hundred and twenty consecutive lines, those from the last of Juliet's to the Prince's 'Where be these enemies? . . .' And so the outcry of the people, the 'ambiguities', the concern to find the 'head' and 'true descent' of the calamity, the general suspicion in which the Prince at last finds himself implicated along with the others, the call

XIV II.ii: the Balcony Scene

XV I.i: the first Brawl

XVI Laurence Olivier as Romeo

XVII Richard Johnson as Romeo

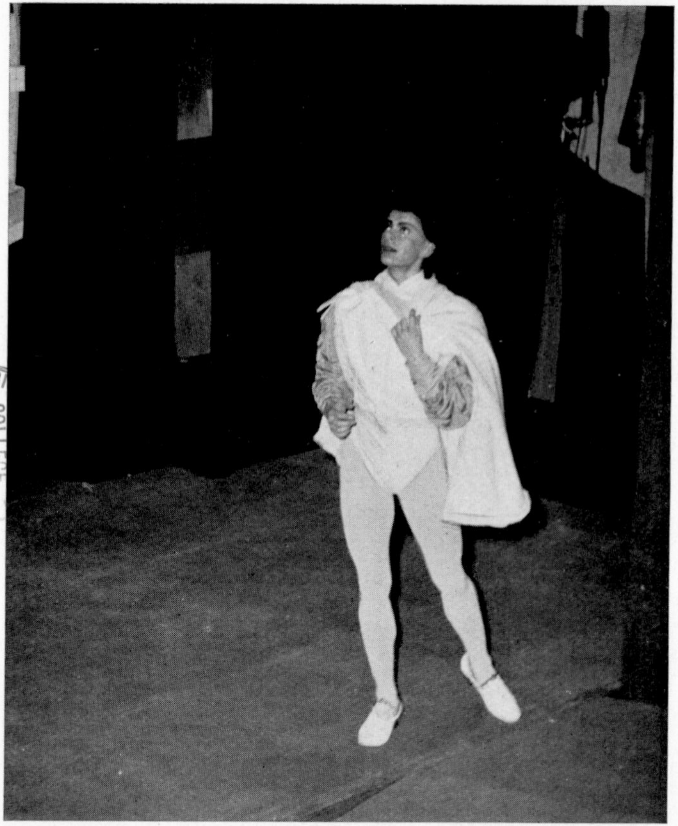

XVIII Michel Bernardy as Romeo

XIX John Stride as Romeo

XX III.i: the Prince after the death of Tybalt

XXI IV.v: Mourning for Juliet

for patience, the demand for 'rigour of severest law', were all sacrificed. The main reason for this was not shortage of time, for the scene was then extended by much interpolated silent business: anonymous servants embraced in pairs, symmetrically placed as a statuesque expression of general grief; mechanically, without being ordered to do so, they moved the bodies of Romeo and Juliet to the catafalque; in a slow procession, accompanied by singing off-stage, the supposedly reconciled families departed with composed neatness at opposite sides of the tomb, without a look at the dead bodies and without recognition of each other. Benvolio and the Nurse were then re-introduced to take silent farewells of the bodies and, finally, to swelling music, the lights faded with impressive slowness until the curtain fell. The ending had been refashioned as a solemn, exotically illuminated dumb-show. In comparison with the animated interplay of words and action that had preceded it, this spectacle seemed empty and meaningless. A production that had at first gripped and moved its audience was at its conclusion pretentious, sentimental and vague.

Again it must be admitted that the discrepancy was not unexpected. Professional producers in recent years have all cut something from the last scene of *Romeo and Juliet.* Glen Byam Shaw directing at Stratford-upon-Avon in 1954 and 1958, cut the dialogue between the Friar and Balthazar as the former approached the tomb, cut lines on the entry of the watch, delayed the Prince's entry, so that he had no need to repeat his question, and eliminated some of his orders; he also cut a few lines of the Friar's explanation and the whole of the depositions of Balthazar and Paris's page. The Stratford production of 1945 cut the Friar's last speech from forty lines to six; that of 1941 omitted the Friar altogether after he had left Juliet; and Peter Brook's production of 1947 deleted everything after Juliet's last words and, then, simply brought on the Chorus to conclude with a few of the Prince's last lines (and yet on this occasion there was time enough in the course of the play for introducing a negro servant, an Arab, a carpet seller, a 'man with a drum' and various other extra attractions).[3]

Directors working in the English theatre do not respond to Shakespeare's presentation of authority and responsibility and of understanding, compassionate grief. This is surely a loss. The Prince's acknowledgement of complicity is Shakespeare's addition to the story

[3] The prompt books of these productions are in the library of the Royal Shakespeare Theatre, at the Birthplace Centre, Stratford-upon-Avon.

as he found it in Arthur Brooke's narrative poem, *The Tragical History of Romeus and Juliet*. Moreover we know that Shakespeare was deeply concerned with the ways in which responsibility is learnt in adversity. The theme recurs at important crises in plays throughout his career: it is found when Richard the Second is imprisoned and when Henry the Fifth prays before Agincourt, and later, when Lear, Pericles, Cymbeline, Leontes and Prospero become suppliants. Such a climax in *Romeo and Juliet* needs the development of the preceding hundred and twenty lines which Zeffirelli cut. And these lines have important dramatic interests to present on their own account. Compared with Shakespeare's source, in which Juliet has two long speeches immediately before her death (and with versions of the play by Otway, Cibber and Garrick, who all invented final speeches for the heroine), Juliet's last moments are hustled in the play; Shakespeare has allowed her only the briefest possible utterances and brought the busy watchmen on stage immediately afterwards. He has given time and words and action at this important culmination of the tragedy to the crowded stage, as one after another of the characters kneel as 'parties of suspicion', and as the two families stand silently listening. The Friar's long speech is so tightly written that it is difficult for a director to do anything but keep it almost intact or cut it out entirely: its highly wrought texture shows that it cannot represent a slackening of interest in the dramatist, but rather a determination to show the manifold ways in which small, over-confident human decisions had worked together with some kind of destiny, that 'greater power than we can contradict'. Shakespeare's complicated last movement of the tragedy shows that however powerful destiny may seem, men and a Prince among men react to catastrophe first in guilt ('And I, for winking at your discords too Have lost a brace of kinsmen. All are punished'), and then with a sifting of responsibility and a demand for justice:

> Go hence, to have more talk of these sad things;
> Some shall be pardon'd, and some punished.

Zeffirelli's change to dignified dumb-shows of grief could not help these words to express the socially responsible particularity of Shakespeare's full text. To present *Romeo and Juliet* satisfactorily, it is necessary to find a style which can sharpen attention on words in still and deeply felt moments and to create a company capable of ensemble playing. Only so can a director sustain the dramatic life of the entire last scene—

make an audience listen to the Friar and observe the physical and emotional involvement of the surrounding figures. And only so can he sustain those earlier moments of authority, responsibility and understanding grief which prepare for this conclusion.

* * *

In part the shortcomings of this production may have been due to a lack of sympathy, for several of the less successful passages are known to be capable of lively presentation. In part it was probably due to a weakness in the metrical control of speech, for most of these moments involve sustained utterance or counter-pointed phrases. It may also be bound up with the timing of the production as a whole.

At the very end the director used a slow pace in order to make the invented conclusion impressive, but this was after he had hurried some speeches which demand time to give the impression of consideration and after he had cut much from the second half of the play: III. iv and IV. iv were cut completely, the beginning IV. ii, the musicians from IV. v, the first twenty-three lines of the important scene of Romeo in Mantua. It looked as if the earlier Acts had been given too easy a rein. Discounting two intervals, the performance lasted two hours and fifty minutes: the first part, up to the end of II. ii, took an hour: the second part, up to the end of III. i, took forty minutes; and this left but an hour and ten minutes for most of Act III and the whole of Acts IV and V. It may well be that Zeffirelli purposely tried to speed up Acts III, IV and V, sensing that the tempo had become too slack.

Often the beginning was slow in order to establish characters and atmosphere. For example, Romeo's first entrance was long and silent, accompanied by shouting and laughter off-stage; it showed his solitary, self-absorbed nature. To introduce Mercutio with Benvolio for II. iv, time was taken to show them lounging in the street and encountering two casual passers-by who left the stage before the first of Shakespeare's words were spoken. After the Prince had pronounced judgement for the death of Tybalt, the stage emptied very slowly until only the Chorus was left, and then he closed the scene by slowly walking the full depth of the deserted stage and, again slowly, lifting his hands in a gesture of despair. These pieces of stage-business, and others like them, should have been cut in the interest of a stronger pace for the whole production; while not contradicting Shakespeare's text, they merely offered superfluous illustration. This economy would also have given more power to gestures and business that were required by the words, and that intimately illuminated and sustained the words; in such invention Zeffirelli had been prodigal.

But the chief cause of slowness was scenic realism. Twice a curtain rose to show the stage covered with smoke, giving a hazy impression, and a singing or chatting crowd of stage-dressing supernumeraries. Two sets of curtains were used within the proscenium (visible in Pl. XV), so that the scenery could be changed on every possible occasion, even if to disclose merely 'another part of the streets' or 'another room in Capulet's house'. Some of the changes mirrored the change of mood implicit in the text: the most effective was to Juliet's bedroom with pale blue walls and a tall bed furnished with the same blue and white, making these colours dominant for the first time and giving a sense of space, femininity and domestic peace. But too many scene-changes were trivial, one set being only more or less commodious than the other, or providing a large and inessential property, like the desk for Friar Lawrence that was placed before an all but meaningless back-drop.

Although the mechanism and scenic realism were often old-fashioned in contrast to the style of acting, the audience and critics generally admired the settings which were designed by Zeffirelli himself. But on reflection we may question their usefulness. With a simpler, but not necessarily less evocative or less changeable setting, the new, alert style of action and speaking might have made an even greater impact and the 'realism' centred in the human behaviour on which the story and tragedy depends. By the same means, the tempo could have been more brisk. This would have answered the motif of 'sudden haste' which is found in Shakespeare's text repeatedly, and with insistence:

> It is too rash, too unadvised, too sudden: Too like the lightning . . . on a sudden one hath wounded me. That's by me wounded. . . . Tybalt, that an hour Hath been my kinsman . . . let Romeo hence in haste. . . . Hie to your chamber. . . . Hie you, make haste . . . hie hence, be gone away! . . . Come, stir, stir, stir! . . . Uncomfortable time, why camest thou now . . .? . . . O mischief, thou art swift. . . . Stay not to question . . . then I'll be brief.

Once the action is under way, such phrases are found in almost every scene and are not without significance. The pace, momentum and general sweep of events can help to represent the 'star-crossed' elements of the love story, and so Romeo and Juliet appear to be fighting with growing urgency against an increasingly complex concatenation of misfortunes that seems to emanate from 'inauspicious stars' beyond man's control.

And—to return to the earlier and even more important point—a simpler setting with a brisker pace would have allowed the director to give the necessary time in Acts III, IV and V for presenting the theme of responsibility and the deeper understanding which men learn through this catastrophe. The young characters of this production were so compellingly alive that the loss is doubly unfortunate: it would be a pity if Zeffirelli's unity of speech and action, his enfranchisement of the elaborate dialogue as the natural idiom of the characters of the play, were to be associated in the public's mind with a tragedy which seemed to have lost its momentum and lifelike qualities half-way through performance.

XII

Acting Shakespeare Today

[*Performances at Stratford-upon-Avon, August 1962*]

*

THE Royal Shakespeare Company's productions at Stratford-upon-Avon in 1962 provide useful examples of contemporary Shakespearian acting, for their achievements were of diverse kinds. A revival of the 1960 production of *The Taming of the Shrew* showed some talents of the company to best advantage. Elaborate comic business obscured the dramatic line of the play as a whole but provided many farcical incidents that could be performed vigorously and ostentatiously. Doors were slammed, heads slapped, plates tossed, postures held, lines underlined or thrown away with controlled gusto. This was a competitive style of production in which everyone was allowed to be assertive and single-minded.

Cymbeline, in contrast, was Vanessa Redgrave's play. As Imogen she varied hasty speech with credible pathos. She always used the simplest means, moving as little as possible and avoiding modifications of pitch or tone, even in long speeches. For the rest, the broadest stroke in the text of the play, the appearance of Jupiter, was notably well done: John Corvin, in gold costume and make-up, descended on a wide-winged copper eagle and spoke his lines with deliberate force.

In *Measure for Measure*, Marius Goring seemed to isolate himself from every other player in creating a straight-backed, tight-skinned Angelo: he concentrated on the expression of suffering by physical tensions. Tom Fleming as the Duke used sharp turns of head and eyes with a vocal decisiveness to represent authority, and Judi Dench as Isabella aimed as consistently for ardour, often narrowing the range of her voice and using gestures repetitively in her search for emphasis. In general the production was remarkable for the way in which the three main characters all used pauses to give an impression of profundity. During the silences the figures on stage often did not move so much as an eyebrow to express feeling, and if they walked across stage it was as simply as possible: the device was used to direct attention to single lines of the text, or placings on the bare set.

As Macbeth, Eric Porter husbanded his resources. In his first scene he gave little outward sign that a 'horrid image' shook his 'single state of man'. The dagger-soliloquy was accompanied by long and impressive pauses, but the first major climax was the banquet scene that concluded the first half of the performance. Here he was a tired and desperate man and, at the end, only anger was added. It was a strong, consistent, closely observed, and limited portrayal.

In a revival of the 1959 production of *A Midsummer Night's Dream*, the farcical performance of *Pyramus and Thisbe* and the Burgomask made the largest impression at the close. And elsewhere there was a marked tendency to choose one of several possible impressions and to work whole-heartedly for that: broad coltish humour in the lovers, an endearingly simple single-mindedness in the mechanicals, and verbal beauty in the fairies. This last attempt was a modification of the previous showing of this production and entailed still moments when Titania, Oberon or the first Fairy stood facing the audience, out of contact with other persons on the stage, to speak lines in a studied manner that was out of tone with the giggles, pouts and posturing of the rest of their fussy performances. The speeches gave great delight, especially to the verbally conscious among the audience.

* * *

Undoubtedly the actors can feel gratified by the 1962 season, for they were often effective, playing strongly for the audience's immediate attention. But if we ask how well they served Shakespeare's plays, their success will appear far smaller. Perhaps the most common and noticeable failure was the inability to give an impression of intelligence. Shakespeare often requires an actor to speak as if he were thinking quickly, cunningly or subtly; sometimes he must say one thing and seem to think about another, sometimes he must seem to enjoy alacrity of mind, or to turn desperately to it because his passions have been inexplicably aroused. On such occasions the pursuit of immediate effectiveness betrays the actors to clumsiness. If a Malcolm punches home his points and tries to appear vigorously concerned when he is falsely describing himself as a tyrant and beast, he will find it very difficult to make it appear that he is using his wit to test Macduff. Yet this is what Brian Murray endeavoured to do; and when the audience response slackened he sometimes redoubled his efforts. Gareth Morgan as Lennox tried to be intense and urgent in order to impress his intelligently ironic speech to the Lord at the beginning of III. vi: but it is surely written to heighten the sense of danger by alert caution, and requires subtle speaking. When Posthumus has been persuaded that Imogen is false, he returns to the stage for a soliloquy which moves rapidly from the general to particular, from the present moment to the past and future, from others to his lady and himself; but Patrick Allen played it forcefully. He showed no intellectual energy or insecurity in his passion, but placed his foot upon a table and pointed towards the audience to make his 'points' with emphasis. He then strode back and fore with firm tread until he stopped with 'Yet' and paused with his finger authoritatively raised before rounding the phrase out with ''tis greater skill In a true hate. . . .' The soliloquy was 'big', as actors sometimes call such renderings, but it was not sharp and varied as the writing; and it was not a revelation of a man at his wits' end, a man who, according to the text, is prepared to 'write against' women as a last resort. In *Measure for Measure* as we have seen there was a general attempt to give an impression of thought by introducing pauses; but this gave a portentous impression, not that of quick intelligence. And for Lucio another method had to be found; for his most biting speeches (in III. ii), he excused himself from suggesting intellectual edge by pretending to be drunk.

The actor who thus pursues effectiveness alone may be said to be afraid of subtlety. How else can we account for the protracted moment at the end of the first scene between Petruchio and Katharine in the Stratford *Taming of the Shrew*? This was played so broadly for sentiment, the lovers gazing in each other's eyes while Petruchio strokes his lady's calves, that the whole 'game' of the play was given away: these two would *have* to love-ever-after. It gave a strong moment of feeling at the beginning of the play and engrossed the audience's interest, but Katharine's final victory was shorn of all its surprise and much of its pleasure; the general strategy of Shakespeare's progressive revelation of the bases of character was defeated at the outset. The Queen in *Cymbeline* also lacked subtlety: from the first she was presented as obviously wicked in appearance and manner; her 'glozing' words were spoken to sound malicious, not to show feigned friendship, and no attempt was made to show 'Who is't can read a woman?' or how she made the King believe at the end:

> Mine eyes
> Were not in fault, for she was beautiful;
> . . . it had been vicious
> To have mistrusted her. (V. v. 62–66)

Snow White would not have been deceived for a moment.

Yet this fear of subtlety and the failure to show intelligence are symptoms of a more basic failure. Shakespeare was surely popular and successful, as present day actors try to be, but the closely wrought texture of his writing and the development of characterisations from play to play show that he sought other qualities as well. His presentation of men and women so that the deepest resources of their beings are progressively revealed—so that their words and actions seem at once appropriate and permanently interesting and their combined 'life' on the stage a mirror held up to our own—was not achieved by pursuing effectiveness for its own sake. When our actors fail to see some of the more obvious devices by which Shakespeare gave his plays this quality of 'humanity' or, seeing them, reject them in favour of simpler ways of catching the audience's attention, they intrude their own interests between the audience and the plays. Our actors are so afraid of not making an immediately strong impression that they are often needlessly limited, presenting silhouettes instead of Shakespeare's characters, momentary excitements instead of a coherent, expressive whole.

The restricted aims of effective acting are most apparent in characterisation. Shakespeare often gave opposing reactions to one *dramatis persona*, so that an actor can suggest different levels of consciousness; but his interpreter today is likely to seize upon one reaction only. In small scale, Shakespeare's technique is seen in Imogen's speech on reading Posthumus' letter in III. ii. Here the text alternates between an extreme practicality that inquires about distances, feigns a sickness, thinks of a franklin's housewife, and a sweeping fancy that travels on a winged horse more nimbly than the sands in an hour-glass. At Stratford Miss Redgrave subdued the first impression in favour of the second, in a rendering that did not swerve from a lightly urgent raptness; she also did not seem to catch at the almost unspoken instability or insecurity which the speech can also suggest, especially towards its close.

On a grander scale, the conclusion of Macbeth's role alternates between angry, valiant resolution and deep reflection, between:

> Bring me no more reports; let them fly all . . .
> The mind I sway by and the heart I bear
> Shall never sag with doubt nor shake with fear . . .

and

> . . . Seyton!—I am sick at heart,
> When I behold—Seyton, I say!—This push
> Will cheer me ever, or disseat me now.
> I have liv'd long enough. . . . (V. iii. 1–22)

Sometimes one mood overwhelms another in an instant, as Macbeth's mind is turned to a new object; so:

> it is a tale
> Told by an idiot, full of sound and fury,
> Signifying nothing.

is followed by '*Enter a Messenger*' and Macbeth leaps to hear *this* 'tale':

> Thou com'st to use thy tongue; thy story quickly.
> (V. v. 26–29)

When he hears what it signifies he answers with 'sound and fury', with the wrathful 'Liar and slave!' And then, his passion being spent, he reverts to the wider view: 'I 'gin to be aweary of the sun. . . .' Faced by Macduff and knowing he was 'not of woman born' but ripped from his mother's womb, he momentarily tries to escape and then finds from within himself a deep-seated pride:

> I will not yield,
> To kiss the ground before young Malcolm's feet.
> (V. viii. 27–28)

From this, the last transition takes him back to vaunting resolution: 'And damn'd be him that first cries "hold, enough!" ' Faced by these diverse demands, Eric Porter at Stratford underplayed the reflective passages and concentrated on presenting furious desperation. He shouted 'I have lived long enough', made an angry point of 'There would have been a *time* for such a word', and directed 'A tale Told by an idiot, full of sound and fury' in large exasperation to 'the Idiot', some god imagined for the moment above his head. 'I 'gin to be aweary . . .' was spoken in order to show how strongly and vehemently he repudiated life; it was another outburst of anger. With sure consistency his death was that of a tired, angry, disarmed fighter: to make this clear he was killed on stage after he had been encircled by the entire army and had lost all his weapons.

As Iachimo in *Cymbeline*, Eric Porter again simplified his role. He taunted Posthumus with relish and in Imogen's bedchamber noted particulars with an amused and watchful exactness. This was all played with a nice and appropriate sense of timing. But Shakespeare presents another reaction from a deeper consciousness within Iachimo, which is clearly revealed for the first time at the end of the bedchamber scene. This villain realises that there is no need to write down particulars:— as Hamlet knows that Claudius' crime is written on the tables of his mind and heart, so Iachimo says that Imogen's beauty is 'riveted' and 'screw'd' to his memory. Next he is aware of the 'dragons of the night' and wishes for day; this echoes Achilles' evocation of 'the dragon wing of night' after the assassination of Hector in *Troilus and Cressida*—but this villain wishes them to be gone. After these hints Iachimo's soliloquy at last makes an explicit statement of fear and guilt, sharply expressed as so many of the deepest feelings in *Cymbeline*:

I lodge in fear;
Though this a heavenly angel, hell is here.
(II. ii. 49–50)

To give credibility to this line and a half, the actor needs to suggest a subtextual uneasiness in the rest of the soliloquy: in this way the last couplet will *seem to be* the necessary resolution of an earlier lack of conviction. If the actor strives to make these final lines ring true from deep within his consciousness, he will be supported by the stage device, appropriate to a 'comedy of menace' and already used memorably in Marlowe's *Faustus*, of an immediate striking of a clock. The audience is suddenly alerted, but Iachimo smoothly accepts the sound as a sign of completion, for he says only 'One, two, three: time, time!' and returns to the trunk. Eric Porter let all this go by unmarked: to give prurience to an expert stealth was his limited objective. His last lines gave the impression that he thought his task had been neatly done, not that he felt a deep and true response which revalued the entire preceding soliloquy, and prepared for the time when conscience rather than the 'force' of a sword, brings him to his knee (V. v. 412–14).

It seemed almost a rule at Stratford that the actors should choose only one face of the character they portrayed. The lovers in *A Midsummer Night's Dream* might have shown more than coltish energy. In *Measure for Measure*, Juliet's:

> I do repent me as it is an evil,
> And take the shame with joy.
>
> (II. iii. 35–36)

was bold and sure, but it could also have indicated the deep involvement with Claudio and the modesty which is implied by her access to such a response, a response so full of feeling that it stops even the Duke's stream of good advice. Yvonne Bonnamy's Mariana pleaded earnestly in the last scene, as of course she should, but not at all pathetically or at a loss for words, as implied in the broken, repetitive phrasing of:

> Isabel
> Sweet Isabel, do yet but kneel by me;
> Hold up your hands, say nothing; I'll speak all.
> They say best men are moulded out of faults;
> And, for the most, become much more the better
> For being a little bad: so may my husband.
> O Isabel, will you not lend a knee?
>
> (V. i. 434–40)

On occasion the direct description of a character by others on the stage was neglected because this 'face' did not agree with the one that had been chosen for emphatic presentation. So Clive Swift made Cloten the clotpoll, the coarse, slow-witted buffoon; but he did not attempt to live up to Pisanio's description of his sudden passion for the loss of Imogen's presence at court, nor show what drove him alone to the forest.

Irene Worth's Lady Macbeth was a simple reading in keeping with the bias of the whole company: but here one 'face' yielded to another—at first determined and egocentric ambition, and then guilt and weakness. One reaction succeeded the other during the discovery of Duncan's murder at the moment when, very effectively with a movement down centre-stage, she fainted. On her next appearance, and even when she appeared crowned for the first time, Lady Macbeth was physically weakened and mentally strained. The sleep-walking scene was no surprise, for as she had spoken 'A kind goodnight to all', on the departure of the thanes from the disordered banquet, she had already shrunk in stature within her great robes, and her mind controlled her voice only by a great, dying effort; she stood a long time without moving and then went slowly to her throne from which she did not rise until after the scene had finished with a blackout. Her few brief words while Macbeth played out the scene were uncalculating responses when speech, of some sort, became unavoidable (see Pl. XXIII). Miss Worth had decided on an effective interpretation and presented it in clear lines. In the earlier passages, she made little of those reactions which contrast with willed ruthlessness:

> Had he not resembled
> My father as he slept, I had done't
>
> (II. ii. 12–13)

and

> I have given suck, and know
> How tender 'tis to love the babe that milks me
>
> (I. vii. 54–55)

were both too tense with determination to suggest, as they did for Mrs. Siddons and many Lady Macbeths after her, the gentler impulses that are for most of the time subdued by cruelty. Nor did Miss Worth show Lady Macbeth's love for her husband; she was closest to him, but still not intimate, after she has asked 'What's to be done?' and has been answered by Macbeth's invocation of 'seeling night' and the assertion 'Things bad begun make strong themselves by ill'; then she leant upon him for support, becoming dependent in a simply physical way. In the sleep-walking scene, Shakespeare has directed that Lady Macbeth is first concerned with her own guilt and then mocks her husband for being afraid; then she remembers the dead man who had resembled her father and so is led back to imagine that earlier moment of horror; this raises a profound and inarticulate sigh, and then, after a silence, almost all her thoughts are of her husband, and her last speech is chiefly spent urging him to come with her, asking for his hand (as she had not done after the real murder):

> To bed, to bed; there's knocking at the gate. Come, come, come, come, give me your hand. What's done cannot be undone. To bed, to bed, to bed.
>
> (V. i. 64–66)

Here, however, Miss Worth continued the single line of her portrayal: 'What's done. . . .' was emphasised by a held, crucified attitude, and on leaving she went towards Duncan's room and not the conjugal bed; and then, realising her mistake, she turned in horror and ran out. Guilt was the last impression; 'To bed, to bed, to bed!' spoke only for fearful haste.

The refinement of this performance, the varied vocal technique and fresh invention which were brought to it, showed all the more brilliantly for the predilection of most of the company towards broader and more obviously strong effects. Vocal control and range were shown, for example, in her quite low-pitched 'You must leave this': she was not urging and encouraging her husband as most actresses play this moment; rather it was followed by a turn away from him and suggested by its terseness a determination (and a failing power) to find new ways of confronting danger for herself. More strongly but still precisely controlled, 'Stand not upon the order of your going. But go at once', was spoken as two phrases, the first a courtesy assumed with difficulty and the second a betrayal of inner tension, pain and hopelessness, a loud and curt 'AT ONCE!' Originality was nowhere more apparent than in 'Give me the daggers!': this was said with nothing of the usual, obvious drama, but with a rapid, quiet simplicity which spoke eloquently for self-reliance and its limitations.

* * *

Perhaps no way of presenting Shakespeare is without its rewards. In a few contexts the pursuit of effectiveness is a quite appropriate approach: some moments do need a simple unreflecting strength. Sudden expressions of sentiment are among these, and when Imogen greets Guiderius and Arviragus in the last scene of *Cymbeline*, Vanessa Redgrave's

O my gentle brothers,
Have we thus met? O, never say hereafter
But I am truest speaker! you call'd me brother,
When I was but your sister; I you brothers,
When ye were so indeed

(V. v. 374–8)

held the audience by its large impression of new-born wonder and spontaneous joy. Broad acting, if it is also unaffected, can transform such a moment, giving to brief words of recognition the emotional authority sufficient to resolve the niceties of the narrative. The grief of Tony Steedman's Siward for the death of his son and the last blessing on his foster children of Paul Hardwick's Belarius were also unusually affecting by clear and large expressions that changed the mood of entire scenes. Such acting was also useful in scenes which even a few years ago were customarily played with some awkwardness. Possibly new plays like Ionesco's *Rhinoceros* or Pinter's *The Dwarfs*, which use fantastic happenings to present the fantastic realities of half-conscious thought, have accustomed actors to playing unrealistic situations boldly. No tricks of lighting and no trap-doors helped to present Banquo's ghost at Stratford, for its phantom presence and power needed no more reality than the added intensity it brought to Eric Porter's acting of Macbeth. Jupiter's eagle was supported on a solid and obvious steel pole (see Pl. XXVIII), but this did not detract from his supernatural reality because the actor's firm and simple acceptance of unhurried formal speech carried a strong conviction and awakened forward interest. And, although Cloten's headless body was an object which raised nervous laughter, the audience was then held in rapt belief and concern as Imogen was roused from her drugged sleep to feel it at her side. Miss Redgrave carried this scene boldly, by accepting the improbability and absurdity of her expression of half-conscious thoughts; as she said:

> . . . it is
> Without me, as within me; not imagined, felt
> (IV. ii. 307–8)

she was struggling to be objective and practical, and only slowly convinced of what she saw and 'felt'. She touched the stuffed and painted canvas which represented the bloody neck and said 'A headless man!' as a quiet, flat recognition, such as comes before full realisation of consequences; she did not gain a fully responsive consciousness until she cried 'Murder in heaven?' The other major difficulty of the soliloquy:

> Where is thy head? Where's that? Ay me! where's that?
> Pisanio might have kill'd thee at the heart,
> And left this head on (ll. 322–4)

was met with comparable clarity, for the question which sounds merely absurd in considered or temperate speech was spoken in full flight of passion, and gave to that expression of feeling the recklessness and directness of imagination—and of thought which is too rapid and instinctive to be sensible.

Imogen's reawaking to hear Lucius questioning her was similarly affecting by a simple and convinced performance. She gazed at him unmoving while he slowly asked:

> What's thy interest
> In this sad wreck? How came't? Who is it? What art thou?
> (ll. 366–7)

and without changing this impression of inward involvement she then spoke slowly, one broken word at a time: 'I am nothing.' Only by telling her story did she seem to gain a full knowledge of what she was speaking. Miss Redgrave accepted both fantasy and pathos as manifestations of a mind overmastered by feeling, and her performance had the strength and simplicity to carry conviction. The Stratford *Cymbeline* showed that Shakespeare is not always served by subtlety; sometimes conviction and immediate effectiveness must come first.

* * *

A further achievement of the 1962 season at Stratford was not gained by its general pursuit of effectiveness. This was the playing of Derek Godfrey, Paul Hardwick and Ian Holm in *The Taming of the Shrew*, as Petruchio, Baptista and Gremio. Occasionally they all acted too broadly and were too indulgent in accepting details of comic business, but this was the second or third season in which these players had appeared in these roles, and their acting had been refined by practice and complicated by further knowledge. Many points were now rejudged by instinct or vigilant self-criticism, and seemed to gain new meaning and deeper effect. Derek Godfrey's

> O, how I long to have some chat with her!
> (II. i. 161)

could now suggest both assurance and something like self-mockery. Both Ian Holm and Paul Hardwick could turn a jest so that it aroused pity as well as laughter, and by making their two old men draw close together in adversity (see Pl. XXIX) they suggested unconscious subtextual reactions and enhanced the whole play by a comic demonstration of a coupling of practical interests to offset the various couplings of love. This was not superimposed on the text, but a revelation of a part of Shakespeare's play which would be missed in less subtle performances and probably in the most painstaking reading of the words

Macbeth at the Royal Shakespeare Theatre, 1962
(Eric Porter as Macbeth and Irene Worth as Lady Macbeth)

XXII I.v: Arrival at Inverness

XXIII III.iv: after the Banquet

XXIV Irene Worth as Lady Macbeth in VI.i: the Sleep-walking Scene

XXV Eric Porter as Macbeth in the last scenes

Cymbeline at the Royal Shakespeare Theatre, 1962 (Vanessa Redgrave as Imogen and Eric Porter as Iachimo)

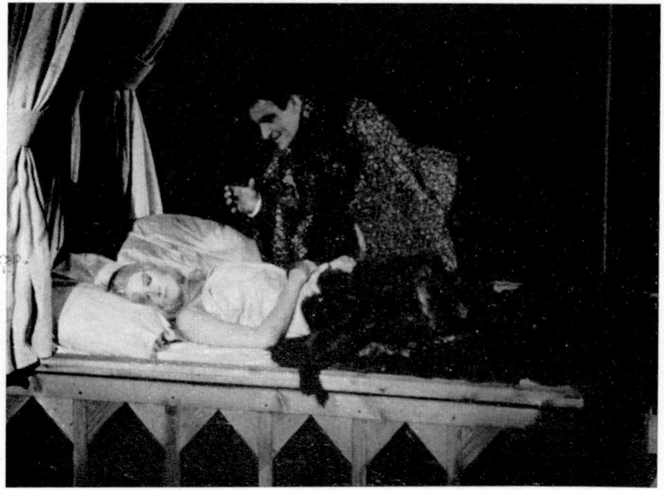

XXVI (above) II.ii: the Bedchamber Scene

XXVII (right) IV.ii: Imogen by Cloten's Corpse

XXVIII (above) *Cymbeline* at the Royal Shakespeare Theatre; V.iv: the descent of Jupiter

XXIX (right) *The Taming of the Shrew* at the Royal Shakespeare Theatre, 1962 (Ian Holm as Gremio Ian Richardson as Tranio and Paul Hardwick as Baptista)

alone. As the plot unfolds, these two characters do, in fact, speak in new agreement and the action does require that they should stand or sit by each other's side. At the latest possible moment in the comedy, Baptista gives money to Katharine; so Gremio had offered money at his instigation to purchase Bianca, but now the money is a gift without conditions. These actors had had practice to make perfect their characterisations, and they were often drawn by the text to discover the various 'faces' of their roles: a single line gave a double impression; subtextual concerns were suggested through certain qualities of the text; gesture effected what words could not. So they were able to present characters responding at various levels of consciousness and to contribute to the general wit and enjoyment of the play.

These few, matured performances were made possible by years of familiarity with a text and with the practical problems of each role in performance. And they point the way to the most necessary condition for improving our Shakespeare productions: his plays require skilled, subtle, strong and imaginative performances, and so actors must work consecutively, patiently and ambitiously.

Often the warning has been voiced. In 1907 Gordon Craig wrote that

> It takes most young actors but five years' acute suffering to become effective, to become theatrical. . . . Beware of this and rather be ineffective.[1]

Much earlier David Garrick wrote to his protegé, Powell:

> You must, therefore, give to study, and an accurate consideration of your characters, those hours which young men too generally give to their friends and flatterers. . . . Study hard, my friend for seven years, and you may play the rest of your life. . . . But above all, never let your Shakespeare out of your hands, or your pocket; keep him about you as a charm. . . .
>
> One thing more, and then I finish my preaching: guard against *the splitting of the ears of the groundlings*. . . . Do not sacrifice your taste and feelings to the applause of the multitude; a true genius will convert an audience to his manner, rather than be converted by it to what is false and unnatural;—*be not too tame either*.[2]

[1] *On the Art of the Theatre* (ed. 1957), p. 40.
[2] *Private Correspondence*, i. 177–8.

The need is obvious, spoken about in many ways and with differing emphasis; but today in England an actor has little chance to prepare a masterpiece. For the beginner, training is huddled into two or three years and then he must make his name and establish himself as the man to be called upon for this type of role, or this kind of play. Unlike a young painter, he cannot expect benefactions and therefore he does not travel in pursuit of new ideas and experience, nor become an apprentice to a master-craftsman. He cannot, like a young poet, singer or dancer, learn the rudiments of his art while practising it in a continuous and responsible way. Even an established actor is unable to plan his career so that he can give two or three year's study to a major role before showing his interpretation to a wide public; he must choose continuous publicity (with its demands to be consistently effective) or the forced pace of underfinanced repertory companies. Somewhere, somehow, more hopeful conditions must be provided for actors to explore and begin to create Shakespearian roles.

XIII

Three Kinds of Shakespeare

[*1964 Productions at London, Stratford-upon-Avon and Edinburgh*]

★

AT the National Theatre, in 1964, those fortunate or persistent enough to obtain a ticket saw a starred performance by Sir Laurence Olivier, an Othello whose words could startle and whose actions were inventive and sensuous. His last speech can serve as an image for the whole production. Othello, naked beneath a simple white gown, closed only at the waist, kneels on a low bed placed down-stage centre with tall hangings around it disappearing into the 'flies' behind the top of the proscenium arch. He clasps Desdemona's dead body to his chest, as if she knelt with him, and he raps out a loud: 'Soft you!' After the following pause his voice is surprisingly quiet, almost soft: 'a word or two before you go'. And then without break, continuing the impulses that had changed his voice, Othello kisses Desdemona on the neck, sensuously engrossed. Then the speech follows with recollected formality: 'I have done the state some service . . .'.

For the production of seven history-plays in a series at the Royal Shakespeare Theatre, Stratford-upon-Avon, in 1964 (the three parts of *Henry VI* freely adapted to form two plays only), a representative image might be a scene change. There is music and a slow, purposeful filing off-stage, nicely judged to illustrate the political factions and the concerns of the characters. The lights change and two large, dark, triangular-based structures turn before a dark, trellised background. And the stage is now a battlefield, with instruments of war, careworn soldiers, and the slow yet alert tempo of battle. Other notable features could be chosen to represent the Stratford production, especially the acting of Peggy Ashcroft and Hugh Griffith, but the deliberate scene-changes are demonstrative of the originality and distinction of this season as a whole.

At the 1964 Edinburgh Festival, Joan Littlewood's production of *Henry IV, Part I* by the Theatre Workshop Company (with rearrangements and cuts and some interpolations from *Part II*) can be represented by the conclusion of its first half. Hal is backing away on the bridge stage that was constructed across the Assembly Hall of the Church of Scotland. Poins remains in the centre. He wears a trim, black velour bowler hat, a single ear-ring, high-heeled, blue suede boots, and dark ski-pants. He bends forward as he listens to Hal's words (addressed to Peto in both quarto and folio texts): 'We must all to the wars, and thy place shall be honourable. . . . Be with me betimes in the morning; and so good morrow, Poins.' The delivery of the words is not remarkable and in the centre of the picture is the listener, not the speaker. Poins is smiling; puzzled; embarrassed, perhaps; ingratiating; there is a servility in his jaunty appearance, an insecurity in his knowing manner.

One element common to these three images is a determined realism, of sensuous embodiment in Sir Laurence Olivier's Othello, of the side-effects of power politics in the Stratford Histories, of psychological observation in Joan Littlewood's *Henry IV*. This element is realistic in the sense that it is meant to awaken in the audience a recognition of actuality. And the realism is determined because it is continuously attempted in contrast to unrealistic elements: the undoubted showiness of the star actor; the simplification of the motives of men involved in power politics; the witty vitality of the highway, tavern and rustic scenes of the Workshop production.

Eccentricity is another feature found in the three productions. But Shakespeare is so large that any enactment tends to seem odd; even those rare productions, that seem on first viewing to fill a play to its very limits, will be thought in ten years' time to have missed whole areas of Shakespeare's invented world. And with eccentricity these 1964 productions had a further object in common: a strenuous search for a 'way to do Shakespeare'. For more than sixty years English directors have been engaged on this quest, but their efforts have recently been intensified and multiplied. (Financial help from the State for two competitive theatres may be a cause of this, or new influences from contemporary dramatists and from theatre directors of other countries, or, perhaps, the thought that a distinctive brand of Shakespeare, a production with a clear image, would gain more attention from the general public.) Today theatre directors are convinced of the need to make Shakespeare 'come alive'. They search, experiment, debate, justify and try to learn.

* * *

The stage-settings at Stratford represent only one part of that theatre's obvious and advertised experimentation. The isolating effect of John Bury's cross-stage platform for *Measure for Measure* in 1962 or the dwarfing effect of his spacious flats, steps and ramp for *Julius Caesar* in 1963, have given way to a more variable design. Sometimes a vast background without local emphasis is seen behind a completely empty, level stage, marked with rectangles in a perspective that enhances the impression of space. At other times, one or two large pieces of scenery, with steps, recesses, doors or windows to choice, come in from either side, giving intimate and localised settings. Trees, greenery, thrones, prison-bars also vary the setting, but large steps or rostra are seldom introduced so that movement can always be free and often wide-ranging. For battles, group entries or other spectacular opportunities (like the lists at Coventry in *Richard II* or the embarkation of Henry V at Southampton) the stage is filled with nimble and well-drilled supernumeraries giving, by action, costume, properties and make-up, an extraordinarily complete attempt at verisimilitude. This mixture of the vast and localised, with this reliance on actors to 'dress' the stage, is a useful solution to the problems of providing a décor for Shakespeare; it is capable of sustaining the audience's interest through most of the seven plays. But these productions used it too indulgently, in that too many items were introduced to support the actors—especially torches, carts and animals; and scene changes or fairly simple entries often took up thirty to sixty seconds before the play could proceed. The scenery accounts in part for the slow tempo of the Stratford productions.

In colour the set had small variations of a basic brown, black and grey, and simple sharp contrasts for costumes and properties. The variations were shrewdly used and associated with differing textures (not unlike a fashionable mode of interior decoration): wood, various metals, gloss, matt and stippled surfaces, coarse fabrics and smooth, leather and silk. By apparently economical (though probably expensive) means the stage varied as widely in tone as in form. Particularly memorable was the austere use of black and white for the Archbishop Scroop scenes or the black and dull tones for Henry IV's bed-chamber. The French court was distinguished from the English by the usual means of colour contrast, but in this neutral set the details of peacock blue and gold were more than usually effective. The only conspicuous omission in the range of effects was wealth and assured regality; Henry IV's words:

> the perfum'd chambers of the great,
> Under the canopies of costly state . . .

bore no relation to what the audience had seen.

The directors of the plays—Peter Hall, John Barton and Clifford Williams, working in collaboration—would not be likely to judge this omission to be important. For another of the experiments of the Stratford season was a continuous emphasis of violence and of the shallowness of politicians' pretensions. The plays became a high-class cartoon, a relentless horror comic. An elevated tone was sustained by restrained colour in the setting, slow tempo and deliberate utterance, but, with this, horror and violence were presented by liberal splashes of blood, and by inventive business that elaborated every opportunity for the exhibition of cruelty and pain that the text suggested, and more that were foisted on to the text. Joan of Arc cut her own wrist like a Tamburlaine with a very large sword; Young Clifford's head was cut off on stage and carried around upon a spear; Clarence was drowned in the malmsey-butt at the back of the stage, rather than 'within' as the words of the text direct. Going beyond the requirements of the stage-directions and dialogue, action was realised as horribly as possible: Richard II struck the dying Gaunt with a whip repeatedly; when he smashed the looking glass he did so with his bare fist and so inflicted pain upon himself; in prison he was tethered by a huge, noisy chain that had to be flung aside to allow movement and which he used as a weapon that threatened to pull himself down in the last struggle with his warders—the sound and apparent weight of that chain may well have been the dominating impression given by the Prison Scene. Fights were arranged with persistent ingenuity, important ones with disparity of weapons to heighten interest, such as Hotspur with a two-handed sword against Hal with sword and buckler, or Douglas using a spiked mace against a sword. Deaths were thoroughly painful; sack was thrown around and splashed liberally; Hotspur and Lady Percy rolled on the floor in their love-fights; Henry IV was given a foul-tasting potion to drink after its ingredients had been ground in a mortar by a monk-like doctor clothed in black. Repetition lessened the effect of these devices, but they were placed importantly at dramatic crises: *Henry IV, Part I* did not end with the king's deceitful and dramatically ironic exhortation:

> And since this business so fair is done,
> Let us not leave till all our own be won

but with Vernon in death agonies, swinging in a noose; he was then cut down and Worcester climbed to take his place. This experiment had a slight connexion with current talk of a 'theatre of cruelty' and the Royal Shakespeare Theatre's experimental programme of that name shown to the public in the L.A.M.D.A. studio in 1963; but it lacked the severity of Peter Brook's innovating production of *Titus Andronicus* or the emotional depth and rigour required by Artaud in his newly translated *The Theatre and its Double*. Its most obvious effect was a grand-guignol grip on the audience (especially in the first four or five plays that each member had seen), and its most assured the verisimilitude given to certain horrible episodes in the text of *Henry VI*, the earliest in date of composition. Among interesting achievements were the mob-violence that accompanied Bolingbroke's judgment on Bushy and Green, building that into a scene of general social interest rather than a further revelation of the emergent ruler, and, more surely within the scope of the text, the very ample provision of exhibits for Falstaff's discourse on a dead man as a counterfeit. Thus the directors' exaggeration of violence by invented stage-business served to accentuate one vein in the text of these plays that has often been obscured by a picturesque accentuation of pageantry and royal panoply.

The shallow, cartoon-like presentation of the major political characters was another continuous feature of these productions, and it, too, was most satisfactory in the plays written earliest. Sharp verbal juxtapositions were pointed for comic effect without concern for the loss in dignity. Burgundy's

> I am vanquished; these haughty words of hers
> Have batt'red me like roaring cannon-shot
> And made me almost yield upon my knees.
>
> (*1 H VI,* III. iii. 78–80)

so relished the rapidity of his change of sides that the audience was encouraged to laugh. So too, the multiple throwing down of gages before Aumerle in *Richard II*, IV. i, quickly deflated the pretensions of the newly loyal nobles. Wars and rivalries became what Shakespeare once called them: a 'comic sport'. But the directors again accentuated one vein in the text, and made Shakespeare persistently anti-heroic and deflationary. Edward IV wooed the widow so slowly that his lechery was foolish as well as his government; and later when Warwick surprises him, '*bringing the King out in his gown, sitting in a chair*' (IV. iii, S.D.), the directors had him dragged out on a mattress where he was lying with a whore and sent both off-stage as nearly naked and foolish as possible—a rhetorically impressive scene was here made to seem like a notorious comic strip. Equally, Henry VI's ineffective attempts at friendship and love were comically played. David Warner in this role, and in the first half of his Richard II, used nervous smiles and a loose-limbed awkwardness to suggest anxious timidity. Richard's commands were under-played so that even these gave an impression of weakness:

> Think what you will, we seize into our hands
> His plate, his goods, his money, and his lands
> (II. i. 209–10)

was said with neither assurance nor effort. Later, when York remarks on his eye 'bright as is the eagle's', Richard's 'We are amaz'd' was quiet and flat.

For the central political characters of the later plays, Hotspur, Hal, Henry IV and Henry V, and for the virtuoso role of Richard III, the lack of psychological subtlety deprived the productions of long-valued qualities. Ian Holm's Richard was childish in his humour; he sat alone after the scene with the two religious men—here soldiers comically disguised—and kicked his heels. At the end, he was more concerned with his own importance than with his fear, stressing, for example, the second personal pronoun in: 'I fear . . . *I* fear'. His character did make a changing impression as the play proceeded, but in one direction only; towards violent fury, expressed by vocal power and tremendously taxing fights. At the end a monster died: he had struck Catesby a blow when he offered help, but his voice began to fail so that 'A horse! a horse!' was weak as well as terrible and mad; and his death pangs were prolonged close to the audience at the centre of a vast empty stage. Here was little intimation of a tragedy, little scope for any reaction to Richard besides aversion.

Hotspur was comic and coarse, so that Lady Percy's praise of his 'chivalry' seemed wholly fantastic (and out of keeping with her own hoydenish behaviour in the first part of the play); and Henry IV's envy of his character, wishing Hal were like him, seemed absurdly misplaced. Henry IV was nettled and sour, with little indication of his ability to rule and his strength of spirit. Hal was coldly played, as if the actor's main task were to prepare the audience for the 'rejection' of Falstaff. When this point was reached it was easily reached, so that the new king's speech was neat and wholly controlled. The major impression of the last scene of this play was left for Falstaff and his fellows to make in the succeeding episode. Henry V was shallow in another way. He was so obviously thoughtful, careful and, occasionally, sharp, that he never attempted to enter the outline depicted by the Chorus of 'cheerful semblance and sweet majesty . . .' or 'A largess universal, like the sun'. The Chorus was allowed to orate and make flourishes about a quite different play, as if the directors thought that all he said had to be ironically wrong.

Although simplification of character was not the most noticed feature of the Stratford productions, it was probably the most regrettable because it obscured deeply observed and imaginative elements of Shakespeare's art. The directors indulged and supplemented the horrible and the curiously picturesque; and they neglected the humane, the psychologically true, the emotional and affective. The rivalries of the Wars of the Roses were presented intelligently and relentlessly as kid's stuff.

A further objective of the whole season—an attempt at a uniform vocal style that respects the poetic qualities of the text—was potentially a safeguard against this sort of simplification. Peter Hall can justly claim in the pamphlet, *Crucial Years* (1963): 'There is no question that the verse-speaking of this Company has improved. It has started to be noticed. . . .' Gone are almost all the glossy tones and meaningless pomposities that could be heard twenty, ten or five years ago. The speaking often echoes 'ordinary speech', and can be both alert and pedestrian. David Warner and Ian Holm have these qualities abundantly, and almost all the company seem to strive to follow them. But, as Peter Hall is aware, this is a noticeable beginning rather than a maturing of the company's style that could lead them into Shakespeare's imaginative world. The early achievements have brought unhelpful side-effects. First, there is a lack of sustained line or rhythm, and a would-be impressive slowness. Long speeches are broken with pauses and far too frequently short speeches are prepared for with silent business, or followed by some such invention. The aim, here, is not psychological subtlety or depth of feeling but effectiveness and psychological actuality for each simplified moment; the broken and slow delivery at Stratford is an aspect of the company's determined realism. And, unfortunately, it combats the excitement of Shakespeare's writing, its ability to draw the audience like a kite in the wind.

Besides rhythm, music and forward pressure, rhetorical energy is lost, and climax. The new style is, in fact, uneconomical. And it is self-important in that the actors seem to think the audience will always wait for them. Hamlet's was good general advice for acting Shakespeare's plays: 'speak the speech . . . trippingly on the tongue'. An actor must, of course, rehearse in slow tempo and study the phrases of his part one by one, but in performance he should not expect the audience to share this trouble. Within a strongly paced production the necessary moments of slow speaking will grow in power, and the whole design gain in eloquence. So, too, the production will gain the subtle influence of a continuous metrical control.

The second side-effect of the new vocal style is a sacrifice of affectiveness. The actors seem to lack temperament and size, as if they tried to be clever at the cost of developing an impression of great feeling. Of course, this was apt for the directors' denigrating attitude to the characters of the plays but two performances that outshone all others were reminders of the limitations elsewhere in the productions of both acting and direction.

These interpretations—acclaimed by rapt and heightened attention and by press-notices—were achievements of temperament and bold psychological conception. Hugh Griffith, as Falstaff, occasionally took his time too much (in common with others) and resorted to repetitive hand movements to sustain interest; but using an individual and comparatively florid delivery he always played up his role. Although the production demanded a Falstaff ripe for rejection, a 'sink of iniquity', he added a visionary's temperament, the surprise, wealth and endurance of an imaginative life. 'The rogue fled from me like quicksilver' (*Part II*, II. iv. 217) was not simply an empty boast, irresponsible and slick, but a ruminative and beloved indulgence, played as if Falstaff for the moment believed in a long-past valour. When he acted Henry IV to Hal's Falstaff in the play-within-the-play, Falstaff became Harry's benevolent father indeed—in his imagination—and peacefully touched the prince's head and face on the concluding: 'And tell me now, thou naughty varlet, tell me, where hast thou been this month?' (*Part I*, II. iv. 416–17; see Pl. XXXVI). Occasionally the general style of the production hampered his performance; the sherris-sack soliloquy was held back from its natural rhythm by realistic business with a tun of wine and a drinking cup, and the Orchard Scene (V. iii, of *Part II*) was interrupted by a dim-witted three-man band fussing around on stage. But this Falstaff had size and a consistent and inventive complexity: at the end of *Part II*, when the new king has left the stage, Hugh Griffith showed the struggle for an imaginary and imaginative survival; and there was a last breakdown when he allowed Pistol to help him to his feet, so accenting the silent exit that Shakespeare has given him.

Peggy Ashcroft's Margaret, in the two parts of the re-arranged *Henry VI* and in *Richard III*, started with an intrusive lisp. (At times it seemed as if this was intended to be a 'funny' foreign accent.) But in the Paper Crown Scene (*Part III*, I. iv) her portrayal of weakness in cruelty, helplessness in victory, brought depth of understanding to the characterisation and a sustained beauty of phrase to the rhetoric; other barbarous episodes seemed trivial and shocking in contrast. The cruel humour of the lines was played close to hysteria: 'I prithee grieve to make me merry' (line 86) was a final textual acceptance of Margaret's previously subtextual impulse towards helpless laughter, an emotional relief and a breakdown of control. Margaret was constantly changing her stance and position as if instinctively; her taunts were controlled and insistent so that only her body, moving repeatedly, could show the inward instability. As York replied in pain and passion, Margaret was silent, after one last and, now, forced laugh. When she stabbed him it was with a quick movement, and then she wept. Then the tears stopped with a wild, painful cry. In this scene the violent was emphasised as much as anywhere, but there was also rhetorical and musical control and a daring, emotional performance revealing depths of unwilled and conflicting desires.

In *Richard III*, Margaret's long scene with the mourning Queen Elizabeth and the Duchess of York (IV. iv) lacked the consistency of style for its shared and concerted rhetoric. But Peggy Ashcroft's first scene, entering alone to Edward's divided court as an old, vindictive woman, was compelling. She spoke from compulsion ('I can no longer hold me patient') and caught the strange verbal exaggerations of her speeches, accentuated them, and added the physical deformities of extreme age and spite. She was crazed and helpless. No one could effectively speak to her except Richard, and he resorted to shock and surprise. She talked to herself as well as to her victims, and to the heavens: 'Can curses pierce the clouds and enter heaven?' she *actually* asked and, with 'Why then, give way', she clapped her hands for attention. She entered, too, into the cruelty she described: 'Look when he fawns, he bites', she warned Buckingham, and then acted the biting and gave a mad laugh. The scene was held back only by the inability to show on the stage a commensurate response: 'My hair doth stand on end to hear her curses', says Buckingham, but in performance the words seemed untrue after the sharp reality, deep feeling and persuasive rhetoric of this Margaret. Peggy Ashcroft's achievement would have been even greater in a company used to ensemble-playing in a similarly ambitious style.

* * *

A director's shaping hand has great influence over a production; but psychological truth, emotional, ambitious acting, and Shakespeare's rhetoric and poetry can be more powerful. In Joan Littlewood's witty and intelligent *Henry IV*, much of what she devised to demonstrate her reading of the play seemed slight tricks beside some superbly right and sustained performances she encouraged among the comparatively minor characters. She presented the king and nobles as cold politicians, uniform in dress and clipped and unemotional in speech. Only Hotspur played by Julian Glover in a manner reminiscent of Stratford performances of five years ago, was allowed to make flourishes and he, lacking any answering voice, seemed to beat the air. The director permitted no uncertain effect here. A neurotic reading of the letter scene (II. iii) where added emphasis and quickening tempo turned assurance into an expression of fear—'a good plot, good friends, and full of expectation; an excellent plot, very good friends'—indicated that Hotspur's grandiloquence was *meant* to sound empty. A single, huge cannon, awkwardly pushed into position behind Henry IV for the battle of Shrewsbury, showed that the king was *meant* to lack stature on his own account. So half the play dwindled at the director's command; through manner of speech and action, costume, stage-movement, this half became an intentional demonstration of inadequacy.

It was hardly surprising that newspaper critics, uncompensated with the picturesque and horror-seeking realism of the current Stratford production, castigated Miss Littlewood. But they rightly excepted from censure the actors of some minor characters to whom she had given more rewarding roles. In the highway, tavern and rustic scenes (including the recruiting episode from *Part II*) there was music and abundant activity to make them generally entertaining, and here the characterisation was more ambitious. Victor Spinetti, the most accomplished actor in the company, was Poins, and there were inventive performances from Murray Melvin as Gadshill and Shadow, and Brian Murphy as Bardolph. Costumes throughout the production were modern, with hints of the 'historical' in cloaks, hats and accessories, and this appearance was matched with modern ways of speech and behaviour. While the politicians suffered by these devices—they were given the fixed poses and grey-and-black colour of newspaper photographs—other characters gained: there was no verse to combat the modern inflections, and lines and incidents normally guyed in performance were acted so that they gave new recognitions of meaning and truthfulness. The wide range of Poins's responses to Hal was revealed. Gadshill's boast that he has nothing to do with 'landrakers, . . . sixpenny strikers, . . . purple-hu'd malt-worms' shed all its footnote fustiness to become the compensating gloss of a slight-bodied rogue, a cheap, street-corner exquisite. His 'Tut', his negative constructions, his eagerness ('She will, she will'), reliance on a group-image ('We steal . . . we have . . . we walk'), and scorn of others, concern with others, posh airs, and scornful dismissals, all ceased to be unusable lumber from Elizabethan London, and became amusing and revealing dramatic lines: 'Go to; "homo" is a common name to all men. Bid the Ostler bring my gelding out of the stable. Farewell, you muddy knave' (*Part I*, II. i. 96–97). At Stratford, Francis was a gormless lout, kicked around for broad comic effect, but in the Theatre Workshop production, played by Jeremy Spenser, his scene with Hal revealed honesty, loyalty, ambition, ignorance—a small, conventional and intense imagination; and all this was given by a performance taking much less acting-time than at Stratford. Richard Gurnock as Feeble, the woman's tailor, was mincingly polite, nervously pulling down his jerkin and smiling with each speech. Not only was this character more 'recognisable' and funnier than his Stratford counterpart but the scene as a whole was more lively and complete; instead of trying to make Feeble's philosophy sound impressive by an answering pause after 'we owe God a death', Joan Littlewood turned Bardolph's 'Well said; th'art a good fellow' into a quick, smirking response to make everything easy again, after this rather too smug and tactless facing of facts. Feeble's good nature was as firmly established, but his philosophising was not produced as if it were philosophy; he was the sort of man who might quote Patience Strong in the barrack-room. 'Faith!, I'll bear no base mind' spoke of inexperience as well as bravery, self-concern as well as honesty; it was of a piece with the whole characterisation.

Falstaff, without the traditional whiskers and ruddiness, was an unsentimental picture of a public-bar soldier. His bulk, high-living and capacity for friendship were as much a part of his fantasy as his valour. But here the dialogue Shakespeare has provided leapt ahead of the characterisation; the verbal energy and colour of the text bore little relationship to the physical image or the tone and rhythm of speech. The search for a contemporary portrayal of Falstaff is not finished; a realism depending on the accurate observation of human behaviour and a general vitality and invention has not filled out this role.

* * *

The production of *Othello* at the National Theatre, undertaken by John Dexter, aimed at grandeur; except for its sombre colours and wide groupings it was reminiscent of a Stratford production five or ten years ago. But it also gave an impression of uncertainty; on recollection, it might seem that the current trend towards realistic stage-movement was represented by some awkward entries and exits, but in performance they often looked like clumsiness. For example, time was wasted in repeated backward turns for Emilia after giving Iago the handkerchief, and the drunken scene was staged in a corner of a largely empty stage so that the actors had to work too hard to give an impression of conviviality.

Characterisation also seemed uncertain. Or perhaps some roles were deliberately scaled down in confident expectation that Laurence Olivier's Othello could best succeed as a solo performance. Frank Finlay as Iago so neglected the verbal dexterity required by the technical difficulties of his speeches that he was often hard to hear from centre-stalls. This looked like miscalculation until it became clear he was not suggesting the danger, evil or, even, energy under his 'honest' appearance; perhaps he wished to seem wholly ruthless and blunt. Maggie Smith as Desdemona was cold and doll-like at first, responding to danger and loss by tension and then simplicity. Either of these narrowly conceived interpretations would have been more successful within their own terms by added scale or intensity.

The interpretation of Othello was not so remarkable as the artistry which presented it. Here was a sensuous man of primitive culture breaking through social propriety and making a great misjudgment. (A conception reminiscent of Alfieri's summing-up of Eddie in Arthur Miller's *View from the Bridge*: 'even as I know how wrong he was, and his death useless, I tremble, for I confess that something perversely pure calls to me from his memory—not purely good, but himself purely. . . . And so I mourn him—I admit it—with a certain . . . alarm.') In token of a movement back to primitive responses, this Othello tore from his breast the crucifix he had always worn and sometimes fondled.

In execution the most original element was Olivier's persistent sensuousness: a full-lipped make-up, cat-like walk, soft and low-pitched passages, caressing movements. In his first scene he entered carrying and smelling a red (twentieth-century) rose. This emphasis continued to the end: in Shakespeare's text Lodovico says:

> Look on the tragic loading of this bed.
> This is thy work.—The object poisons sight; . . .

and immediately commands 'Let it be hid'; but here the implicit stage-direction was not followed; rather there was a very slow fade with lights focused on the two dead bodies, Othello's chest naked. Olivier also gave a sustained impression of physical power even in relaxation, as if Othello practised weight-lifting weekly in a gymnasium.

His verbal delivery was equally accomplished and more ambitious. At first his speech had remarkable ease, allowing a low, self-amused and quick laugh on 'Upon this hint I spake'. But in 'Farewell the tranquil mind . . .' which was given immediately before the single interval, two hours after the performance began, Olivier revealed a tremendously increased range of voice. He spoke the repeated 'Farewells' with lengthened and varied vowels, and gave an illustrative expressiveness to the succeeding evocations of 'big wars . . . shrill trump . . . rude throats . . . dread clamours'. He strongly marked a rhythm that grew more insistent throughout the sustained passage so that vocal virtuosity was combined with a compelling performance. At this point, too, his postures became more studied or artificial, often held for several lines and occasionally restraining Iago in an unmoving grip. With 'ne'er ebb to humble love', there was a long silence after 'humble' while Othello forced himself to say the word 'love' that had stuck in his throat; this silence was full with the impression of physical struggle and when at last the word came it was, convincingly, quiet. This device was similar to the many pauses in the Stratford productions, but Olivier used time more sparingly, worked hard to deserve each split second, and by controlling the tempo and shape of each speech and episode counteracted an occasional slowness with a display of both temperament and art.

The central performance of the National Theatre's *Othello* was a demonstration of the huge opportunities Shakespeare has provided for an actor who is at once realistic and histrionic. While several small performances at Edinburgh brought a more immediate recognition of psychological truth, and the Stratford Falstaff and Margaret more imaginative reach and emotional depth, Olivier's performance was supremely inventive, sustained and astonishing. As so often in the past, an actor rather than a director had created his own kind of Shakespeare.

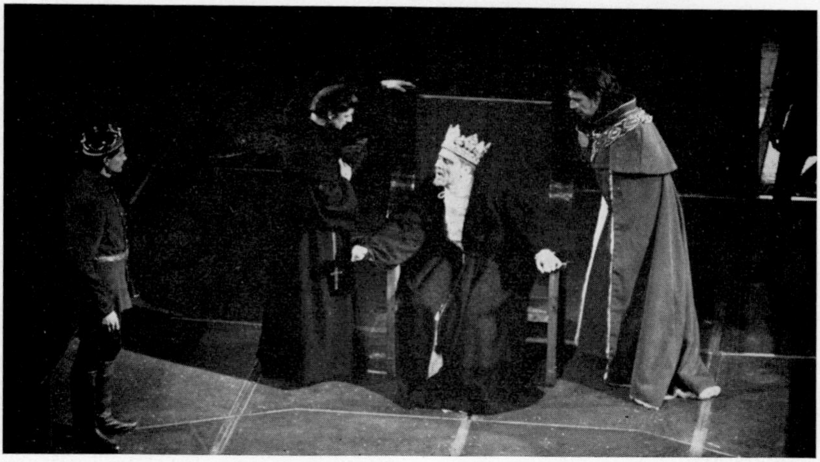

XXX Henry IV in his palace, with his doctor (to left)

XXXI Henry V, with his army and Montjoy

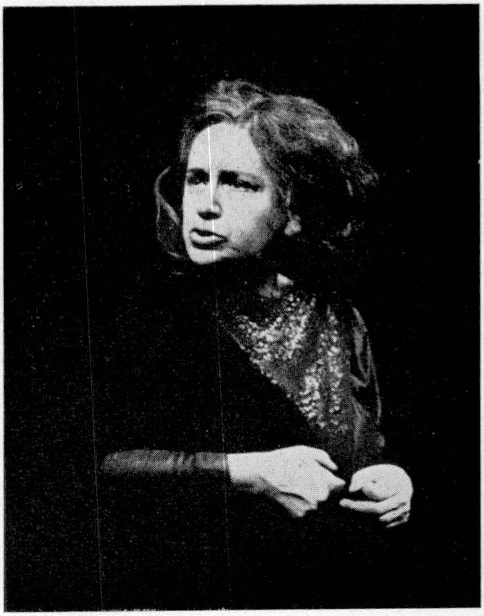

XXXII & XXXIII Peggy Ashcroft as Queen Margaret in *3 Henry VI* and *Richard III*

XXXIV Hugh Griffith as Falstaff

XXXV David Warner as Henry VI

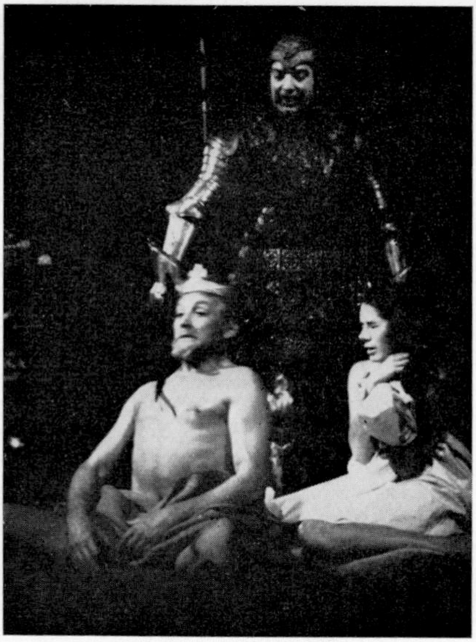

The History Plays at the Royal Shakespeare Theatre, 1964

XXXVI Falstaff and Prince Hal in *1 Henry IV*, II.iv

XXXVII Edward IV, with a whore and Warwick

XXXVIII Falstaff with Poins in the Theatre Workshop Production, Edinburgh, 1964

XXXIX Roy Dotrice as Hotspur

XL Richard III and Richmond in the last scene of *Richard III*

XLI Laurence Olivier as Othello in I.ii

XLII *Othello*, IV.i: 'What would you with her, sir?'

Production at the Shakespeare Memorial Theatre, Stratford-upon-Avon, 1955: designed by Malcolm Pride

XLIII *Twelfth Night*, I.i

XLIV *Twelfth Night*, I.v

Production at the Shakespeare Memorial Theatre, Stratford-upon-Avon, 1958: designed by Lila de Nobili

XLV *Twelfth Night*, I.i

XLVI *Twelfth Night*, V.i

XLVII Laurence Olivier as Othello dead, with Desdemona (Maggie Smith)

XIV

Directions for Twelfth Night

★

AFTER the first dozen *Twelfth Night*'s there are still surprises, new guises for the old masterpiece. Directors colour it golden, russet, silver or white; blue for dreams, and sometimes pink; or they allow red and even purple to dominate. They can make it sound noisy as a carnival, or eager, or melodious, or quarrelsome like children; it can also be strained and nervous. In 1958, Peter Hall at Stratford-upon-Avon hung the stage with gauzes and contrived what *The Times* called a 'Watteauesque light'. And critics report that a year previously, at Stratford, Ontario, Tyrone Guthrie contrasted Feste and Malvolio in 'psychological terms', allowing the final song of the 'wind and rain' to be 'as plaintive and wonderful as a Jewish lament.' Two years before that, at the English Stratford, Sir John Gielgud brought 'a faint chill to the air' of his production; the comics were on their best behaviour in deference to a pervasive 'charm'; *The Observer* said that the polite word for this would be 'formal', and the exact word 'mechanical'; it seemed as if, during rehearsals of the last scene, Sir John had stopped the actors and commanded, 'Be beautiful; be beautiful'.

This play might have been designed for an age when each director must make his name and register his mark. Yet there is one difficulty: in most productions some part of the play resists the director's control. In Sir John's elegant *Twelfth Night*, Malvolio yielded Sir Laurence Olivier a role in which to exploit his impudent and plebeian comedy, and in his last line—'I'll be revenged on the whole pack of you'—an opportunity for the cry of a man unmade. The grey and urban setting of the Old Vic's production in 1950 was enlivened by an untrained ballet of sailors and riffraff, but Peggy Ashcroft's clear, white voice was an unechoed reminder of other directions the comedy can be given. More commonly, without such trained stars to cross the director's intentions, robust comics usurp more attention than their part in the last Act is allowed to satisfy, or an intelligent Sebastian will deny his own words, a too gentle Orsino devalue Viola's ardour. There is need for vigilance: Margaret Webster, who sees *Twelfth Night* as 'filled with impermanence, fragile, imponderable'; has found that:

> The director will have to balance and combine his ingredients in carefully graded proportions, compensating for weaknesses, keeping a moderating hand on excessive strength. This play, above all, he must treat with a light touch and a flexible mind, keeping the final goal clearly in sight.[1]

What happened, one wonders, before there were directors to give directions?

For if we refer back, from the theatre to the text of the play, we shall observe a similar lack of simplicity and uniformity. Malvolio can be a 'turkey cock', a common 'geck and gull' who is told to 'shake his ears'; or a fantastic who asks what 'an alphabetical position portends' and speaks repeatedly 'out of his welkin'. Yet Olivier's petty, ambitious vulgarian is also true to the text when he addresses his mistress with 'Sweet lady, ho, ho!' and with tags from popular ballads. Even Michael Hordern's tortured Malvolio at the Old Vic in 1954, 'dried up, emaciated, elongated . . . (as) an El Greco'—his hands, reaching out of the pit in the scene where Feste visits him as Sir Topas, the curate, suggested to one critic 'the damned in the *Inferno*'—is authorised by Feste's disguise, by his own first words of 'the pangs of death' and 'infirmity', his account of how 'imagination' jades him, and his physical and psychological isolation at the end. And yet again, Olivia's high regard for Malvolio—she 'would not lose him for half her dowry'—justifies Eric Porter's performance at Stratford-upon-Avon in 1960, as a solid, efficient steward waking with practical good sense to worlds unrealised.

Actors seeking to express their originality will find that 'new' interpretations rise unbidden from a straightforward study of the text, Sir Toby is usually a domesticated Falstaff, but at the Old Vic in 1958 with tumultuous 'gulps and shouts', he was seen as a plain 'boor'; and for this there is plenty of support in his name, Belch, and in his talk of 'boarding and assailing', making water and cutting 'mutton'. And the same year, at Stratford-upon-Avon, Patrick Wymark made him young and spry with a sense of style; for this, 'she's a beagle, true-bred' was most appropriate language, and his easy confidence in 'consanguinity' with Olivia and expertise in swordplay were natural accomplishments.

[1] *Shakespeare Today* (1957), p. 205.

One might imagine too, a melancholy Sir Toby, tried in true service and knowing from experience that 'care's an enemy to life': his tricks upon Sir Andrew would then be a compensation for his own retirement, his wooing—off-stage and presumably brief—of Maria, a just and difficult tribute to her service for him; lethargy comes with drunkenness and he 'hates a drunken rogue'; he needs company, even that of a fool, an ass, and a servant.

Olivia is another role which can be seen to be of different ages—either mature years or extreme youth; and she can be melancholy or gay. Maxine Audley at Stratford-upon-Avon in 1955 presented a gracious lady, truly grieving for the death of her brother and strong enough to recognise an absolute passion for a boy; this Olivia had the 'smooth, discreet and stable bearing', the majesty, to which Sebastian and Orsino testify. And three years later, at the same theatre, Geraldine McEwen presented her as kittenish and cute, saved from triviality by fine timing of movement and verse-speaking, the dignity of 'style'. And yet another Olivia may be suggested by the text: a very young girl, at first afraid of meeting the world and therefore living in a fantasy capable of decreeing seven-years of mourning; then a girl solemnly repeating old saws with a new understanding of their truth;

> Even so quickly may one catch the plague. . . . I do I know not what, and fear to find Mine eye too great a flatterer for my mind. . . . What is decreed must be . . . how apt the poor are to be proud . . . youth is bought more oft than begg'd or borrowed,

and forgetting her 'discreet' bearing in breathless eagerness:

> *How* does he love me? . . . *Why*, what would you? . . . not too *fast*: soft, soft! . . . Well, *let* it be, . . . That's a degree to love. . . . Yet *come* again. . . . I have sent after him: *he says* he'll come. . . . *What* do you say? . . . *Most wonderful!*

Feste, the fool, can be melancholy, or bitter, or professional, or amorous (and sometimes impressively silent), or self-contained and philosophical, or bawdy and impotent. Sir Andrew Aguecheek can be patient, sunny, feckless, gormless, animated or neurotic. (In 1958 Richard Johnson gave an assured performance of this knight as a 'paranoid manic-depressive, strongly reminiscent at times of Lucky in *Waiting for Godot*'.) Orsino can be mature or very young; poetic; or weak; or strong but deceived; or regal and distant. The text can suggest a Viola who is pert, sentimental, lyrical, practical, courageous or helpless. Shakespeare's words can support all these interpretations, and others; there are few plays which give comparable scope for enterprise and originality. The characters, the situations and the speeches are protean.

This is evident in a director's ability to alter the trend of his production, even in the very last moments, to achieve what Miss Webster has called his 'balance', to arrive at his chosen 'final goal'. If sentiment needs reinforcing, Viola (as Cesario) can be given a down-stage position and a preparatory pause as the arrangements for her duel with Sir Andrew grow to a comic climax, and thus her 'I do assure you, 'tis against my will' can be, not the usual laugh-line, but a reminder of her other full-hearted struggles of will and passion; this momentary seriousness, the more impressive for its incongruous setting, was managed with great grace by Dorothy Tutin at Stratford, in Peter Hall's productions of 1958 and 1960. Still later in the play, there is another opportunity for the strong re-emphasis of Viola's depth of feeling: Peggy Ashcroft mastered this in 1950, and J. C. Trewin has well described its effect in performance:

> At the end, as Sebastian faces his sister, he cries: 'What countryman? What name? What parentage?' There is a long pause now before Viola, in almost a whisper (but one of infinite rapture and astonishment) answers: 'Of Messaline'. Practically for the first time in my experience a Viola has forced me to believe in her past. . . .[2]

More simply and without affecting any established characterisation, the balance of a production can be altered by the Priest's lines in the last scene, with their special idiom and assured syntax and timing:

> A contract of eternal bond of love,
> Confirm'd by mutual joinder of your hands,
> Attested by the holy close of lips,
> Strength'ned by interchangement of your rings
> And all the ceremony of this compact
> Seal'd in my function, by my testimony;
> Since when, my watch hath told me, toward my grave,
> I have travell'd but two hours.

If these lines are spoken in a weighty and measured way, they can restore a sense of awe, an awareness of general and timeless implications, to a

[2] *John O'London's Weekly*, 8 Dec., 1950.

dénouement which has become too headlong and hilarious for the director's taste. Or, at the last moment, Orsino can give 'guts' to an over-pretty production: the sight of Antonio permits an evocation of the 'smoke of war' and 'scathful grapple', and can legitimately bring a harsh quality to his voice which has hitherto been tuned to softer themes. When he invites Olivia to live 'the marble-breasted tyrant still' and turns to Cesario with:

> But this your minion, whom I know you love,
> And whom, by heaven I swear, I tender dearly,
> Him will I tear out of that cruel eye
> Where he sits crowned in his master's spite.
> Come, boy, with me; my thoughts are ripe in mischief:
> I'll sacrifice the lamb that I do love
> To spite a raven's heart within a dove

the director can call for physical as well as verbal violence towards Viola. The lines imply that Orsino cares more for his seeming boy than for the lady of his dreams and fancy, and thus they may be acted fully and strongly; the release of passion in a desire to kill Cesario shows the true object of that passion, and its power. (This reading of the subtext is authorised by Shakespeare, as by Freud and Stanislavski, for Orsino has just acknowledged that a 'savage' jealousy 'kills what it loves', not what it *thinks* it loves.) If the production is, at this stage of the play, too solemn rather than too sentimental or hilarious, there are opportunities in plenty for lightening the whole last Act: Olivia's 'Where goes Cesario?', after Orsino's outburst, can easily be spoken to invite laughter; and so can her 'Most wonderful' as Viola and Sebastian confront each other. Nearly all Sebastian's lines can be tipped the same way, as 'I do perceive it hath offended you' . . . 'Fear'st thou that, Antonio' . . . and (about the mole on the brow of Viola's father) 'And so had mine.' Antonio's 'An apple, cleft in two is not more twin' can be directed so that it implies laughter rather than rapt amazement, and Orsino's final 'Cesario, come' can be a jest at the whole contrivance of the last Act, or even at Viola's expense, rather than recognition of his own long, half-hidden affection for his bride-to-be.

The opportunities for swinging a production round into line with a chosen mood—to make it 'what they will', to reverse roles as in a 'Twelfth Night' revel—have encouraged directors to tackle *Twelfth Night* and to experiment widely in the search for original interpretations. But a second practical consequence of the freedom of interpretation is of greater importance: this play challenges us to provide a longer and deeper study than is normally given to a text in the theatre. We may be assured that the diverse ways of playing the characters and controlling the mood are not finally irreconcilable. The experience of seeing many independent productions and reading about many more does not create a multitude of separate memories; each new revelation reflects on earlier ones and, in the mind, a single view of the play is continually growing in complexity and range, and in understanding. We may believe that a single production might, one day, represent to the full our single, developing awareness. Our knowledge of *Twelfth Night* and of human behaviour may assure us that an Olivia is both mature and immature, according to which side of her personality is in view; a Sir Toby energetic *and* melancholic, vulgar *and* well-schooled; and a Viola lyrical *and* practical, *and* helpless. The world of the play is gay, quiet, strained, solemn, dignified, elegant, easy, complicated, precarious, hearty, homely; the conclusion close to laughter, song, awe *and* simplicity. And this is an understanding which begs not to be hid, but to be realised on the stage.

Of course, in the theatre it is temping to simplify too early, in order to be effective and make a 'strong' impression. But with such a play as *Twelfth Night* we are drawn by another possibility, a more demanding course: five years' study, a repeated return to its problems in a succession of productions under different conditions and for different audiences, might make possible a production which would be original, not by one-sidedness, but by answering more fully than before to Shakespeare's text and combining the excitement of many interpretations. The time necessary to make this attempt would be an expensive investment; and it would be a risky one—for the speculator may not be capable of living up to the developing demands of his enterprise. Yet the business is a practical possibility, and must be considered. An exclusive pursuit of immediate effectiveness and originality leads to immature and insecure achievements, in theatres as in other fields of activity; a play like *Twelfth Night* offers, therefore, an opportunity and a challenge which it would be salutary merely to envisage, regenerative to attempt. Shakespeare's stage-cunning, human understanding and poetic imagination, which are all implicit in the text would be fine assets.

* * *

The necessary conditions for such an achievement would be a concern for, and skill in, all the arts of the theatre—this is required for any sort of theatrical success—but, more peculiarly, a constant return to the details of Shakespeare's text. Here the popular misconception that close textual study is a dull and pedestrian activity, restricting originality and encouraging an exclusively verbal kind of drama—may inhibit the right kind of work, and must be denounced: a prolonged and careful study of Shakespeare's text, in association with other theatre skills, can awaken and enrich a production in all elements of a play's life. If we trust Shakespeare's imagination, we know that *Twelfth Night* was conceived as a whole with each apparently discordant element reconciled to its opposite: and our only clue to that original resolution is the printed words. Every opportunity for visual realisation or elaboration, for movement and variation of grouping, for temporal control, for subtlety of elocution or stage-business, for creation of character and mood, emotion and expression, that the text can suggest should be searched out, tested, practically evaluated and, finally, given its due place in the responsible and mature production which each successive, partial and conflicting production of such a play as *Twelfth Night* invites us to consider, and to hope that one day we may help to stage or witness.

The combination, or growing together, of elements from new interpretations of roles is, perhaps, the best charted part of a difficult task; it calls for a developing sympathy and understanding, and a grasp of the progressive and formal presentation of character, but it does not require, at the beginning of rehearsals a single limiting choice; moreover the actors are always in obvious contact with Shakespeare's words. Perhaps the problems of a textually responsible production will be most perplexing in choosing the stage setting, especially if the play is to be performed on a picture-frame stage with the full range of modern equipment.

Twelfth Night has received many visual interpretations: the elegant, controlled and overtly dramatic, as a Tiepolo fresco, is a common one; or domestic with dark shadows, like the Jacobean interiors in Joseph Nash's *Mansions of England in the Olden Times*; or Italianate, free and colourful in the fashion of the *commedia dell'arte*. Or the stage may be spacious and clean, like one modern notion of what an Elizabethan platform stage was like, or pillared, tiered and substantial, like another. Some designers have introduced the satins and laces of Restoration

England, and others the boaters and billows of the theatre of *Charley's Aunt*. The main difficulty is that all these, and others, are in some degree appropriate, usually in different parts of the play; and yet it would be distracting to a modern audience to move from one to another during a single performance, even if this were technically possible. If a mature production of *Twelfth Night* is to be considered, this problem will have to be solved in a single way—the more urgently because the proscenium arches and lighting devices of modern theatres have made the visual embodiment of a play, in setting, costumes and effects, a dominating—often *the* dominating—element of a production.

A resource to the text in the search for a comprehensive style and single stage setting does not involve the director in an antiquarian production which tries to reproduce original stage conditions; those are, in any case, irrecoverable, in their full complexity which involves specially trained actors and historically accurate audiences, as well as theatres which no longer exist. The study of the text can be of help in utilising the modern technical devices of a picture-frame stage, and in answering the expectations of any particular audience. The verbal imagery can, for example, give valuable help towards deciding which setting is most appropriate; it can tell the director the kind of visual images which were associated with the action and characters in the author's mind and which he may usefully transmit to the audience in visual stage terms.

Illyria, the world of *Twelfth Night*, is obviously a land of love, music, leisure, servants, a Duke and a Countess; it must have dwellings, a garden, a seacoast and a 'dark house' or temporary prison. Its institutions include a church and a chantry, a captain and officers of the law, an inn; and there must be doors or gates. Thus far the choice of a setting is not circumscribed; it might be English, Italian, French, Russian (before the revolution), or, with some adaptation, American or Utopian; medieval, renaissance or modern. But incidental details of speech and action at once limit the setting to something resembling, or representing, English countryside and domesticity. In the first scene there are mentioned a bank of violets, a hunt, sweet beds of flowers, and these are followed by wind and weather, a squash and a peascod, a willow, the hills, a beagle, roses, a yew, a cypress and box tree, and more flowers; familiar living creatures are a hart, a sheep-biter, a horse, a trout, a turkey-cock and a wood-cock, a raven, lamb and dove, and hounds; daylight, champaign (or open fields), harvest, ripeness, and oxen and wain-ropes easily come to mind; the songs of nightingales, daws and owls have been heard. The characters of the play do not talk of an elegant or fanciful scene, although the violets and beds of flowers might be interpreted in that way; their wain-ropes, sheep-biter and daws belong to a countryside that knows labour and inconvenience, as well as delights. Speaking of horrors and danger, they are neither sophisticated nor learned; they refer to tempests, the sea, fields, mountains, barbarous caves, and hunger. The domestic note is almost as persistent as that of the countryside: early in Act I, canary-wine, beef, a housewife and a buttery-bar are mentioned; even the Duke, Orsino, speaks of knitters in the sun; there is talk of pilchards and herrings (fresh and pickled) and of vinegar and pepper. If a director is to attempt a responsible production of the play, he should give substance to these references in his setting—not in an illustrative way which provides objects for the actors to point at, but in a manner which echoes, extends and, where appropriate, contrasts with the dialogue and stage business. This is the mental and emotional world of the *dramatis personae* as revealed by their language, and the stage picture can help to establish this, not insistently, but with subtlety.

It is the world of the play's action too, and its visual recreation will, therefore, aid the director towards an appropriate rhythm and acting style: an Italianate setting, which is often chosen, suggests the wrong tempo—the wrong temperature, even—and insists on distracting contrasts between dialogue and visual effect. An English summer takes three months to establish itself, through April, May and June, and so does the action of this play—as Orsino states explicitly in the last scene. It would be convenient, therefore, to show this passage of time in modifications to the setting during the course of the play: the first Acts green and youthful, the last coloured with roses in bloom and strong lights; the same setting but at different times of the year. In the first scene Orsino would be seeking the earliest violets; later 'beauty's a flower', 'women are as roses', 'youth's a stuff will not endure' would sound properly precarious in view of the visual reminder of the changing seasons; a 'lenten answer' would seem more restrictive and 'let summer bear it out' a fuller and more inevitable judgement. Orsino might stand in white, as the young lover in Nicholas Hillyarde's miniature (dated about 1590), over against frail, twining roses: this association represented for the painter his motto—'*Dat poenas laudata fides*', or 'My praisèd faith procures my pain'—and it might serve in much the same way today. 'Midsummer madness' and 'matter for a May morning', which are spoken of in Act III, would be in key with the setting, and the talk of harvest, the grave and the immutable yew-tree would sound in significant contrast.

The course of single days might also be suggested in the lighting of the stage picture. Talk of hunting in the first scene establishes the time as early morning. In the third, Maria's remonstrance to Sir Toby about returning late 'a'nights' belongs to the first meeting of a new day, and then coming 'early' by one's 'lethargy' implies preprandial drinking. In II. iii, the chaffing about 'being up late', Malvolio's chiding about 'respect of . . . time', and 'its too late to go to bed now' all suggest midnight; so one 'day' is completed in due order. (Again Feste's song in this last mentioned scene, about 'present mirth' and 'what's to come' and 'youth's a stuff will not endure', will be more poignant if it seems indeed to have been sung just before the 'night-owl', nature's reminder of death, is roused.) The following scene, II. iv, is clearly a new day with its first lines of 'good morrow' and 'we heard last night'; and the truth that '. . . women are as roses, whose fair flower Being once display'd doth fall that very hour' is more fully expressed if spoken in the transitory light of dawn. The next scene, II. v, beginning with 'Come thy ways . . .' and with news that Malvolio has been 'i' the sun practising behaviour to his own shadow this half hour', is still early morning. Act III, Scene i, which follows with Feste speaking of the sun shining everywhere, may be at noon, and later, when Malvolio supposes Olivia invites him to bed, his outrageous presumption would be more apparent if it were obviously not that 'time of day'. At the end of IV. ii, Feste visits Malvolio in prison and sings:

I'll be with you again,
  In a trice,
  Like the old Vice,
Your need to sustain;
Who, with dagger of lath,
In his rage and his wrath,
  Cries, ah, ha! to the devil. . . .

—here stage lighting could simulate a sudden, passing storm, such as interrupts an easy summer's afternoon in England; it might culminate in thunder. This would be an elaboration impossible to stage in an Elizabethan theatre, but it would be appropriate in a play which is continually concerned with the summer countryside of England, with 'beauty that can endure wind and weather', and which ends with a song of the rain that 'raineth every day'. Sir Toby and Maria could take shelter from the storm, while the fool is left to bear it out and 'pursue the sport'. The sun would shine fully again for Sebastian's 'This is the air; that is the glorious sun; This pearl she gave me . . .', and for the high afternoon of the ending of the comedy. Towards the close shadows might lengthen and, as the marriages are postponed till 'golden time convents,' the sky might become golden with a sunset's promise of another fair day. Then as the other characters leave, to enter perhaps a lighted house, Feste might be left in the grey-green light of early evening to sing alone of time and youth, and of the beginning of the world and the conclusion of a play.

(There is in fact a double time scheme in *Twelfth Night*: three months for the development and fulfilment of the action, and two consecutive days for the sequence of scenes. The representation of both schemes in the setting and in the lighting may help an audience to accept this double sense of time which suits, on the one hand, the rapid fairy-tale transitions and the 'changeable' characterisations, and, on the other hand, the play's suggestion of the season's alterations and the endurance and maturing of affections.)

Such lighting effects require an outdoor setting for almost all the play. And this may be convenient for the action: Olivia's house might be shown to one side, with a terrace and garden before it, a main entrance and a way to the back door; and there might be a dovecote, small pavilion or gazebo on the other side of the stage to do duty as Malvolio's prison. There would be some inconvenience in staging the carousing scene between Feste, Sir Toby and Sir Andrew in a garden, but there is plenty of reference to outdoor affairs in its dialogue and the two knights could fall asleep around their table at the close of the scene and be discovered there next morning to be awakened by Fabian. The scenes at Orsino's court could also be in the open air, and could be set by bringing in tall cypress hedges to mask Olivia's house and garden, and to reveal part of the sky-cloth or cyclorama at the end of a long walk or vista in some spacious park. It would be appropriately affected for Orsino to seek the shade of such a walk in the early morning; there could be a stone seat on one side, and on the other a sculpture of Venus, or some such deity. For the brief scene outside Olivia's gate (II. ii) and for the Sebastian scenes, 'somewhere in Illyria' (II. i and III. iii), a 'wall' could be let down from the flies, with a gate in its centre: this would locate the action outside Olivia's estate and, if her house and the taller trees were visible over the top of the wall and through the gate, the audience would relish the physical proximity of Sebastian to his journey's end.

There remains one, apparently unrelated, scene (I. ii) which begins 'What country, friends, is this?' This might also be played 'outside Olivia's garden', but Viola's mysterious entry into the play from the sea asks for a different visual presentation. It would be possible to play it in front of gauzes let down to hide the transition from Orsino's park of I. i, to Olivia's garden of I. iii; these might be lightly painted and lit to suggest a seashore, touched, perhaps with fluorescent material low down, as if catching the surf of a strange sea. If Orsino had been contemplating a statue of Venus in the previous scene that figure might be caught by a higher light as the gauzes came down, and then, in a moment of darkness, Viola might take its place to rise from the sea as the stage is relit. If this were effected tactfully, this scene could easily take its place in the chiaroscuro: its sea-effects might be echoed later as Feste is also isolated in the 'storm' of his 'vice' song; and echoed differently at the end of the play, as he is isolated in the evening. Moreover the myth-like transition and transference would be in keeping with the 'romantic' attraction of the lovers and the solution of their stories—the dream, or fantasy element, of the play.

The colours of setting and costumes could be those of an early English summer: clear, light blues, greens, yellows and pinks, and plenty of white. The buildings could be the honey-coloured stone of the English Cotswolds, with marble ornaments for Orsino's park. Olivia would, of course, wear black while in mourning, and Malvolio always—the only character to take no colour from the sun.

* * *

Such is one solution of the visual problems of *Twelfth Night*, and one which tries to answer the demands of the text in terms of the realism of the picture-frame stage—which is perhaps the furthest removed from Elizabethan practice. Other stages and other visual styles would call for different solutions. This way of staging the play is worth consideration chiefly as an example: for if any production is to be undertaken with a belief in the unity and imaginative quality of Shakespeare's text, its choice of setting must answer the same demands and others like them, as more are revealed through further study of the text and further experiments in eccentric productions.

The quest for a responsible direction for *Twelfth Night* will not lead to a series of stereotyped productions: changing stage-conditions, actors and audiences will prevent that. Nor will we rest content with our achievements, for the 'idea' of the play, which grows in our minds as we meet it frequently in many guises, is most likely to remain several steps beyond our most truthful production. The desire for an authentic direction will not be satisfied easily, but those who try to respond to it will grow more aware of the wealth of Shakespeare's imagination and perhaps more expert in their attempts to give his masterpiece its theatrical life.

APPENDIX

*Theatre Research and the Criticism of Shakespeare and His Contemporaries**

★

> My approach to playwriting and the drama itself is organic; and to make this glaringly evident at once it is necessary to separate drama from what we think of today as literature. A drama ought not be looked at first and foremost from literary perspectives merely because it uses words, verbal rhythm, and poetic image. These can be its most memorable parts, it is true, but they are not its inevitable accompaniments.

SO Arthur Miller introduces his *Collected Plays*,[1] and proceeds to demonstrate that we must think of his development as a dramatist in terms of a full theatrical experience, including the management of time, visual backgrounds and relationships, and the kind of 'questions' which are asked and answered each time an actor walks on to the stage. He convinces us that his plays need a theatrical criticism, not a mere adaptation of literary criticism.

There are many reasons for believing that the same is true of Shakespeare's plays. Clearly he was a man of the theatre, more so than Mr. Miller: he was actor, 'instructor' of actors, manager and theatre-owner, as well as author, and he never took the trouble to publish his plays with notes, special stage-directions, preface or dedication as most of his contemporaries did on occasion, the more literary ones many times. He surely cultivated 'literary' qualities in his writing, but the experience of watching one of his plays in rehearsal demonstrates forcibly how the text is awakened, coloured, emphasised, extended in performance, in relation to visual and temporal elements inherent in it. The need for a theatrical criticism of Shakespeare seems self-evident, for even the consciously literary dramatists of the present century, as Yeats or Eliot, have obviously modified their writing in response to the

* Based on a paper read to the Society for Theatre Research, 15 March 1960, and later published in *Shakespeare Quarterly*, xiii (1962).

[1] *Collected Plays* (1958), pp. 3–4.

experience of seeing their works in performance; a critic of plays must understand and account for such things.

Yet it is said on all sides that Shakespeare is an exception to this rule. In his most perceptive book, Professor L. C. Knights has claimed that:

> in recent Shakespeare criticism, the *verse* has moved well into the centre of the picture, . . . because *linguistic vitality* is now felt as the *chief* clue to the urgent personal themes that not only shape the poetic-dramatic structure of each play but form the figure in the carpet of the canon as a whole.[2]

For our greatest dramatist, so this theory goes, words are the heart of the matter, and many critics have followed this literary lead. The result is that many books are written about Shakespeare's doctrine, themes, ethic, philosophical patterns, images, moral ideas, and few about his dramas, plays, varieties of theatrical experiences. And the chief clues to this philosophic Shakespeare lie, necessarily, in the variety of his verbal images, the structure of his complex words, his 'linguistic vitality', rather than in his theatrical technique, his use of time, movement or isolation. Almost all the criticism of Shakespeare—and the criticism of lesser writers tends to follow suit—uses specifically literary techniques and terminology, is based on literary perceptions, and leads to literary definition.

There are many reasons for this attitude. Critics, trained in literary disciplines, are apt to think that theatrical experience is coarse and vulgar, to be measured only in terms of popular appeal—as if the brave colour of Van Gogh's sunflowers were all the finesse of which the visual arts were capable. More informed is the belief that theatrical experience is too complex and unmanageable to be talked about profitably: among its obvious difficulties are antiquarian considerations, the lack of terminology, diversity and conflict of opinion, and dispersal of interest among many trivial phenomena. Professor Wilson Knight, a critic who has himself acted Shakespeare's major roles, produced plays and attended many performances, has averred after much study:

> my experience . . . leaves me uncompromising in my assertion that the literary analysis of great drama in terms of theatrical technique accomplishes singularly little. . . .

Professor Knight believes that it is necessary to 'write of Shakespeare

[2] *Some Shakespearean Themes* (1959), p. 14; the italics are mine.

. . . as a philosophic poet rather than a man of the stage'.[3] And the majority of twentieth-century critics agree with him, when judging Shakespeare's plays or those of his contemporaries.

In this situation in the play of criticism it seems appropriate for theatre research to make an entrance. There are many ways in which it can help to define the theatrical experience provided by the text of a play, to remind the critic of its visual and temporal elements as well as the verbal, and so to lead towards a full theatrical criticism. Literary criticism has set the pace and revealed the subtlety and range of one part of Shakespeare's imagination; theatre research can help to reveal and define other parts.

* * *

In a simple and obvious way it can sharpen the critic's eye. By recovering, ordering and assessing the records and reviews of past performances, theatre research can help the critic to see what stage actions, movements and visual relationships are implied by the author's text. For instance, Gordon Crosse's *Shakespearean Playgoing, 1890–1952* (1953) by describing past productions shows the potential force of Banquo 'keenly' watching Macbeth in Act II during the discovery of Duncan's murder (p. 64). This is an important fact, critically. Banquo's silent watch can make an audience aware of Macbeth's equivocations —his concern to make his foul seem fair—throughout the scene in which he appears most successfully to cast his guilt on others; it adds force to Banquo's 'In the great hand of God I stand' with which he rejoins the general dialogue; and its immobility contrasts with Macbeth's new rapidity, with his actions implied in 'Let's briefly put on manly readiness'. In short, the theatrical effectiveness of Banquo's silent presence, which in reading the play it is easy to forget, is an important indication of the design of the tragedy, showing how continuous was Shakespeare's concern with the responsible, theocentric world against which, and over against which, Macbeth is shown living and fighting. The same record of past performances can again act as visual prompter for the critic in describing the force of Macduff's standing apart in Act V, Scene vi, when the other characters talk stirringly of imminent battle:[4] the fact that he breaks a conspicuous silence to say:

[3] *The Wheel of Fire* (4th ed., 1949), Preface, p. vi.
[4] Cross, op. cit., p. 88.

Make all our trumpets speak; give them all breath,
Those clamorous harbingers of blood and death

shows that he, unlike the others, has been thinking of the cost of battle in terms of 'blood and death'; and that Shakespeare was still, as in the earlier scene in England, concerned to show the particular, personal loss which Macduff alone has sustained in the death of his wife and children, to remind the audience here, at the last moment, that Macbeth has broken bonds of private affection as well as those of social, political and religious order.

The usefulness of research into theatre records as a prompter for those who try to understand the full theatrical implications of a dramatic text could be illustrated in thousands of instances. Two more may suffice here. A review[5] after the performance of *The White Devil* in London on 6 March 1947, points to the importance of a one-line part in this play—which many have read, but few have been able to see. It describes the sense of embarrassment which Webster achieved by introducing a young, anonymous page to contradict Cornelia's attempt to shield her son from Bracciano's anger, with a simple 'This is not true, madam'; attention is thus drawn away, rapidly and without warning, from the centre of a very 'dramatic' situation, and a silence follows. This is not a trivial point, though it might easily be overlooked in reading: it illustrates Webster's power of using violent and crowded scenes for sudden, and therefore striking, manifestations of an individual's lies or hypocrisy, the 'variety' of a 'busy trade of life'; and it prepares the audience for another young, unsubtle voice at the end of the play, that of Giovanni as he metes out justice without knowing the full complexity and danger of his task.

A further example of theatrical prompting is one which does not depend on the record of a single review. Almost any production of *Much Ado About Nothing* will furnish reviews commenting upon the speaking of Beatrice's words 'Kill Claudio', and they will often be contradictory. Read together, as they may be by a theatrical researcher, they show how precarious the comic and sentimental issues are at just this point in the play; how, in performance, these two words can trigger off great and opposing reactions, sometimes causing laughter, sometimes concern. Again this has more than incidental significance: it marks how powerful the 'covered fire' of passion is, beneath the easy wit and

[5] *The Sunday Times*, 9 March, 1947.

rapid movement of Benedick and Beatrice; it shows that Shakespeare was concerned with the danger and the absurdity of the way in which they love while refusing to say they love.

Sometimes the reviews and accounts of past productions can clarify the balance of a whole play. A reading of *Measure for Measure*, for example, may suggest that little importance attaches to Lucio: his jokes seem stale or obscure, his part in the development of the action slight. There are several well-known criticisms of this play which barely mention him: H. B. Charlton's chapter in his *Shakespearian Comedy* (1938) refers to him briefly on two occasions only, once calling him a 'most fallible mortal', and once dismissing him as 'sewage'. But accounts of performances show again and again that the actor of Lucio attracts considerable attention. *The London Chronicle* of 1758 testifies fully:

> The part of Lucio . . . is, as far as I can judge, both for humour and nature, by many degrees superior to any character of the same stamp, introduced upon the stage since. And notwithstanding the audience have seen it so often inimitably performed by Mr. Woodward, the unanimous applause they gave to Mr. Obrien, who appeared in it the above night [October 10], was a convincing argument that they thought he displayed very great theatrical talents.

Theatre research can tell the critic, at least, that Lucio is a fine opportunity for an actor, and a full criticism of the play must take this into account: his dismissal in the last scene is not an easy or slight incident.

The study of cast-lists and playbills—now greatly simplified for the eighteenth century by C. B. Hogan's *Shakespeare in the Theater* (1952, 1957)[6]—can in itself serve the literary critic by indicating the range of interpretation a part or a play has received, and how it has found favour in one century as opposed to another. While modern literary critics extol *Antony and Cleopatra*, and place it among the finest of Shakespeare's works, it will sharpen our comprehension of the nature of Shakespeare's achievement in this tragedy to know that in the eighteenth century it was in the repertory only for one year, 1759, and not revived. Similarly the critic may be given a useful train of inquiry when he has to explain to himself why *Richard II*, displacing Theobald's version of the play in 1738 and 1739, was not revived again

[6] And more recently *The London Stage, 1660–1800* (1960–5), by W. van Lennep, E. L. Avery, A. H. Scouten, G. W. Stone, Jr., and C. B. Hogan.

in that century. When it is argued, as by Dr. Leslie Hotson,[7] that Shakespeare intended Malvolio to be a laughing-stock or comic gull, and that a modern, sentimental concern for the underdog is alone responsible for the more sympathetic, or 'straight', interpretation of the role, a consultation of theatrical records can show that two comic actors, Charles Macklin and Thomas King, were succeeded as Malvolio at Drury Lane in 1777 by the 'straight' actor, Robert Bensley: King played major roles in the company for twenty years after this time, but he never took back Malvolio from Bensley; so the player of the Gravedigger, Stephano and Touchstone was replaced by the player of Antonio (in *The Merchant of Venice*), of Banquo, the Ghost in *Hamlet*, Henry IV, Prospero, and Wolsey. Malvolio was more than a comic butt, long before the contemporary cult of the misunderstood. Feste's thrusts at him

> . . . with dagger of lath,
> In his rage and his wrath

are not, necessarily, a duel with a character who has a comic's resilience; it may well be a real storm among the 'matter for a May morning'. And Malvolio's final appearance, baited before his mistress and his fellows, may be meant for laughter only after it has been, as Fabian says, 'justly weighed'; it may be a sober moment before 'golden time convents' and 'fancy's queen' happily entertained. Theatre research shows that this is an old, as well as a modern, interpretation.

Cast-lists, reviews, illustrations, prompt-books, memoirs, can all, together or separately, show the range of possible interpretations of dramatic texts, and also help the critic to discriminate between them. Michael Langham's production of *Hamlet* at Stratford-upon-Avon, with Alan Badel as the prince, is fully documented in the Royal Shakespeare Theatre Library, with press-cuttings, photographs, and prompt-book. For this production, the reviews were in notable accord: it was a careful, responsible presentation of an anti-romantic, unglamorous prince who has 'of late lost all his mirth', who pities and sometimes hates himself; it showed, with much imaginative detail, a man in a situation stronger than his power to comprehend, who cannot communicate easily until he loses himself in action. The interpretation has some support from modern literary criticism, so that the reviews and prompt-book make particularly fascinating reading. First, all

[7] *The First Night of 'Twelfth Night'* (1954), p. 119 etc.

reviewers—even the favourable ones—agree that interest was not always sustained; this might be due in part to the actor rather than the interpretation, but further reading can prove that this charge was a new one against Mr. Badel. Photographs and prompt-book show, moreover, that the stage was particularly bare, the action continuous and swift; several reviewers noticed this, but nevertheless still insisted on the incomplete hold of the play. Reading further we can see that in order to keep the pace rapid, or because the passage did not seem necessary to this interpretation, the dialogue between Hamlet and Horatio at the beginning of Act V, Scene ii, was completely cut; there was nothing of Rosencrantz and Guildenstern 'going to't' and not lying near Hamlet's conscience, nothing of the question 'is't not perfect conscience' to requite Claudius; the last scene started with Hamlet's regret that he had forgotten himself towards Laertes. These adjustments, necessary for Mr. Langham's interpretation of the play, and the strangely unanimous verdict of the reviewers, academic as well as journalistic, can help the critic to judge this anti-romantic reading of the play in its full theatrical life.

Few theatres performing the plays of Shakespeare and his contemporaries in English maintain comprehensive archives like the Shakespeare Memorial Theatre, but persistent research can often bring the consequences of any particular interpretation into vivid light. Professor Moelwyn Merchant's discussion of illustrations and settings for *Henry VIII* and *Coriolanus* in his pioneering and perceptive book, *Shakespeare and the Artist* (1959), shows the varying visual emphases of different readings of these plays. Professor Sprague's description of the stage business as various Falstaffs have tried to lift the dead Hotspur on their backs draws attention to the picture which Shakespeare has contrived, in which the Spirit of Comedy, with difficulty, carries the Spirit of Heroism from the field of battle; a literary critic might never guess from a reading of the play that the sheer physical difficulty of a fat man lifting a 'dead' weight necessarily holds this picture for the audience's attention, nor how some interpretations encouraged low comedy while others strove to avoid laughter.[8] Occasionally a single piece of evidence will, luckily, suggest the theatrical consequences of a particular interpretation. For example, *Twelfth Night* was presented by Daly in high romantic style, heartfelt and tender, and a delighted description

[8] Cf. A. C. Sprague, *Shakespeare and the Actors* (1944), pp. 90–91.

of one scene in the *New York Herald Tribune* of 28 November 1894, illustrates how much against the quick-moving and complicated action of Shakespeare's play this one-sided reading can be:

> The scene is Olivia's garden. The time is evening. Viola, disguised as the minstrel Cesario, having received an intimation that perhaps her brother, Sebastian, has not been drowned, has spoken her joyous soliloquy upon that auspicious thought, and has sunk into a seat, in meditation. The moon is rising over the distant sea, and in the fancied freshness of the balmy rising breeze you can almost hear the ripple of the leaves. The lovelorn Orsino enters, with many musicians, and they sing a serenade, beneath the windows of Olivia's palace. The proud beauty comes forth upon her balcony, and, parting her veil, looks down upon Viola. . . . Not a word is spoken and not a word is needed. The garden is all in moonlight; the delicious music flows on; and . . . the curtain slowly falls. It was a perfect triumph of art, in the highest and best vein.

So much for the romantic opportunities Shakespeare missed in his 'romantic comedy', as it is often called. The new song, the contrived entrances and the dominance of scenic effects mark the distance from Shakespeare's text that a sentimental interpretation can stray.

Sometimes it is possible to go, with book in hand, to theatrical records to test a new interpretation. Derek Traversi, in his *Shakespeare From 'Richard II' to 'Henry V'* (1958), has searched for what he calls 'meanings' in the 'language and verse' of these plays, and has pronounced (pp. 49 and 107) that Prince Hal is 'the central figure' of *Henry IV, Part I*, and that 'the last word of the play has really been spoken' with the end of the *pen*-ultimate scene. 'Are these things true in the theatre?', we may ask the theatre researcher: 'Is the last scene often cut, or does it pass unnoticed by reviewers and actors?', 'Do surviving illustrations or stage-directions in prompt-books give Hal, and not Falstaff or Hotspur, the central place?' Theatre research cannot always answer such questions unequivocally, but it can always ensure that our search for answers is not exlusively literary. It can extend the critic's response towards the visual and temporal elements of a drama, and give hints of its form and pressure in performance in varying ages, under varying stage-conditions and according to a wide range of interpretations. Experience is of course needed to read the records: stage conditions and audiences and actors are never similar to those of the first performances of plays; good reviewers must be distinguished from those who are prejudiced or inefficient; evidence is never complete. But the records are responses to the essential fact of dramatic illusion and so, even when clear information is denied, the critic from reading them may grow in perception of theatrical experience, and in power to describe the theatrical possibilities of any particular play, or scene, or word, or silence, or grouping, or movement, or gesture.

* * *

If this recourse is available, it seems unfortunate and inexplicable that it is so little used, and that critics are content to write of Shakespeare as a 'philosophic poet *rather than* a man of the stage'. Why is criticism so consistently literary, so seldom theatrical?

The main reason is probably that the evidence for theatre research is so dispersed. There are collections like those at the Lincoln Centre, the Harvard Theatre Collection, and the Birmingham Reference Library, and some private collections to which a student may have access. But it is not easy to attempt complete surveys, and easy to fall into error. Consequently potential theatre researchers are often discouraged. The Arden Shakespeare has a tradition of including stage histories in each volume, but in recent years the editors of *Richard II, Henry VI, Parts Two* and *Three, Othello, All's Well,* and *Henry IV, Part One* have all shrunk from this responsibility, their volumes appearing without this customary aid to the student. When stage histories do appear they are often erratic and sometimes absurd. That in the Variorum Edition of *Troilus and Cressida*, published in 1953, is a bad example: divergent opinions on a production are quoted without comment; other productions are represented by one part of a single review; an amateur *reading* one evening at University College, London, of an *abbreviated* version under the auspices of the British Empire Shakespeare Society is noticed, while two major full-scale productions (involving Sir Donald Wolfit, Miss Pamela Brown and Mr. Paul Scofield) are not even listed; and all is presented in a 'take-it-or-leave-it' manner, which transcribes comments on little local difficulties (like the late arrival of helmets for an amateur production in Boston, Mass.), and sometimes relies wholly on statistics, sometimes on worn-out journalese.

It is easy to see the compilers' difficulties. And one must recognise the diverse claims that are made upon them: they try to satisfy readers interested in the personality and art of great actors, those interested in the development of taste or scenic design, of lighting techniques or of acting techniques, those following the stories of theatre buildings, of dramatists, managers, directors. Because the literary critic may not be aware of all these demands, he may become impatient of even the best among stage-histories, and find theatre research a discipline too bewildering for use. Herbert Marshall's introduction to the 'pictorial record' of *Hamlet through the Ages* (1952) lists some of the questions which prompted the compilation and editing of this book, unfortunately still unique:

> What would we not give to know really how Duse acted, or Irving produced or how Shakespeare's company played at the Globe? How did an Antoine production compare with Molière? Or Saxe-Meiningen with Reinhardt or Piscator? How did Gordon Craig's Shakespeare production compare with Granville-Barker's? (p. xi.)

and in all this conjecture, the literary critic will not find one of his own questions explicitly stated: theatre research seems oblivious to his needs. Professor Sprague is a literary critic as well as an original theatre scholar, yet his list of criteria for considering pieces of stage business in his book on *Shakespeare and the Actors* would not reassure another literary critic turning to theatre research for the first time:

> in deciding to include rather than reject a piece of business, I have usually been guided by one or more of the following considerations: that it possessed artistic merit in itself; or served to illustrate, or to enforce, the meaning of the lines; that it was early in time; that it had a place in the acting tradition of the play. (p. xvii.)

The phrase 'meaning of the lines' will sound familiar to the literary scholar but it will not sound adventurous, or likely to tell him anything he could not discover for himself; and little else in this list seems to be connected with his particular interest in the plays themselves.

So considerable difficulties prevent a fuller use of theatre research. But there is little need to spend time denouncing shoddy stage histories, inaccurate and unhelpful: new ones should be encouraged, and steps must be taken to ensure that they answer the questions of the literary critic more fully or, perhaps, more obviously than is the custom. Among all the various and important demands made upon the theatre researcher, those of the critic need to be attended to more closely. He is, in a word, interested in the play itself, the play which the author wrote and its inherent theatrical life. Of course, details about Forbes-Robertson or Irving acting Hamlet can tell an experienced reader about the play itself; but there are other facts which speak more directly and with less chance of misinterpretation. These could, and should, be found in stage histories and other works of theatrical research, and given some prominence.

* * *

Four precise suggestions may clarify the needs of a literary critic. The first is very simple, and could be followed almost mechanically. It is that the theatre researcher should always record those occasions when he comes across a group of unconnected reviews or accounts of performances which concur in remarking upon any one particular detail of a play. The concern of many reviewers and actors, over many years, with the words 'Kill Claudio' is an example of such a fact: that this crisis (seldom mentioned in books of criticism) has great difficulty and ambiguity in the theatre should be clearly recorded by its historians, for the literary critic will never learn the fact by a rigorous analysis of its not very complex words. There is a somewhat similar concurrence of interest upon a few lines in Webster's *The White Devil*. This play has been given three professional productions in London in the present century, in 1925, 1935 and 1947; each production gave a different emphasis, and yet after each of them a number of reviewers independently noted the deep impression made by a few of Flamineo's words:

> I have a strange thing in me, to th'which
> I cannot give a name, without it be
> Compassion.

The reviewers spoke of 'human feeling' or 'imaginative agony', and, although one of them considered it an 'irrelevant' moment, they all testified to its power.[9] Now this is a most important fact for the critic, for these lines provide an eccentric moment in the presentation of Flamineo and so, in reading, they might be passed over lightly, or judged to be due to forgetfulness on Webster's part of the sort of character he had created. Nor does their theatrical power influence our 'reading' of Flamineo's role only: it can modify our view of the play as a whole. Clearly the heroine, Vittoria Corrambona, is committed to a life of pleasure, passion and courage, instigates two murders,

[9] For details, cf. *The White Devil* (Revels Plays), ed. J. R. Brown (1960), pp. lx–lxi.

and pleads not guilty to her evident adultery; she has some moments of alarm, when she cries 'O me accurst' or 'O me! this place is hell', but it seems, in her own words, that 'nothing but blood could allay' the demands of life as she found it. Only at the very end does she suggest that she could imagine any other way of life; then, in her dying words, she gives a quite contrary impression:

> O happy they that never saw the court,
> Nor ever knew great man but by report.

This sentiment is so out of key with the rest of her part, that a responsible and imaginative editor, M. W. Sampson, has suggested that the two lines belong to Zanche, the waiting-woman, and not to Webster's heroine. But if Flamineo's single and brief recognition of compassion is clearly of great power in the theatre, perhaps Webster intended Vittoria's single regret to have a similar power. Another character in the plays says that

> . . . affliction
> Expresseth virtue, fully, whether true,
> Or else adulterate,

and in *The Duchess of Malfi* Webster has alluded to the commonplace that at death a man speaks truly, like a Hotspur or Laertes. So perhaps Flamineo, witnessing the winding of his brother's corpse, and Vittoria facing death itself are both meant to 'come to themselves' (the phrase is Webster's), and speak their inmost, truest, thoughts and feelings. Theatre history, if it records the simple fact of the reviewers' concurrence of interest in Flamineo's speech, can give notable support to such an interpretation, a view of Webster possessed, not so much with death, as with an inescapable, inward guilt and compassion.

It might also be worthwhile to record remarkable agreements among accounts of even a single production. For example, when *Henry IV, Part One* was performed at Stratford-upon-Avon in 1951, at least two reviewers agreed that the short episode presenting Glendower, and Mortimer and Hotspur with their wives, was the 'most moving scene' in the whole play (they used, independently, the same words);[10] and almost every other reviewer paid special attention to this scene. Now in critical accounts of *Henry IV*, the so-called Welsh Scene often goes entirely unnoticed—as in Harold Jenkins' consideration of the play's

[10] *Punch* (18 April, 1951) and *The Manchester Guardian* (5 October, 1951).

Structural Problem (1956) or in L. C. Knight's investigation of its 'themes'[11]—or else the scene is mentioned briefly for its incidental satire—as by Mr. Traversi. The fact is that most literary critics cannot hear the music called for by the text, nor observe the new restfulness of the characters, relaxing to listen to that music; and so they have missed the visual and temporal stillness of this scene (the more impressive in that it contrasts with the movement and tensions of the rest of the play), and hence they have also missed its potential importance in the dramatic whole. The unanimity of the reviewers in paying tribute to the playing of this scene in the 1951 production should be recorded in order to direct the literary critic's attention towards a significant feature of the play's theatrical life, a scene which gives a still centre in personal affection, to the round of wars, distrust and self-aggrandisement.

A second suggestion is more general: that theatre historians should not restrict their attention to performances of major characters. The effectiveness of the page in *The White Devil* is an example of the interest, for a literary critic, of a one-line part. A reader researching for information about great acting, or stage business, or theatre fashions may pass by such a detail without thought, but whenever such a small character gains apparently incommensurate attention, the literary critic can use the information; it tells him about a detail of the play's theatrical life which a reading of its text can seldom indicate.

A third suggestion is linked to this: a critic is especially interested in impressions arising from a character's silence, and in visual and temporal effects. None of the examples in this present discussion has involved a famous and lengthy speech: the various and sometimes contradictory meanings of the actual lines of a play, the literary critic can tease out for himself—indeed he is often over-cunning in this respect. But he does need visual prompting, and some help in measuring tension and noting changes of dramatic focus. So it is especially important for theatre historians to record visual relationships between characters (irrespective of invented background or business), and unambiguous impressions of haste, slowness, boredom and expectation. Interest in the silent presences of Banquo and Macduff are examples of the value of such detail.

The last of these suggestions is that theatre historians should pay

[11] Cf. *Some Shakespearean Themes* (1959).

special regard to the effect of plays seldom performed but of obvious literary and theatrical importance, and to those parts of famous plays which can seldom be seen in performance. An instance of the latter is the scenes depicting Aumerle's rebellion and discovery in the last Act of *Richard II.* Most critics must form their judgements of these tricky, comic-and-pathetic-and-tense scenes wholly from their reading of the text, for they are seldom performed. They should be able to turn to theatre research; but neither of the two stage-histories of *Richard II* is of any help. That in the Variorum edition of the play, published in 1955, does not mention the scenes; that in the New Cambridge Shakespeare, published in 1939, seems to infer that Benson's 1896 production at Stratford-upon-Avon presented them, but gives no further information. Finding that Professor Sprague has no comment in his *Shakespeare and the Actors*, the literary critic may pursue the question back to the Variorum and find three references to descriptions of the Benson production, and his hopes will rise; but one reference is back again to the New Cambridge Shakespeare, and the other two, when followed up, yield no information about the Aumerle scenes. The literary critic must instigate a search on his own behalf if he wants to learn about the theatrical effect of the fifth Act of *Richard II* as Shakespeare wrote it. A mere reference to two or three reviews which the theatre researcher will have read would not take much space in a footnote, and would be eagerly followed by the literary critic. The clown scenes in *Othello*, the Spy Scene in *Coriolanus*, the Lancelot-Jessica-Lorenzo Scene in *The Merchant of Venice* are further examples of rarely performed parts of Shakespeare's plays in which the literary critic will be, or should be, especially interested.

* * *

These suggestions are not meant to set a limit to a critic's interest in theatre research; they are, rather, sprats to catch mackerel. Once an initial distrust is overcome, there is material for the critic in the wide range of theatre research. Studies of the structure and management of all types of theatre, descriptions of acting techniques and intentions, histories of scenic design, biographies of actors, analyses of audiences—all these can enrich the critic's knowledge of the theatrical life of plays, of their author's visual as well as verbal imagination, and his handling of time, emphasis, expectation, suspense; so they can lead the critic towards the fully theatrical criticism which the works of any author who chooses to write plays, and not poems or novels, necessarily demand.

Theatre research has so many demands made upon it that a request for further information needs, perhaps, further recommendation. The general importance of the issue may provide this—a recognition that the study of Shakespeare as a 'philosophic poet rather than a man of the stage' is symptomatic of an intellectual attitude which divorces literary criticism from the theatre. The men who work in our theatres experiment along their own lines of interest, inquiry, and financial advantage, and critics and university scholars and students along theirs; despite honourable exceptions, rarely do they help each other, or know each other's language. Yet they could help each other and learn from each other, and so immeasurably enrich our theatre. For this to happen literary critics must learn to consider the full theatrical life of the plays they study, so that they can analyse and judge a play as well as a poem, and speak of an image of life as well as of a theme, or pattern, or moral statement. If they could do this, directors, actors and audiences would recognise their own interests in the critics' deliberations, and would share in them. Here theatre research can help, for, if it can respond to the first inquiries of literary critics, it can do much to establish and refine a consideration of plays in the element for which they were written.

INDEX

Index